D1248488

National Communism in Western Europe: a third way to socialism?

Contributors

Manuel Villaverde Cabral is professor at the Instituto de Ciências Sociais, Lisbon, Portugal, and a former visiting fellow at St Antony's College, Oxford.

Howard Machin is lecturer in French government at the London School of Economics and Political Science.

David McLellan is professor of politics at the University of Kent, Canterbury.

Annette Morgan is lecturer in politics at Brunel University, London.

Peter Morris is lecturer in politics at Nottingham University.

Paul Preston is reader in modern history at Queen Mary College, University of London.

Leonard Schapiro is emeritus professor of political science at the London School of Economics and Political Science.

George Schöpflin is joint lecturer in East European politics at the London School of Economics and Political Science and the School of Slavonic and East European Studies, University of London.

Sidney Tarrow is professor of political science at Cornell University, New York.

Vincent Wright is professor of political and social science at the European University Institute, Florence, and co-editor of the journal, *West European Politics*.

National Communism in Western Europe:
a third way to socialism?

edited by
Howard Machin

Methuen
London and New York

First published in 1983 by
Methuen & Co. Ltd
11 New Fetter Lane, London EC4P 4EE

Published in the USA by
Methuen & Co.
in association with Methuen, Inc.
733 Third Avenue, New York, NY 10017

Typeset in Hong Kong by Graphicraft Typesetters
Printed in Great Britain by
Richard Clay (The Chaucer Press) Ltd, Bungay, Suffolk

British Library Cataloguing in Publication Data
National communism in Western Europe.
1. Communism–Europe–History
I. Machin, Howard
335.43'094   HX694

ISBN 0-416-73430-8
ISBN 0-416-73440-5 Pbk

Library of Congress Cataloging in Publication Data
Main entry under title:
National communism in Western Europe.
Based on papers presented at sessions of the West
European studies seminar of the University of London.
Includes index.
Contents: Communism and national communism in West
European politics/Howard Machin–Theoretical roots
of liberal, democratic national communism/David
McLellan–West European communist parties and
international communism/Peter Morris–[etc.]
1. Nationalism and socialism–Europe–Congresses.
2. Communist parties–Europe–Congresses.   3. Communism
–Europe–Congresses.   I. Machin, Howard.
HX550.N3N326   1983   335.43'4'094   82-24945

Contents

Contents

Preface

During the past few years several sessions of the West European Studies Seminar of the University of London have been devoted to an examination of the evolution of communist parties in Western Europe. Some scholars have contributed comparative analyses; others have provided detailed national case studies. A picture of the considerable diversity of national strategies of the major communist parties emerged from these discussions. Most of the contributors revised and up-dated their papers to form this book, but as each writer took the approach he or she considered most fruitful, there is no 'conclusion' to this deliberately disparate collection.

Many people contributed to this series of seminars and assisted in compiling this collection. I would like to express my thanks for the special help of Anthony Atmore, Ian Nish, James Joll, Gordon Smith, Jonathan Geldzahler and Eileen Gregory.

Howard Machin
October 1982

1

Communism and national communism in West European politics

Howard Machin

For most of their sixty tortured years of existence the communist parties in Western Europe have been troubled by their dual identities as parts of an international organization and as national political parties. On the one hand, as local units of the international communist movement, these parties have sought to serve the cause of world socialism, by supporting the 'motherland of socialism' and the positions of the Russian leaders in international affairs. On the other hand, West European communist parties have striven to achieve socialism in their own nation-states by representing the working classes and attempting to gain power in their countries' political systems.

As long as the communist parties of the world remained united and firmly directed from the Kremlin, relatively few problems arose from the tensions between the two identities. No one seriously questioned the need to accord top priority to Moscow's foreign policy requirements before the Second World War. By 1960, however, the situation had changed dramatically. The Soviet occupation of Eastern Europe, the division of Germany, the Cold War, the Yugoslavian heresy, the Sino-Soviet split, the death of Stalin and the invasion of Hungary in 1956 had altered the faces of Western Europe and of international communism. In Iberia, the Salazar and Franco dictatorships were firmly established and the few remaining communists were in exile, hiding or prison. In West Germany, the communist party was first discredited and marginalized by the division of Germany and the unpopularity of the Soviet-imposed regime in the East, before being declared unconstitutional in 1953. Only in Italy and France did the communist parties remain important political forces. In both countries, they had won wide respect for their heroism in resistance and had even participated in government until 1947. Subsequently, however, their predictions of capitalist pauperization had been confounded by the unprecedented economic growth of the 1950s, whilst their support for Soviet policies had led to their ostracism during the Cold War and their discredit after the Hungarian invasion and the denunciation of the crimes of Stalin. During the same period, the Soviet Union had gained an empire, but lost its unchallenged leadership of the international communist movement. Soviet leaders, preoccupied by the superpower status of their country, showed no enthusiasm for the international destabilization which could result from the return to government of communists in Italy or France. Within international communism, in contrast, Moscow's ultimate deterrent of excommunication was no longer operational – the parties in Yugoslavia and China had survived it quite well.[1]

By the mid-1960s, many West European communist leaders were starting to realize that their close identification with Russian-style socialism, together with their uncritical support for Soviet foreign policies, was a liability, rather than an asset, for their goal of winning power at home. At the same time, Soviet leaders appeared to gain nothing from this support or, indeed, to show any gratitude for it. The Italian Communist Party was no nearer to power than in 1948, the French Communist Party was clearly weaker, and Soviet foreign policy had gained nothing from their sacrifices. Henceforth, it was slowly to become acceptable for West European communists to consider the national prospects of their parties as having at least the same importance as the Soviet-defined goals of international communism. Over the next two decades, the West European branches of the international communist movement were to be nationalized.[2]

In the third chapter of this collection, Peter Morris describes and evaluates the process of development of distinct national strategies within the parties of Western Europe. These strategies represented neither a complete innovation nor a total break with the Soviet bloc. International policy choices had always been modified, to some extent, for national political needs. There were also old friendships between Western and Soviet leaders, and old patterns of behaviour (notably that of waiting for Soviet leadership) which were slow to change. Furthermore, in many areas of international politics, there was complete agreement between the West European and Soviet communist parties. The West Europeans, for example, had no ideological reasons or domestic political pressures to abandon their support for national liberation movements or their criticisms of 'American imperialism'.[3]

Thus, as Annette Morgan demonstrates in Chapter 5, whilst public opinion focused on the divisions between European and Soviet communists, 'international communist solidarity' was not destroyed, but merely transformed. It must be noted, however, that despite the continuing consensus on many questions, the Soviet leaders were far from enthusiastic about the 'dissident' views of the West European parties, especially when these implied at first tacit, and later open, criticism of the Soviet model of socialism. Leonard Schapiro, in Chapter 4, provides a full analysis of Moscow's hurt and angry reaction to this development of national communism in Western Europe.

The other chapters of this volume are detailed case studies. David McLellan examines the impact of national communism on communist ideology, the downgrading of Leninist dogmas and the re-evaluation of Antonio Gramsci and Rosa Luxemburg. George Schöpflin provides a concise analysis of developments in Poland up to and after the introduction of martial law and their diverse impact on the West European parties. Manuel Cabral, Paul Preston, Sidney Tarrow and Vincent Wright examine the recent changes of attitudes and behaviour of the communist parties of Portugal, Spain, Italy and France respectively. These studies illustrate the considerable difference of conditions, analyses and strategies of the four parties concerned. They also demonstrate the transitory and fragile nature of the friendship and the coincidence of positions of the Italian, Spanish and French parties in the mid-1970s: the phenomena which won such international interest as 'Eurocommunism' in the mid-1970s.

The interest in Eurocommunism

After two decades of stability West European politics appeared on the brink of major changes in the mid-1970s. In two of the most populous and prosperous liberal democracies, France and Italy, it seemed that communists might soon enter government, albeit as coalition partners, as the result of free democratic elections. The Italian Communist Party made consistent gains in local elections and a 4 per cent gain in the 1976 legislature elections, which led many observers to conclude that Christian Democrat leaders would sooner or later be obliged to accept the appointment of communist ministers. In France, it was the national opinion polls, together with local election results after the near-miss of the communist-supported Mitterrand in the 1974 presidential race, which led to hopes and fears of seeing communist ministers – in alliance with socialists – after the 1978 legislative elections. In both cases, the arrival of communists in ministerial office implied changes in both foreign and domestic policies. Hence in Washington and Moscow as well as in Brussels, Bonn and London there was curiosity and anxiety about the precise nature of these policy shifts.

The attitudes and actions of two other communist parties were also major international preoccupations, but for rather different reasons. In Spain, after the death of Franco, it was unclear whether democratic government would be established, and if so in what form. One unknown factor was the strength of and support for the hitherto clandestine communist party if free elections were organized. Similar uncertainties existed in Portugal, where, after the fall of Caetano, military leaders and civilian politicians wrestled with the huge problems of decolonization and democratization. In both these countries, the communists had led resistance to the dictatorships and had strong links with factory workers' organizations. Until the first 'normal' elections were held, it remained unclear whether the Spanish and Portuguese parties would be minor opposition forces, allies in government or precipitators of new authoritarian regimes.[4]

It was not only this coincident proximity to power-sharing which caused such curiosity and concern. Many commentators and scholars were also interested in the apparent transformation of the behaviour and analyses of West European communists and sought to discover whether or not these changes were real or illusory; Soviet, European or national in inspiration and co-ordination; and whether they could produce the anticipated electoral victories. On the left, many observers and critics concluded that effective changes were indeed taking place, although spokesmen of the more revolutionary schools condemned these trends as revisionist treachery of the proletariat, whilst social democrats welcomed them as progressive and liberal, but insufficient. More conservative commentators generally concluded that communists were changing tactics and policy stances only in order more effectively to gain support. Behind these dangerous disguises (such writers deduced) the basic goals and belief of international communism remained unchanged. Liberal democracy and capitalism were still the enemies to be destroyed.

This debate was both widened and confused by the contributions of spokesmen and intellectuals from the different Eurocommunist parties concerned and from the Soviet Communist Party. These people were far from unanimous, or consistent, in their views about whether or not Eurocommunism existed and, if it did, about its precise nature and composition. Furthermore, the actual dealings of the Western communist leaders with each other and with Soviet leaders led many observers to ask whether the phrase 'international proletarian solidarity' still had any meaning. They also asked whether the liberal, nationalist critiques from the Western parties might even influence Soviet policies on human rights and relations with East European satellites. In short, the idea of a Eurocommunist transformation challenged existing beliefs about the nature of communism, the role of communist parties in West European capitalist countries and the international communist movement as a whole.[5]

Coinciding national approaches and the Eurocommunist syndrome

Between 1974 and 1977 the ideological modifications, national strategies, relations with other communist parties and foreign policy positions of the Italian, Spanish and French communists became so closely parallel to each other that a new style of communism seemed to have developed – Eurocommunism. This period of coincidence of national approaches to domestic and international politics reinforced the friendships between these parties but increased the suspicions of Soviet leaders. It also sharply differentiated these parties from the Portuguese Communist Party which remained much closer to Leninist orthodoxy, Moscow and its own historical tradition. Moreover, there were many differences between the positions and analyses of the Spanish, French and Italian communists. None the less, the similarities between their approaches to making communism more national, liberal, democratic and European were sufficient to justify their description as a 'Eurocommunist syndrome'. Each of these four modifications merits a brief examination.[6]

National communism

The French, Italian and Spanish parties shared the view (together with many other non-Soviet bloc communist parties) that there was no single model for constructing socialism. They emphasized that the method of moving towards socialism – and the ultimate style of socialism itself – must depend on the history, culture, traditions and institutions of a country, as well as its level and type of economic development. This meant that socialism could be built without a violent revolution or a rigidly policed economy and society in a one-party system. It was a short step from this denial of the uniqueness of the Russian model for socialist construction to an open criticism of the less attractive aspects of Soviet government, notably the treatment of dissidents.

A further implication of this national communism was the conclusion that no socialist country should interfere in another's politics. Communist parties should advise and help each other, but no ruling party had a right or a duty to impose by force its own model of socialism on another country's party which had chosen a different model. Hence, for the Italian and Spanish parties at least, the Soviet military interventions in Prague in 1968 and in Kabul in 1979 were an unacceptable face of Russian imperialism. The Soviet pressure on Polish leaders in 1981 was also seen as objectionable.

Finally, this notion of national communism led the French, Spanish and Italian leaders to an increased emphasis on the national interests of their countries in international affairs and, if need be, in disagreement with the Soviet Union. This led the Italian communists as far as giving support for Italy's continued membership of NATO. In fact, none of the three parties allowed national interests to create constant open conflict with the Soviet Communist Party but all had periods of tension and acrimony with it, albeit at different times and over different issues.

Liberal communism

The French, Italian and Spanish communists all included the defence (or indeed the widening) of civil liberties as an element of their new national strategies. This meant that those freedoms (of speech, of the press, of association and of religion) which had formerly been derided as bourgeois illusions were henceforth treated as basic human rights. Thus, a large degree of social and political pluralism was accepted as both inevitable and desirable (although, through cultural hegemony, the truths of scientific socialism would eventually triumph!). The results of this liberalism were very extensive. In the first place, it led to a recognition of the legitimacy of some form of multi-party political competition. A second result was the acceptance of the role of individual initiatives in the economy, and especially in agriculture:

the state, through a programme of nationalizations and economic planning, must dominate the economy and destroy capitalism, but in the new economic order small farmers and businessmen should play an important, productive role, with considerable freedom of action. Of course, both these results were expected to bear electoral fruits.

There were two other results of the new liberalism which created difficulties for all three parties. The first was the problem of dealing with internal party dissensions. If the communist defence of freedom of speech were to have any credibility with the electorate, it must surely include freedom of speech within the communist party itself. In Spain, France and Italy those communists who opposed the new, liberal options, and those who were critical that these options had not gone far enough, demanded the chance to present their views within their party channels. Liberal communism seemed to limit the prospects for the disciplined, monolithic party practices of the past. The other worrying result of defending liberal values was that it meant criticizing one of the major opponents of such values, the ruling Communist Party of the Soviet Union. It was difficult to condemn concentration camps and torture for political dissenters in Chile, Argentina or Northern Ireland and not include Soviet Russia. Open attacks on Russian repression of dissidents merely exacerbated the tensions between Moscow and the communist leaders in Paris, Madrid and Rome.

Democratic communism

The third coincident element of the national strategies of the three West European parties was their espousal of the democratic norms of Western bourgeois democracies. The French, Italian and Spanish communists' new method of winning and retaining power was by repeated electoral victories in free elections. This meant they rejected violent revolution, and election rigging, political repression or other 'Prague coup' techniques once in office. It also implied that they accepted all election results, including defeats, and hence acknowledged the possibility of relinquishing power and permitting party 'alternance' in government. Finally, this democratic approach to socialist construction affected both alliance strategy and internal party organization. Henceforth, electoral alliances and coalition pacts were based on pragmatic tactical convenience rather than basic principle, and in all three countries only fascists and irredeemable capitalists were seen as totally unacceptable allies. Henceforth, too, internal party democracy became much more apparent (although not always more real) than in the past. Indeed, many Spanish and Italian communists now saluted debate, lively criticism and free elections within the party for making better judgements and avoiding errors. Some even called into question the basic features of democratic centralism on which their parties had been constructed. To Soviet minds these positions must have appeared depressingly close to the Dubcek 'errors' of 1968 in Prague.

European communism

The feature which distinguished the national liberal, democratic analyses and strategies of the three West European parties from other non-ruling communist parties outside the Soviet bloc was their recognition of similar cultural inheritances and of common economic and political interests. A dominant Catholic Church, late and rapid economic development, and an experience of right-wing authoritarian government were important elements in the history of each country. Several leaders of the Spanish, Portuguese and Italian parties had spent some of their years of exile in France. All three countries had been firmly committed to the Western side in the Cold War: in practice, this resulted in an increasingly inextricable inter-linking of their economies through the European Community and of their defence systems through NATO. These close links with the rest of 'bourgeois' Western Europe had originally been opposed by all three communist parties, and 'nationalist independence' arguments had been frequently used by party spokesmen. The Italian Communist Party was the first to realize that membership of the European Community was both popular and an advantage for the Italian economy and hence dropped its opposition. The French party followed this example very reluctantly several years later. A joint group was formed in the European Assembly. The support of the Spanish Communist Party for Spain's application to join the community was based not only on its popularity and the economist arguments but also on the hope that the Common Market would help preserve democracy in Spain. Hence, with more or less enthusiasm, all three parties came to accept European integration as a fact of life. The gradual modification of their attitudes towards the Atlantic Alliance followed a similar pattern with the Italian communists again taking the lead.

The other aspect of 'Europeanization' was the increased frequency of contacts between the leaders of the three parties. Bilateral and trilateral meetings and statements became so common that some observers began to speculate that Eurocommunism might be co-ordinated into something more than merely a temporary meeting of interests and policies.

Finally, it should be noted that all three parties at different times identified themselves as 'Eurocommunist' and 'Eurocommunism' as a good thing. The French were most reluctant to do so, but eventually admitted their closeness to the Italian and Spanish parties and their strategies. Subsequently both the Italians and the Spanish appeared concerned lest this term identify them too closely with the French.

The results of Eurocommunism and the divergence of national paths

None of the strategies pursued by the four communist parties in this study bore the anticipated results. Despite its ruthless tactics, the Portuguese party failed to retain or regain power, or even to achieve a dominant position within the left. None of the 'Eurocommunist trio' managed to return to power as major coalition partners after major gains of votes and seats resulting from popular liberal, democratic, pro-European policy promises. The Italian Communist Party entered the parliamentary majority in the 'historic compromise' of 1976, but left it in 1979 having gained neither major policy changes nor seats in the government nor electoral popularity. Both the party and its trade union allies lost members, whilst the number of votes for the party declined in subsequent local and national elections.

The Spanish Communist Party signed the Pact of Moncloa and gave repeated proof of its moderation and liberalism during the waves of Basque terrorism. Despite its boast of being the most open and democratic party in Spain, and its support for the new democratic system, membership fell by 50 per cent between 1978 and 1981, its trade union movement weakened, its votes stagnated at 10 per cent of the poll in 1979 and fell to 3 per cent in 1982.

The French Communist Party formed a firm alliance with the French Socialist Party in 1972, but broke off this arrangement in 1977 when it became clear that the socialists had made spectacular gains in members, votes and seats, but the communists had merely stagnated. Between 1977 and 1981, the French party seemed to revert to a more Leninist view of socialism and to supporting Moscow's foreign policy. The result was even greater losses of support. The paradoxical result was that in 1981 the French Communist Party became the first communist party to participate in the government of a major West European state precisely because its weakness and unpopularity, demonstrated by huge losses of votes and seats, showed it was no longer a serious threat.

The failure of each communist party was essentially a distinct national failure within a separate national political context. The different effects of the international economic crisis, the threats from the army and Basque nationalists in Spain, the impact of the Red Brigades and radicals in Italy, and the impact of the presidential system in France were all key factors in the separate communist declines. None the less, there were some common factors affecting the three Eurocommunist parties.

The first of these was decline in coherence resulting from internal dissension within each party. National policy choices and greater party democracy meant in all cases that those who remained loyal to the Soviet model and to Soviet foreign policy could (and did) articulate their opposition to the new party line, and attempt to use the new party democratic channels to reverse, slow down or block these changes. At the same time, there were those who expected much greater and faster changes. The overall result was that, if the parties appeared more democratic than ever before, they also seemed to be less organized, disciplined and effective.

A second common factor was the absence of policy innovations in the liberal democratic strategies. This is perhaps clarified by considering the analogy of the market. For years these communist parties had been offering one political 'product' and advertising that all the other 'products' on the market (whether social democrat, liberal or conservative) were not only inferior but actually lethal to the consumers. In a sense, the revised positions of the communist parties involved scrapping their previous products, admitting those of other producers were not dangerous, and marketing their own 'brand' of their rivals' product. Past consumers of the previous communist 'product' were doomed to disappointment whilst there was little incentive for other consumers simply to transfer from one 'brand' to another. In short, liberal, democratic, national and European reforms made the parties look more like - but not more attractive than - their national competitors.

The other common factor was the weight of history. For most simple citizens and active politicians, the image and identity of a political party are created not simply by the personalities of its leaders and its present analyses and policy promises, but also by its past. All three parties have long Stalinist pasts and their present leaders have not yet disowned these unpopular aspects of their organizational development. Until these parties attempt to make clear that they have broken with their own pasts – which may imply denouncing some key aspects of communist identity – their claims of renewal and their wishes to be treated 'like other parties' will continue to be treated with widespread suspicion.[7]

All three communist parties, however, have pursued their liberal, national and democratic policies so far that it is very difficult to envisage a return to the patterns of the past. Each of the parties has recruited many new members and militants during the last decade, many of whom support the new style of communism. Those who nostalgically inclined to the 'good old days' of Stalinist discipline and dogma have less and less numerical weight and political influence. Furthermore – in France at least – communist voters have demonstrated their willingness to desert the party when it deserted the new path and its alliance with the socialists. Communist leaders in Western Europe seem trapped in an insoluble dilemma: further advances towards more liberal, democratic and nationalist forms of communism pay no dividends, but a return to past policies and strategies brings losses of votes and members – although these may well be the circumstances which permit communist participation in government.

Notes

1　J.W. Friend, 'The Roots of Autonomy in West European Communism', *Problems of Communism*, 29 (5), pp. 28–43.
2　For the most recent account of this development see Peter Lange and Maurizio Vannicelli (eds), *The Communist Parties of Italy, France and Spain: Postwar Change and Continuity* (Cambridge, Mass., 1981).
3　Cf. Chapter 5.
4　See Neil McInnes, *The Communist Parties of Western Europe* (London, 1975).
5　Cf. Philip Elliott and Philip Schlesinger, 'On the Stratification of Political Knowledge: Studying "Eurocommunism" and Unfolding Ideology', *The Sociological Review*, 27 (1) (February 1979), pp. 55–81.
6　This description is very similar – coincidentally – with that of Georges Lavau, 'Eurocommunism Four Years On', *European Journal of Political Research*, 7 (4) (March 1979), pp. 357–74.
7　Cf. Elliott and Schlesinger, op.cit.

2

Theoretical roots of liberal, democratic national communism

David McLellan

In his book *Eurocommunism and the State*, Santiago Carrillo tells us that there exists

> A new tendency, which has arisen mainly in the advanced capitalist countries, which remains faithful to the principles of Marxism, which takes to itself, in a critical way, the gains made by the revolutionary movement so far, which strives to incorporate in the successes of theory the analysis and elaboration of structural, economic, social and cultural changes, and which demands democratic roads and independence in order to work out its own strategy.[1]

This paper aims to explore the claim that the main tenets of Eurocommunism remain 'faithful to the principles of Marxism'. Of course, no clear answer can be given to the question, both because there is disagreement over what constitutes 'classical Marxism' and also because the notion of continuity of meaning in a tradition is itself a problematic one. Nevertheless a few general points can usefully be made. What characterizes Eurocommunism from a theoretical standpoint is that 'it seeks to achieve the transformation of capitalist society in socialist directions by constitutional means, inside the constitutional and legal framework provided by bourgeois democracy'.[2] In considering the intellectual roots of this idea, I shall consider four main areas in roughly chronological order: firstly, the works of Marx and Engels themselves; secondly, the Second International thinkers and principally Karl Kautsky; thirdly, Soviet Marxism–Leninism and Stalin; and fourthly, Gramsci.

In an effort to legitimate their views, Eurocommunism theorists have naturally turned to Marx, but with inevitably meagre results. It is well known that Marx wrote little of any systematic nature on the state and considered this to be the major lacuna in his legacy and one, moreover, that only he could remedy.[3] There are, of course, the interpretations of such non-Marxist writers as George Lichtheim who argued that Marx developed from a Jacobin revolutionary in 1848 to a radical democrat in his later years; or the neo-Hegelian views of Shlomo Avineri who considers Marx's views on the transition to socialism as a sort of *Aufhebung* of bourgeois democracy. But Eurocommunists have on the whole eschewed such general interpretations and concentrated on evident connections between democracy and socialism in some of Marx's remarks around 1848. For example, in the *Communist Manifesto* he declared that 'the first step in the revolution by the working class is to raise the proletariat to the position of ruling class, to win the battle of democracy'.[4] (It is true that Marx advocated liberal democratic reforms in Germany in 1848, but this was in a country that had not yet achieved a bourgeois revolution and obviously cannot be applied to present Eurocommunist positions.) More immediately striking are Marx's remarks on the importance of political culture as when, for example, in his Amsterdam speech of 1872 he said:

> The workers must one day conquer political supremacy in order to establish the new organization of labour ... but we do not assert that the attainment of this end requires identical means. We know that one has to take into consideration the institutions, mores, and traditions of the different countries, and we do not deny that there are countries like England and America and if I am familiar with your institutions, Holland where labour may obtain its goal by peaceful means.[5]

I myself do not think that too much weight should be attached to such statements: the anti-statist views that Marx developed as a result of the experience of the Commune[6] and his criticisms of the German Social Democratic Party (SPD)[7] show a different approach. In any case, the immense growth in state power since Marx's time with the expansion, and often interlocking, of its bureaucratic,military and industrial sectors preclude the possibility of his offering contemporary Marxists any direct advice on political options. From a very different point of view, it is worth mentioning an affinity between Marx and current Eurocommunism which is stressed not by the Eurocommunists themselves but by their left-wing critics. These writers – Marcuse, André Gorz and the Italian Autonomisti – reject the view that the secularized, rationalizing, instrumentalist view of the world ushered in by capitalism can possibly lay the material foundations for communism. Yet there is in Marx, at least in some of his moods, and certainly in the Eurocommunists, a view that socialism is a question of the relations, and not of the forces, of production.

Although Eurocommunism has not found much support in Marx, it has claimed a clear ally in Engels, who survived Marx by twelve years. Engels, particularly after the lifting of the anti-socialist laws in 1890, was faced with the problems of the correct political tactics for an increasingly mass party. Circumstances prevented Engels from exercising his very considerable gifts as a practical politician, living as he did in enforced isolation from the leaders of the SPD. Towards the end of his life, the growing electoral success of the social democrats led him to stress the evolutionary rather than the revolutionary side of Marxism and declare the tactics of 1848 to be outmoded in every respect. In his Preface to a new edition of Marx's *Class Struggles in France*, written in 1895 shortly before he died, Engels stated that the growth of social democracy 'proceeds as spontaneously, as steadily, as irresistibly and at the same time as tranquilly as a natural process', and continued:

> We can count even today on two and a quarter million voters. If it continues in this fashion, by the end of the century we shall conquer the greater part of the middle strata of society, petty bourgeois and small peasants, and grow into the decisive power in the land, before which all other powers will have to bow, whether they like it or not. To keep this growth going without interruption until it of itself gets beyond the control of the prevailing governmental system, not to fritter away this daily increasing shock-force in vanguard skir- mishes, but to keep it intact until the decisive day, that is our main task.[8]

Such passages, regarded as Engels's political 'testament', certainly played a role in influencing the leaders of the SPD, though it should be noted that Engels agreed (very reluctantly) to excise certain more revolutionary passages under pressure from the Berlin leaders.

In the 'revisionist' debate in the SPD, Engels's (edited) political testament was much quoted by Eduard Bernstein. Naturally, Eurocommunists do not quote Bernstein in their favour as he is re- garded as a theorist of social democracy. Nevertheless, his general point that the expansion of democracy required a long period of eco- nomic and political stability, and that, as against the crisis theories of Marx, Rosa Luxemburg and Lenin, this stability was both possible and desirable, has a lot in common with Eurocommunist views. But it is in the theories of Kautsky, the 'pope' of the Second International, that leftist critics find the origins of Eurocommunism. Ernest Mandel, for example, writes that 'What is incontestable is that Eurocommunism today is repeating the reasoning of social democracy yesterday word for word.[9] Kautsky distinguished between a policy of assault and one of attrition – *Ermattung*. Rather than risk in a precarious attack everything that the party had built up over decades, the workers should gradually undermine and wear down their enemies until they could join battle under much more favourable circumstances.[10] There is, indeed, a strong parallel between Eurocommunist ideas on the extension of democracy and Kautsky's advocacy of a combination of Soviets or workers' councils and parliamentary democracy in which decisive power was retained by parliament as the guardian of constitutional liberties; and the parallel could be extended to Kautsky's criticism of the Bolsheviks as falling short of this model. But the parallels between classical social democracy and Eurocommunism are by no means as striking as many have claimed. Kautsky's political theory tended to preserve the SPD from playing any practical role in government. In sharp opposition to the Eurocommunists, Kautsky was opposed to any form of coalition politics. In his major theoretical work *The Road to Power* he wrote, for example:

A proletarian party which shares power with a capitalist party in any government must share the blame for any act of subjection of the working class. It thereby invites the hostility of its own supporters, and this in turn causes its capitalist allies to lose confidence and makes any progressive action impossible. No such arrangement can bring any strength to the working class. No capitalist party will permit it to do so. It can only compromise a proletarian party and confuse and split the working class.[11]

The reason for this difference is that although Eurocommunists and classical German social democrats share the same electoral politics, the Eurocommunists do not share the SPD's fatalistic, rather mechanistic view of the role of economic crisis in bringing about the transition to socialism. The cataclysmic views of the Second International led them to a passive political stance which relegated all positive attempts to build socialism till after the revolution, whereas Eurocommunists have a much more coherent and interventionist perspective in which bourgeois democracy is gradually actively transformed into socialism. There are more plausible candidates than

Kautsky as intellectual precursors of Eurocommunism. One of them would be Antonio Labriola, the one Marxist of the Second International whose avoidance of mechanism, or indeed any philosophy of history, and whose emphasis on the importance of superstructural elements foreshadow Gramsci. In more directly political matters, Italian Eurocommunists have cited not only Luxemburg's criticisms of the Bolsheviks' treatment of the Constituent Assembly, but also the ideas of the Austro-Marxists, particularly Adler and Otto Bauer, on the combination of workers' councils and National Assembly in which (unlike Kautsky) the weight of power was concentrated in the former.

But whatever affinities there may be between Eurocommunism and the Marxism of Marx, Engels and the Second International, the main current that has formed Eurocommunism is, for all their rejection of Moscow's political hegemony, Soviet Marxism. Although some have claimed to see in the debate between Eurocommunists and their left-wing critics a re-run of the Kautsky–Lenin debate, the Eurocommunists are quick to quote Lenin in their own defence. Khrushchev in 1956 ascribed to Lenin the idea of a peaceful transition to socialism and it is possible to read certain of Lenin's tactical statements in mid-1917 in this sense. Lenin writes, for example, 'The transfer of all power into the hands of the true majority of the people, that is, the workers and the poor peasants, can nowhere take place so easily and so peacefully as in Russia.'[12] And later in the same year Lenin wrote, 'Certain comrades have to come to ask if we have not contradicted ourselves: we were preaching the transformation of the imperialist war into civil war and here we seem to be speaking against ourselves.'[13] He implies that in this period of transition 'civil war is for us transformed into class propaganda which is peaceful, long and patient.'[14] But what is at issue here is really Lenin's views of bourgeois democracy. Before 1914 Lenin seemed to agree with Kautsky that the aim of the proletariat should be to take state power, not destroy it. And he was far less vigorous in his criticism of the reformism of the SPD than were such activists as Luxemburg or Karl Liebknecht. But with the change of perspective exemplified in his *Imperialism* and its political counterpart *State and Revolution*, Lenin's views on bourgeois democracy hardened: imperialism was the negation of democracy, the Soviet was the political form best suited for the transition to socialism, and, with the dissolution of the Constituent Assembly, Soviet democracy was seen to exclude representative democracy. In the early 1920s Lenin's view was that any gain the workers might achieve within the framework of bourgeois democracy was negligible. Even the

modification of his position in *Left-Wing Communism* only amount-
ed to using the political creations of the bourgeoisie with a view later
not to transforming but to destroying them.

The Eurocommunist view is that if Lenin himself changed his political perspective in 1917 as a result of his new analysis of capitalism
then they are entitled to do the same in the 1970s. Carrillo writes of
Lenin's views:

> These are applicable to Russia and theoretically to the rest of the
> world at the time. They are not applicable today because they have
> been overtaken in the circumstances of the developed capitalist
> countries of Western Europe. What has made them inapplicable is
> the change in economic structures and the objective expansion of
> the progressive social forces, the development of the productive
> forces (including nuclear energy), the advance in socialism and de-
> colonization and the defeat of fascism in the Second World War.[15]

But there is little doubt that the Spanish Communist Party's (PCE)
decision to drop Leninism from its self-definition is more honest.
Lenin considered that the bourgeois state was an instrument of class
domination which relied above all on coercive force and, as such,
was incapable of democratic transformation. On a slightly different
subject, the optimistic Eurocommunist view of the bourgeois state
also undermines another cardinal principle of Leninism – the hierarchical and clandestine operation of the party. As the PCE is
finding, it is impossible in the long run not to apply to your own
party the sort of democracy you are advocating in the state at large.

But what is this new stage of capitalism which, according to Eurocommunism, justifies its adoption of a new political stance? The
answer is: state monopoly capitalism. And, in spite of Lenin having
declared imperialism to be the 'highest' stage of capitalism, a Leninist
pedigree is also claimed for the theory of state monopoly capitalism.
Lenin certainly detected a tendency to state monopoly of capital
(which he connected with imperialism) and referred to this state
monopoly capitalism as the 'antechamber' of socialism.

> Socialism [he says] is merely state capitalist monopoly which is
> made to serve the interests of the whole people and has to that ex-
> tent ceased to be capitalist monopoly. There is no middle course
> here. The objective process of development is such that it is impos-
> sible to advance from the monopolies without advancing towards
> socialism.[16]

But it is clear that for Lenin state monopoly capitalism was not a separate *stage* in capitalist development and that there was no question of its being gradually transformed into socialism, the destruction of the state apparatus being one of the cardinal principles of *State and Revolution*. It is rather the theories of Rudolf Hilferding and later Bukharin on the ability of capitalism to organize itself, at least inside national boundaries, that pre-figured the concept of national roads to socialism. The emphasis of Stalinist economists such as Jenö Varga on the struggle over the distribution of surplus value among the capitalist sectors led to the rather shaky theoretical underpinning of the popular front strategies in the 1930s.

Current Eurocommunism claims that the popular front strategies of those years, originating with the French Communist Party in 1934, afford a valid precedent for its policies. For it gave many communist parties their first experience of participation in, and adaptation to, the liberal-democratic and parliamentary regimes for their respective countries. This policy, whose main architects were Georgi Dimitroff and Maurice Thorez, was officially sanctioned at the 7th Congress of the Comintern July 1935. In face of the expansion of fascism, it was necessary, so the theory ran, for the communists to defend bourgeois-democratic freedoms by forging alliances with non-communist socialists and even with the more liberal wing of the bourgeoisie. The dubious identification of fascism and bourgeois democracy that had prevailed at the 6th Comintern Congress was revised: the destruction of fascism would not immediately yield the dictatorship of the proletariat. This had to be prepared by a transitional strategy which involved the defence and, where necessary, restoration of bourgeois democracy and the concomitant rights of the workers. Only thus could the ground for socialism be adequately prepared.[17]

This rather opportunistic change of policy was based on the view that the nature of capitalism itself had changed. Analysis of contemporary capitalism, Varga claimed, revealed 'a new element in the development of capitalism: monopoly profit, the artificial rise of the share of monopoly profit in the total profit at the expense of the income of the smaller capitalists and the "independent producers" still operating'. A new analysis was needed, for 'the economic theory of Marx in general and his theory of crisis in particular are based upon industrial capitalism. Present-day capitalism, however, is monopoly capitalism.'[18] The fundamental Marxist concept of the contradiction between capital and labour tended to be replaced by an examination of the unequal distribution of profit among capitalists. The economy was dominated by monopolies rather than by capital itself and it was the monopolies that were the chief enemy of the working class – a view which obviously chimed in well with much social democratic and even liberal thinking.

It could be added, in more general terms, that the theory of state monopoly capitalism is a contemporary answer to the abiding question haunting Marxists in the industrial West: why have Marx's expectations of capitalist breakdown in the advanced West so far failed to materialize? Before the Second World War, this failure had been explained in terms of Lenin's theory of imperialism and its corollary – the labour aristocracy; or later in terms of the rise of fascism. The theory of state monopoly capitalism performs the same function against the phenomenon of the post-war capitalist boom. But it was only after the Second World War that a fully fledged theory of state monopoly capitalism emerged. This theory, particularly well developed among French Marxists, stated that the increasing economic concentration in advanced capitalism had given rise to a powerful monopoly sector. To maintain a high rate of profit this monopoly sector has more and more recourse to political measures – the extension of the state productive sector, diverting state savings to the advantage of trusts and generally using the resources of the state to undertake the devaluation of capital that would formerly have occurred through bankruptcy. This co-operation between state and monopoly capital means that state policy is increasingly dictated by the needs of monopoly capital – needs which are at variance with those of small capitalists.

For the state is no longer viewed, on this account, simply as an external support for capitalist reproduction; it is an active agent at the very core of the process: 'the state now intervenes as the organiser of the capitalist mode of production'.[19] In classical Marxism, capital was devalued by bankruptcy; under monopoly capitalism it is devalued by nationalization which means that commercial viability is no longer a necessity and thus contributes to the raising of the level of profit in the private sector. In addition, the state contributes substantially, through its various welfare services, to financing some of the costs of private production. Thus

> the state is more than ever the instrument of the political and economic domination of the monopolist bourgeoisie ... This is what makes the seizure of state power absolutely indispensable for the forces of labour and democracy. It is a first, although not sufficient, condition of any fundamental change in society.[20]

For the democratization of the state deprives the monopolist bourgeoisie from using the state to further its own interests. The decline in the power of monopoly capitalism over the state implies more power for the working class and its allies to create the pre-conditions for a passage to socialism.

As Carrillo writes:

> The development of technology puts the very principle of private enterprise in crisis, because only a few giants are in a position to dispose of the immense sums of capital it requires. The capitalist state steps in to make good private capital failures, using public funds to prop up those industries which are unable to finance themselves or obtain sufficient private credit. Together with the injection of capital, the same things happen with the reduction of charges for public services, the lowering of taxes or the giving of export premiums. But when all is said and done, the resources which the state deploys are those of society. Without consultation, society as a whole supplies the needs of capitalist development. In this way, the social character of the economy reaches colossal proportions. The least and humblest contributor is providing for monopolist concerns with profits which get no further than their owners. This role gives the capitalist state, as an instrument of monopoly capital, a decisive power of intervention in economic life.[21]

These views cannot be said to have theoretical roots in the works of Marx and Lenin. There are four aspects of state monopoly capitalist theory which are alien to their approach. Firstly, these theories tend to take competition as their starting-point and concentrate on the struggle over distribution rather than analysing production; secondly, the state is viewed as an instrument isolated from capitalist relations of production and presented as an agent of a particular social group – capable, therefore, of being used by other social groups; thirdly, the emphasis on national roads to socialism is evidently at variance with the internationalism of Marx and Lenin; and fourthly, their views on the tendency of the rate of profit to fall and the consequent crisis are presented in a mechanistic manner as being automatic and inevitable. All these items do, however, have their origin in the Stalinist version of Marxism, however uncomfortable to Moscow the political programme that is currently being deduced from them. For obviously, if the main enemy is monopoly capital, there is room to advocate a democratic transition to socialism based on an alliance with other parties of the left and even of the centre which represents the intermediate strata and non-monopoly capital: the state of 'advanced democracy' will wrest the state from the hands of monopoly capital and democratize it in the interest of all sectors of society exploited by monopoly capital.

Finally, I would like to discuss the most acclaimed intellectual precursor of Eurocommunism – Antonio Gramsci. Gramsci has been portrayed, in a truly vast output of literature by the PCI (the Italian party), as sanctioning its post-war policies of minimizing class conflict by appealing to national interest and proletarian 'responsibility' and forming alliances with the lower middle class and peasantry against the common enemy of monopoly capital. (It should be noted that the Gramsci appealed to by the PCI is, of course, not the pre-prison Gramsci who would have had little sympathy with most of their ideas, but the Gramsci of the *Prison Notebooks*.) By appealing to the authority of Gramsci, past general secretary of the party and martyr to fascism, the party has tried to invest its novel policies with the appearance of continuity and even of orthodoxy. While Palmiro Togliatti was still alive, Gramsci was held by the PCI to be a thoroughgoing Leninist and his originality to lie in applying strictly Leninist principles to Italy. Since 1964, however, there has been a shift in the PCI's attitude, admitting that Gramsci had a different conception of revolution from that of Lenin and even allowing that Gramsci's own teachings may be in need of modification and development. This picture of Gramsci is reinforced, though for opposed reasons, by the PCI's political opponents. The socialists – Giuseppe Tamburrano is the most striking example – have seen Gramsci as the antithesis of Lenin with his emphasis on party democracy, freedom of expression, and general attachment to humanist and cultural values. According to some far left critics, on the other hand, Gramsci's stress on reforms, consensus and stages is akin to the evolutionary views of the Second International.

Amid all this welter of evidently biased claims to Gramsci's legacy, it is difficult to get a clear picture of his ideas. It is nevertheless fairly evident firstly that Gramsci *was* indeed deeply opposed to what he saw as the mechanical internationalism of Trotsky. He wrote:

> To be sure, the line of development is towards internationalism, but the point of departure is 'national' ... it is in the concept of hegemony that these exigencies which are national in character are knotted together; one can well understand how certain tendencies either do not mention such concepts or merely skim over it.[22]

This advocacy of national roads certainly seems to foreshadow the PCI's *Via Italiana*. Secondly, Gramsci's opposition to the Comintern's 'third period' and his advocacy of anti-fascist alliancies (which caused some of his prison comrades to accuse him of having become a social democrat) sound like the policies adopted by Togliatti around the end of the war. Thirdly, Gramsci certainly outlined a different revolutionary strategy in the West as opposed to the East: this was implicit in his contrast between wars of position and wars of manoeuvre. Leninist strategy was not applicable to Italy.

But however true these general points may be, there are two main areas where there seems to be at the very least a tension between Gramsci and current Eurocommunist policy. Gramsci's enthusiam for a (temporary) period of parliamentary government and for the formation of a historical bloc of proletariat, peasantry and lower middle class were evolved in a period of triumphant fascism and a routed communist party. His politics were therefore historically very specific and it is very doubtful whether he would either have advocated such measures in post-war Italy where the communist party enjoyed such success or extended the 'national' democracy of the party to include even large-scale industrialists and proprietors. At a more rarified level his critique of Bernstein and his whole attitude to the dialectic show him to be opposed to the evolutionary reformism of the Second International type. Secondly, Gramsci was not a pure reformist. For all his advocacy of inter-class alliances and his rejection of the idea of a minority revolution, Gramsci never denied the possibility of violent insurrection – an idea which was so readily accepted in the political climate of the Third International that it did not need stressing. It would be a mistake in interpreting Gramsci not to see that his support for reform and for the formation of a historical bloc by no means excluded revolutionary insurrection. His contempt for parliamentary democracy is more akin to Lenin's *State and Revolution* than to Togliatti. It would be equally wrong to suppose that Gramsci saw the war of manoeuvre and war of position as mutually exclusive. Although the war of position was basic in bourgeois society, the war of manoeuvre must always be ready to be used in accordance with the demands of the situation.

The 'gradualist' interpretation of Gramsci proposed by the PCI is therefore misleading. But it does contain some truth. For it is arguable how far the PCI itself is a thoroughly reformist party. Its own pronouncements foresee the supersession of present reforms by more thorough-going socialist solutions. And in its desire to attain these solutions through popular participation, extended democratization, and the creation of a national proletarian culture, it certainly draws heavily on Gramsci.

In conclusion, I would just like to add that, although this chapter has been concerned with political *ideas*, I fully realize their derivative nature. What I have been discussing is, in a broad sense, ideology; and although ideas are not a mere reflection of reality (they also establish the parameters of possible action), a more detailed treatment than has been possible here would explore similarities of ideas in connection with similarities of circumstance and establish a deeper analysis of the relation between theory, practice and reality.

Notes

1 S. Carrillo, *Eurocommunism and the State* (London, 1977), p. 172.
2 R. Miliband, 'Constitutionalism and Revolution: Notes on Eurocommunism', *Socialist Register*, 1978, p. 159.
3 Cf. Marx to Engels in Marx–Engels, *Werke* (Berlin, 1957 ff.) vol. 31, p. 364.
4 K. Marx, *Selected Writings* ed. D. McLellan (Oxford, 1977), p. 237.
5 ibid., p. 594. See also, in a similar vein, Marx's letter to Hyndman, ibid., and Marx-Engels, *Werke* vol. 34, p. 498. These passages are specifically appealed to in the writings of current French Eurocommunists. See, e.g., L. Seve *et al.*, *Les communistes et l'état* (Paris, 1977), p. 44.
6 See the Preface to the second German edition of the *Communist Manifesto* in *Selected Writings*, p. 559.
7 See Marx's 'Circular Letter', *Selected Writings*, pp. 573ff.
8 Cf. Carrillo, op. cit., pp. 92ff.; cf. also K. Marx, F. Engels, *Selected Works* (Moscow, 1962), vol. 1, pp. 135ff.
9 E. Mandel, *From Stalinism to Eurocommunism* (London, 1978), p. 34.
10 Cf. K. Kautsky, *The Dictatorship of the Proletariat* (Ann Arbor, 1964), pp. 70ff.
11 Kautsky quoted in Miliband, op. cit., p. 168.
12 V. Lenin, *Collected Works*, vol. 25, p. 116.
13 V. Lenin, ibid., p. 203.
14 V. Lenin, ibid., p. 496.
15 Carrillo, op. cit., pp. 9f.
16 Lenin, op. cit., p. 357.
17 See further G. Dimitroff, *Der Kampf um die Einheitsfront* in *Ausgewählte Werke* (Berlin, 1958), vol. 2, pp. 498ff.
18 ibid.
19 *Traité marxiste d'économie politique* (Paris, 1971), vol. 2, p. 29.

20 *Traité marxiste d'économie politique* (Paris, 1971), vol. 1, pp. 84f.
21 Carrillo, op. cit., pp. 20f.
22 A. Gramsci, *Selections from the Prison Notebooks*, ed. Q. Hoare and G. Nowell Smith (London, 1971), pp. 240f.

3

West European communist parties and international communism

Peter Morris

A discussion of the type of relationship that exists between the communist parties of Western Europe and the Communist Party of the Soviet Union (CPSU) presents no difficulties to many politicians and commentators in the West: they see this relationship as one of complete dependence of the former on the latter. The belief that all communists place the strategic interests of the Soviet Union above the national interest of the country in which they happen to reside is held by groups and individuals who themselves hold wildly dissimilar views of what does constitute the national interest. Henry Kissinger, Harold Wilson, Vanessa Redgrave as political actors, Stephen Haseler and Ernest Mandel as political analysts, all agree that for the Western communist parties subservience to the superpower of the East is the basic reason for their existence.[1] Agreement, of course, stops there – social democrats and conservatives equate communism with the Soviet Union, the natural enemy of the West, while radicals blame the Soviet Union for having used the Western parties to prevent social revolution in Western Europe, especially after the Second World War. Nevertheless radicals and conservatives are at one in their belief that, for historical and doctrinal reasons, the communist parties of Western Europe are, ultimately, the agents of a foreign power. That is what communist internationalism means.

This argument has an important consequence: that there is no point in a chapter with the title of this one unless it is to demonstrate that things do not change. Proletariats and their dictatorship may come and go; Marxism–Leninism may be in one moment and out the next; NATO may cease to be the enemy and become the shield of socialism in Italy – none of it matters because the basic subordination to the Soviet Union remains. The judgement rests on a total assessment of the 'communist phenomenon' and in particular on the belief that, since leopards do not change their spots, the phenomenon is the same in the 1980s as it was in the 1920s. Its implication is that, in a situation in which the Soviet Union challenged the supreme national interests of Western countries, the Western communist parties would side with the aggressor. Whether or not this implication is correct cannot be proved until the crisis occurs. It is, however, reasonable to assume that the reaction *might* vary from communist party to communist party; that this assumption is reasonable suggests in turn that the 'communist world' is no longer a united world. After all, a longer period now separates the Russian Revolution from the present day than separates the Russian Revolution from the Paris Commune, and it would be surprising if nothing had changed over sixty years. This chapter will try to show that the types of contact that the Western parties have with each other and with Moscow have indeed changed over time and that the language of communist discourse is not what it was. It cannot prove that the new language is 'sincere', only that a shift has apparently taken place in the Western communists' perspective of their place in the international communist movement and their place in their national communities.

All communist parties and governments are supposed to be united by the identical place in the productive process held by the proletariat whose interests they represent. This fundamental unity is itself supposed to transcend the division of mankind into national units and is at the basis of communist internationalism. Thus the history of communist parties necessarily involves – in a way that the history of European conservative and liberal parties does not – international as well as national politics. It is well known that in 1914 the alleged international solidarity of the European working class collapsed in the face of competing national solidarities. The collapse was a traumatic shock to the leaders of pre-war revolutionary movements – Lenin could not believe it when told that the German social democrats had voted war credits. What 1914 demonstrated to Lenin was the absolute necessity of a political organization that, unlike the Second International, would ensure that the revolutionary mission of the European working challenge was never again perverted by its leaders. When the Russian Revolution broke out, many in Europe both on the left and the right agreed with Lenin that it was only a beginning and that an international uprising of the working class was imminent. The international nature of the revolution was accentuated by the Bolsheviks' own belief that the Russian Revolution would be secure only when socialism was installed in an advanced industrial country like

Germany. Thus confidence in an impending global transformation and anxiety about the immediate future led to the creation of the Third International. In 1918 communist parties had been founded in Germany, Austria, Hungary, Finland, Greece, Latvia and Holland; in March 1919 the first meeting of the new International took place in Moscow; and in 1920 at the Hotel Lux in Moscow, the International acquired its institutional form as the Comintern and laid down the famous twenty-one conditions for membership. These conditions extended Leninist forms of organization to the whole movement and required all communist parties to subordinate their activities to Comintern decisions.[2] The urgency – and the realism – of this international imperative seemed to be vindicated by the flags on a big red map which every day charted the progress of the red armies towards the West. The world party of revolution would bring about the world union of Soviet Socialist Republics.

In this scheme, the external boundaries of the former Tsarist Empire were temporary – the future would be one of minimal units of national groups and a universe of communism.[3] What happened, of course, was the failure of the world revolution and the consolidation of Bolshevik power into the Soviet state. This sentence offers an explanation of what in turn happened to the Comintern, namely the degeneration of the world party of revolution into the defender of one country, right or wrong. Kolakowski argues that Lenin and Trotsky did not envisage the Comintern as 'an instrument of Soviet state policy. The idea that the Bolshevik party itself was no more than a section or branch of the world revolutionary movement was at the outset taken quite seriously. But the way in which the Comintern was organised soon dispelled such illusions.'[4] From the beginning, the Comintern demanded of its members unconditional support for the cause of the Russian Revolution, and Soviet Russia had a deciding voice in the executive committee which governed the International between congresses. These congresses, originally intended to be held every year, became biennial in 1924; after 1928 only one other congress was ever held, in 1935. The permanent representatives of other communist parties at the Moscow headquarters of the Comintern became, in effect, Soviet functionaries. Yet it was not organizational centralization nor even financial dependency that came to characterize the communist parties; rather it was the utter subordination of national policy to the dictates of Moscow. This process did not occur overnight but it was manifestly established by the 1930s. As far as the parties of Western Europe are concerned, the most famous example of subordination is the virtually overnight switch in 1939 from a strategy of union with all democratic forces against fascism to one of entente with fascist regimes against the liberal democracies. In 1943 the Comintern itself was abolished since it appeared to constitute an obstacle to good relations between the Soviet Union and its own allies in the fight against Hitler. Abolition, however, implied no relaxation in the tightness of Moscow's control, and in 1947 the coming of the Cold War led to the establishment of the Cominform, an organization of the seven governing communist parties in Europe (USSR, Poland, Yugoslavia, Romania, Bulgaria, Czechoslovakia and Hungary) plus the two largest non-governing parties (France and Italy).

This identification of communist interest with the state interests of the Soviet Union is indissolubly linked to the awful figure of Joseph Stalin and to his famous declaration that 'an internationalist is someone who is ready to defend the USSR without reserve, without hesitation and without condition'.[5] Proletarian internationalism was (and is) the polite name of the war game. Stalin certainly regarded the Comintern, as an institution, with murderous contempt. Many of its officials in Moscow were effectively stateless persons and perished in his purges or in the Nazi camps to which he abandoned them as part of his détente with Hitler. Yet it is clear that the path down which the Comintern would travel was already marked out before Stalin asserted his domination of the communist world. Thus the problem of the Comintern is only part of the wider problem of the relationship between Leninism and Stalinism, a problem that gives rise to a furious debate both inside and outside Marxism. The debate involves much more than the nature of the impact of Stalin on the other parties of the Third International – but it is that impact which is relevant here.

Stalinism did not mean that Stalin was able personally to control all aspects of the international communist movement. The two most prominent cases of communist leaderships going their own way in defiance of his instructions are Mao's refusal to collaborate with Chiang Kai-shek after 1945 and Tito's spectacular break in 1948. The drama of Tito's challenge has led to an overestimation of its uniqueness; other communist leaders after 1945 believed that their right to rule included the right to independent judgement, as for example in the plans for a Balkan Federation of Communist States and in the interest shown by Czech and Polish communists in Marshall Aid. This belief was quickly dispelled; yet it had existed and even the leaders of non-governing parties could, on occasion, thwart Moscow's intentions. In 1951 Palmiro Togliatti, secretary-general of the Italian party (PCI), was able to resist Stalin's attempt to kick him upstairs as secretary of the Cominform.

Stalinism, moreover, coincided with two periods when the non-governing parties proclaimed a political tactic very different from that of the USSR. The popular front period (1934–9) saw communist parties seeking alliances with many non-communist organizations and advocating policies hardly compatible with the image of Soviet reality. The Spanish communists formed a Peasant Anti-Collectivist League; the French communists wrote respectful letters to 'Monsieur le President Daladier', assuring him of their deep commitment to the maintenance of private property. After the war, communist parties participated in bourgeois-led governments of national reconstruction in Italy, France, Belgium, Luxembourg, Austria, Greece, Norway, Denmark, Iceland and Finland. The PCI played a large part in the drawing up of the new Italian constitution while Thorez, leader of the French Communist Party (PCF) worked enthusiastically for the Ecole Nationale d'Administration. It is precisely this 'co-operativeness' that leads Ernest Mandel to accuse the communist parties of being mainly responsible for the successful recasting of bourgeois Europe after 1945.[6] But it was more than just co-operation. Communist leaders in both Eastern and Western Europe asserted after the war that the Russian road to socialism was not necessarily the royal road. The PCI began its 'long march through the institutions'; the British Communist Party (CPGB) published in 1951 the *British Road to Socialism*; Thorez in 1946 gave his famous *Times* interview in which he claimed that the French communists would use 'different methods from the Russians in finding their own way towards greater democracy, progress and social justice'. Similar statements were made by communist leaders in Czechoslovakia and Poland.[7]

These statements sound a lot like what would later come to be called Eurocommunism, which is precisely why so many people reject the term. The experience of Eastern Europe in general, and Czechoslovakia in particular, demonstrated the utter worthlessness of all the talk about 'different roads', 'reconciling socialism with liberty' or whatever. The 1948 Prague coup continues to haunt all attempts to construct a genuine alliance between communist and non-communist forces, and François Mitterrand, once the leading European advocate of such alliances, said in reference to the fate of Jan Masaryk, 'I have no taste for defenestration'. More generally, Western communist politics showed – and this is as true of the co-operativeness of 1941–7 as it is of the intransigence that followed – that the non-governing parties continued to place the defence of the Soviet Union above all other considerations. Some of them went further and participated in the worship of Stalin and of his infallibility that characterized the communist world. Santiago Carrillo, secretary of the Spanish Communist Party (PCE), pointed out in 1976 that the institution most frequently used to describe by analogy the Communist International is the High Medieval Church; and it is not surprising that this analogy has become one of the most ubiquitous clichés in political writing.[8] Examples of the deification of the man and his system are legion – all those poems by Louis Aragon, men going to their death praising their executioner, Maurice Thorez rejoicing in the title of 'Best Stalinist in France' (one thinks irresistibly of Henry VIII as Defender of the Faith). The names most often associated with the last period of Stalin's rule, Andrei Zhdanov and Trofim Denisovitch Lysenko, still have an awful resonance about them. Not all the Western parties imitated the practices of the Soviet world but those that did – notably the PCF and the PCE – showed the intensity of their faith by organizing trials of the 'traitors' in their midst that paralleled those of Eastern Europe, and by exalting the capacities of their leaders. The style of communist behaviour in this period can be gauged from the letter which the central committee of the PCF sent to the ailing Thorez in 1952:

> Notre parti tout entier, faisant de cette année l'année d'études individuelles de tes études y trouve les armes et les moyens de conduire véritablement les Français à la victoire nationale contre le fascisme et les fauteurs de guerre. A chaque pas chacun de nous se demande: qu'en penserait Maurice Thorez? ... Nous te demandons d'avoir confiance en nous.[9]

Such language defies translation and belief. Yet the identification of communism with the Soviet Union was not, at least for the two largest communist parties of Western Europe, an obstacle to their electoral strengths, though it plainly isolated them within their communities. The PCF held on to the bulk of the spectacular gains it had made in 1945 and the PCI vote increased steadily. The fundamental point is, however, that even if the Western communists' intransigence had ruined their domestic position, they would have maintained it for the simple reason that it was their essential contribution to the defence of the Soviet Union. Two former communist intellectuals, Dominique

Desanti and Georgio Ceretti, make the point that what to outsiders seemed a slavish subservience was to them the reason for their existence.[10] Stalin was the Soviet Union, the Soviet Union was socialism; whoever attacked – literally or verbally – the first and second was attacking the third.

The identification of Western communism with the Soviet Union is horrifying to the majority of policy-makers in Western Europe and the USA, partly because of their assessment of communism as a social system but more because of their dread of Russia's strategic ambitions. Western leaders have no difficulty at all in signing defence agreements with communist states which are in conflict with the USSR. And the fact that communist states are in conflict shows that the view of 'world communism' as a monolithic, timeless entity is unreal. In 1960 the second world conference of communist parties made the assertion that 'there are no objective causes in the nature of the socialist system for conflicts and contradictions between peoples and states belonging to it' and thus proved the importance of the subjective in history.[11] Even before Stalin's death, Tito asserted his independence of the Soviet bloc; in the 1960s the Sino-Soviet split developed in such a way that the Russians appeared to have 'lost China' as thoroughly as the Americans had done. Tito's spectacular break owed less to disagreement over what constituted a properly socialist strategy (the Yugoslavs had led the attack on French and Italian 'revisionism' in 1947) than to his refusal to allow the Russians to control his administration. The importance of the break lies in the fact that Tito, a European communist leader, was able to challenge the Soviet Union, be supported by his own communist party, and survive.

Thus communist governments showed that they could successfully escape Soviet control. But this was not the only change to occur in the communist world. The year 1956 is remembered for the Suez crisis, during which Khrushchev threatened to bomb London, and for the Soviet invasion of Hungary, which demonstrated the fiction of a Socialist Commonwealth of Nations and the reality of a Soviet Empire controlled by force. Hungary in particular pushed the Western communists even deeper into the political ghetto which they had entered in 1947. The CPGB lost many of its most able members, for example John Saville and E.P. Thompson; the Italian Socialist Party broke off its electoral pact with the PCI, which lost 200,000 members in a year; the PCF excelled itself with nauseating articles about Budapest smiling through its tears the day Soviet tanks rolled in. Nevertheless 1956 is a crucial year in the history of the communist movement because of the two speeches which Khrushchev made to the 20th Congress of the CPSU. In a public address, he reaffirmed the possibility of peaceful coexistence between East and West based on the economic and diplomatic invulnerability of the Soviet Union. It would be too much to see this speech as heralding the end of the Cold War, but it did suggest a thaw in international relations whose first manifestations were the Soviet withdrawal from Austria (1955) and the dissolution of the Cominform (1956). And if the Soviet fortress was no longer embattled but *imbattable*, the activities of non-governing parties no longer needed to be so obviously directed to its defence, and the 'different roads to socialism' (which Khrushchev had conceded to Tito in 1955) became open to others as well. With this public address went another one, the now famous 'secret speech', in which Khrushchev for the first time placed responsibility for some of the crimes of Stalinism not on Beria, not on some anonymous cult of the personality – but on Stalin. The secret speech, which was leaked to the Western press in 1956, was an admission not only that the man whom all communists had worshipped was a tyrant but that the political and social system which had been regarded as Marxist perfection was not perfect at all. A Marxist analysis of Stalinism could not be limited to Stalin.

The conventions that had dominated international communism were, therefore, disintegrating in the 1950s. The political supremacy of the CPSU within the movement was challenged; the absolute identification of the USSR with 'real' socialism was challenged; and the strategic need to subordinate everything to the protection of the threatened homeland was no longer so vital. By the 1970s the diplomatic relations between communist states demonstrated 'the same range of positions – alliance, neutralism and hostility – that have marked historic relations among non-communist states; containment and power balances are now operative principles within as well as outside the communist movement'.[12] Moreover East–West relations showed, if not an international end of ideology, an attempt to transform détente from a practice to a policy. It must be stressed that none of the Western communist parties was primarily responsible for the changes in the political and diplomatic practices of communist and non-communist states and that the leaders of all of them, including initially Togliatti, attempted to stop Khrushchev's secret speech being made public. Nevertheless, the changing international and communist environment was bound to have consequences for the perceptions of the non-governing parties, enabling them to revise their assessments of their place in the international communist movement and also in domestic politics. It is with this revision that we are concerned.

All communist parties, except possibly the Albanian, devote much time and energy to public displays of the close links that bind them one to another. Part of the ritual of communist conferences has always been the sending of expressions of fraternal solidarity to the host party from other parties. Between conferences, telegrams speed back and forth between parties commemorating famous victories, shared struggles and so on. Such contacts are not purely triumphalistic. When the PCI omits any reference to proletarian internationalism in its telegram of congratulations on the PCF's fiftieth birthday, when the PCE refuses to invite the Czech party to its 1978 conference, when the French communist leader Georges Marchais declines to attend the 25th conference of the CPSU, a ritual is being given a political edge. The purpose is, however, primarily symbolic, to demonstrate the international unity of communism.

Such contacts have never, even in the days of monolithic Stalinism, constituted the sum total of the inter-party contact. The Comintern produced a whole generation of communist officials who knew each other and about each other, a familiarity which, particularly after the Spanish Civil War, proved fatal to many of them. The controversy over Marchais's alleged visit to a Moscow party training school in 1955 shows how promising young officials from the Western parties could expect to meet each other. A sense of the cross-national familiarity of communist officials and intellectuals comes over very strongly in Desanti's *Les Staliniens* (an account of her life as a PCF publicist after 1945), and John Saville has described the closeness with which he and his friends followed the Italian communists' reaction to the 1956 Congress of the CPSU.[13] There are other areas in which the international contacts between communist élites were made manifest in the 1950s. Desanti sees the origin of the so-called Marty Affair in the PCF in an article published in an English communist journal, the *New Diplomat*, while another former PCF official, Annie Kriegel, has emphasized the international dimension of the show trials that occurred in several communist parties, both governing and non-governing, in the early 1950s.[14] Kriegel sees, in particular, a connection between the Prague trials of 1952 and the virtually simultaneous denunciation of two PCF leaders, André Marty and Charles Tillon. Later on, it appears that the PCF leader Thorez intervened to obtain the release of one of the victims of the Czech trials, Arthur London, whose wife was the sister-in-law of another French communist, Raymond Guyot. The communist élites of the 1940s and 1950s had their natural share of internal and cross-national rivalries – Thorez versus Marty, Togliatti versus Secchia, Togliatti versus Thorez – and these could spill over into the Soviet leadership as well. The identification of the PCF with the CPSU in 1956 did not prevent Thorez from conspiring in 1957 with the anti-Khrushchev group led by Molotov.

All these types of contact – from the triumphalist to the clandestine – have obviously continued. What is new after 1956 is the emergence of a formal, apparently open diplomacy based on the premise that the theoretical equality of all communist parties, which had never been devised by the CPSU, is a real one, and that agreement must be negotiated, not imposed. If the Sino-Soviet split provided the occasion for this change, the PCI took the initiative in making it, at a series of world conferences of communist parties that marked what was once called the epoch of conciliar communism. The first of these conferences held in 1957 proclaimed the 'invincible camp of Socialist states headed by the Soviet Union' while the second, in 1960, marked the public beginning of the Sino-Soviet split. This split, which originated in the Chinese rejection of Khrushchev's doctrine of peaceful coexistence, rapidly got worse. Peking started to call Khrushchev a bald-headed coot and Moscow attempted to 'expel' the Chinese from the international communist movement by means of another world conference. Just as in 1947 Moscow had used another party – ironically the Yugoslav – to head the attack on French and Italian revisionism, so in 1963 it arranged for the PCF to propose another world conference. In a series of private meetings between Soviet and Italian communist leaders, the PCI revealed its objections to the idea and in July 1964 Togliatti visited Russia to try to persuade Khrushchev to alter his plans for an expulsion of the Chinese. When Khrushchev refused to see him (preferring to go on a junket with Roy Thomson) Togliatti wrote down his objections in a memorandum. Immediately afterwards he died of a stroke and his successor, Luigi Longo, decided to make the memorandum public. The result was the so-called Yalta Testament, which Keith Middlemas calls one of the key documents in post-war communism.[15] The testament said nothing that the Italians had not said before but it said it publicly; the largest communist party in Western Europe expected to be treated as an equal of the CPSU. The PCI was on the Russians' side in the dispute with China but it was not prepared to underwrite a Soviet action – 'expulsion' of China – of which it disapproved. The world conference was postponed and repostponed as the PCI position was adopted by the communist parties of Britain, Holland, Sweden, Norway and Iceland. Only seventy-five of the eighty-six communist parties attended the conference which was eventually held in Moscow in 1969. Five of these refused to sign the final communiqué and twelve more formulated reserves. For the first time, the disagreements were made public.

By 1969, as we shall see, the areas of disagreement between Western communist parties and the CPSU had spread far beyond the question of what to do about China. Also, a practice of bilateral and regional contact had developed between parties in which, once again, the Italians were prominent. As early as 1957 Togliatti re-established ties with the Yugoslav League of Communists and in the 1960s he and his successors visited many communist party leaders inside and outside Europe. These journeys were not just the traditional visits 'learning about the problems and successes of building socialism'. Though such visits continued to take place, the purpose was now to assert as well the autonomy of communist parties and countries within the movement. The deaths in 1964 of Thorez and Togliatti enabled the leaderships of the PCI and the PCF to move closer together; Waldeck Rochet and Longo met in Geneva in 1965 and set up a joint committee to initiate collaboration between their parties. Regional conferences of Western communist parties were held in the mid-1960s (Brussels 1965, Vienna 1966) and again in the 1970s (Brussels 1974, Stockholm 1976, Vienna 1977, Brussels 1978).

It would be quite wrong to assume that these contacts and these conferences were necessarily unwelcome to the USSR. Writing in the early 1970s Donald Blackmer said that the CPSU welcomed bilateralism as a way of restoring 'communist unity'[16] and in 1980 the French and Polish parties took the initiative in 'proposing', plainly at Moscow's behest, a conference of European communist parties that had as its sole purpose the affirmation of support for current Soviet policy at a time of great international tension (Afghanistan and theatre nuclear weapons). Yet this conference, which was held in Paris in April 1980, succeeded only in emphasizing what an earlier conference of European communist parties held in Berlin in 1976 had already demonstrated – the extent to which the CPSU had apparently lost control of several of the largest Western parties. In 1976 the signing of a joint communiqué by all the parties was made possible only because the CPSU accepted the omission of hitherto sacred texts. By not attempting to answer the question 'Are there any longer a number of basic laws applicable in all circumstances to the achievement of a socialist society?', the communique revealed the diversity within the communist parties; and the Eastern press showed the dangers of this diversity by systematically censoring the Berlin speeches of Berlinguer, Marchais and Carrillo. The disagreement was doctrinal and, therefore, to many critics irrelevant. What is impressive about the 1980 conference is that a move designed expressly to underwrite the Soviet position in an area not of Marxist doctrine but of great power politics, was boycotted by some of the largest (those of Spain and Italy) as well as some of the smaller (Holland, Iceland, San Marino, Great Britain) parties of Western Europe.

The shorthand word most frequently used to describe the 'changes' in Western communist parties is, of course, Eurocommunism. The history of the word has been very well charted by Elliott and Schlesinger, who show how a term invented by an opponent of Western, or any, communists, the Yugoslav journalist F. Barbieri, was adopted by many communist parties, both inside and outside Europe.[17] Barbieri started with the assertion of many Western communist parties that they no longer do what the Russians tell them and with their pledge that they will extend rather than crush civil liberties. He denied both the assertion and the pledge, arguing that 'a Eurocommunist Europe would definitely mean the Sovietisation of Europe'.[18] Thus Barbieri invented a word but denied the existence of the phenomenon for which the word was a shorthand. Within a short period, however, the most prominent leaders of Western parties accepted the word – Berlinguer at the 1976 conference, Carrillo in his book *Eurocommunism and the State*, Marchais at the March 1977 summit of the PCI, PCE, PCF.[19] The political values for which Eurocommunism was a shorthand had been stressed in a series of joint declarations, of which the most prominent were those signed by the PCE and the PCI (June 1975); PCF and PCI (November 1975); PCF and PCE (also November 1975); PCI and CPGB (April 1976); PCF and CPGB (May 1976). The Italian, Spanish and British parties also signed declarations with the Japanese communists, and other parties which have got in on the act include those of Mexico and Switzerland.

What gave 'Eurocommunism' its wider currency was plainly not the doctrine in itself. The activities of the British or Belgian parties have never warranted leading article status in *Newsweek*; the fact that the Irish communists continue to defend the Soviet invasion of Czechoslovakia, whereas the San Marino communists asserted a sturdy independence at the 1969 world conference of communist parties, is of little interest to those who do not read the (excellent) background reports of Radio Free Europe. 'Eurocommunism' appeared at a time when it seemed quite likely that for the first time in nearly thirty years the PCF and PCI would enter their national governments, and would do so through the impeccably democratic method of the ballot box. The PCI obtained its highest ever vote in the Italian general election of 1976; all the opinion polls in France predicted that the communist-socialist alliance was going to win the parliamentary elections of March 1978; even the PCE - smaller in terms of votes - was playing an important part in post-Franco Spain. The performance of these parties suggested that Western communism was on the verge of a breakthrough that had potentially dramatic consequences for the national and international *status quo*.

It was this that gave to the word 'Eurocommunism' its political sex appeal, an appeal which was of very short duration. From the first, many commentators agreed with Barbieri that the notion was meaningless. Others pointed to the inconsistencies within the policies of the parties that called themselves Eurocommunist, ignoring the fact that those parties always explicitly denied that Eurocommunist implied an overall codification of policy, still less an organizational centre.[20] The behaviour of the PCF after 1977 in national politics and after 1979 in international politics, seemed to prove that all its Eurocommunist statements were worthless - and so why should we believe anyone else's? More generally, by the late 1970s the political climate of Western Europe had changed. Not only did the PCI fail to capitalize on its 1976 electoral success (for the first time since the war its percentage share of the national vote fell in 1979), but there was a revived pessimism in Europe about the possibility of combining social change with political liberty. This possibility had provided the impetus for Eurocommunism; its decline, and the heightening of East-West tension that occurred after 1978, meant that the word lost not only credibility (which some would say it never had) but also topicality.

The fact remains, however, that the language of Western communist parties did change both in their dealings with the Soviet Union and in their statements of domestic political aspirations. At its most basic, the change took the form of criticism of certain internal practices of the Soviet Union. This began very quickly after the secret speech of 1956, with Togliatti's recognition, which he made clear to Carrillo, that a Marxist analysis of Stalinism could not be limited to Stalin. By 1963, PCI analysis of Soviet repressiveness (e.g. the ban on the publication of *Dr Zhivago*) had ceased, in Blackmer's words, to be emotional and outraged and had become normal and conscious; part of the Yalta Testament dealt with the suppression of basic freedoms in the socialist countries.[21] The PCF too started gingerly to disassociate itself from the cruder forms of Soviet intolerance. Party intellectuals like Roger Garaudy and Louis Aragon criticized the Soviet thesis on atheism and Zionism, and Thorez himself condemned the anti-semitism of a Moscow pamphlet, *Judaism without Disguise*. (It is a measure of the extent of communist conformism that F. Fëjto should call Moscow's subsequent withdrawal of this document 'an unprecedented occurrence in the history of the communist movement.[22]) In 1964 the PCI, together with other Western parties, though not the PCF, criticized the manner in which Khrushchev was removed from power. Condemnation of judicial and political intolerance and a willingness to analyse rather than eulogize Eastern Europe has obviously continued in the 1970s. The Italian and British Communist Parties both run institutes which research into the socialist countries and the PCE leadership, notably Carrillo, engage in flamboyant criticism of the USSR.[23] What appeared significant in the mid-1970s was the willingness of the PCF to distance itself from the Soviet paradise. As late as 1973, the French communists published a brochure which spoke of the authentic democracy of a country where people could vote at eighteen, where everyone participates in decision taking, where a Lip Affair could never happen because the unions would not allow it, and so on.[24] This sort of language disappeared from the public pronouncements of PCF leaders and the publication of *L'URSS et Nous* in 1978 was, for all its insufficiencies, a landmark in the disengagement of the PCF from socialism with a Russian face.[25]

Critics argue that it means nothing. They point out that none of the Western parties, not even the PCE, has pushed criticism so far as to deny that the USSR is a socialist state and that, once again, the PCF has revealed the whole thing to be a sham by withdrawing much of its earlier criticism on the grounds that it had been 'misinformed'. French television viewers of the 1980 Olympics were able to watch Marchais talking about the political liberty he saw everywhere in Moscow and comparing the journalists who sought to interview Russian dissidents with prostitutes. Marchais is not alone among French communists in his assessment of the Soviet Union. A recent poll suggested that 44 per cent of PCF sympathizers agree with the party line that the record of the socialist states is 'globally positive' and there is also evidence that many of the party's members strongly disliked the critical tone of *L'URSS et Nous*.[26] It would be wrong, moreover, to assume that the PCF alone continues to admire the Soviet Union as a socialist society. Ten years after the Russian invasion of Czechoslovakia, only a third of PCI members are prepared unreservedly to condemn it; in at least three of the Western parties – those of Spain, Britain and Greece – the leadership's criticism of Soviet policies had led to the creation of splinter parties, whose members demand total loyalty to the Soviet Union.

Anti-communists believe that the exercise of power by Western communists, should it ever happen, must involve the same political tyranny that characterizes communist government in Eastern Europe. They may not desire tyranny but they cannot avoid it. Kolakowski is quite sure that Berlinguer is sincere in his belief in the possibility of reconciling socialism with liberty but claims that he just cannot achieve it. It was all very well for Togliatti to condemn in the Yalta Testament the 'restrictions and suppressions of democratic freedoms in Stalin's Russia'; what he advocated – 'a return to the Leninist norms that ensured within the party and outside it a wide liberty of expression and debate on culture and art, as well as in the political field' – may seem no better than the alternative. Whether or not Western communists can exercise power in a way that respects the Western democratic tradition is, as already suggested, beyond the scope of this chapter. What is clear is that the larger Western parties have sought to construct national strategies for achieving and exercising power that go beyond a mere flexibility of tactics. Of such flexibility no good Bolshevik could ever disapprove, yet the Soviet Union and its more faithful side-kicks, like the leaders of Czechoslovakia and Bulgaria, did disapprove strongly of the Eurocommunist declarations of the mid-1970s.[27] The 'historic compromise' of the PCI is not just the popular front tactic brought back to life but the product of an Italian analysis of Italian social and political reality. *Eurocommunism and the State* depends on a sustained critique of the Soviet model of socialism not only for Spain but also for Russia. The Union of the Left strategy in France (a proposed governmental alliance between communists, socialists and Left radicals) may evoke the dear, dead days of Third Republic political romanticism, but it was much more a response to the political conditions of the very unromantic Fifth Republic. The response was plainly not imposed from outside and indeed led, in the mid-1970s, to a serious conflict of interest between the CPSU and the PCF, over the latter's support for the socialist Mitterrand against Giscard d'Estaing.

To say all this is not to say that the Western communists have become social democrats. The PCF intended to dominate the Union of the Left as a good communist party should, and smashed it when it ceased to be advantageous to the party. Questions of national political alliances, of the value of representative democracy as a separate form of political organization rather than as a political tactic, of the proper economic organization of a socialist state continue to divide communist parties one from another. The differing attitudes towards the EEC of, on the one hand, the PCI and PCE and, on the other, the PCF, CPGB and PCP show the extent of the disagreement. Within the European Parliament, the PCF and PCI form one group but have been split on many issues. Nevertheless the fact that Western communist parties interpret their national political environments in different ways does not mean that their strategies for socialism are imposed from outside. It is this assertion of the national that makes the events of 1968 in Czechoslovakia so important. There was, of course, considerable sympathy within the leaderships of most Western communist parties for the Dubcek experiment which became a symbol of the socialism with a human face that they already claimed to be their own. Longo in May committed the PCI to the success of the Czechoslovak reform programme, so too in June did Waldeck Rochet, leader of the PCF. As the disagreements between the Czech and Russian leaders worsened, French and Italian communist leaders flew to Moscow to warn against an armed intervention and Waldeck Rochet emphasized the concern of Western parties by proposing, this time on his own initiative, a conference of all the European parties. The Soviet-led invasion in August showed, of course, the Russians' contempt for the views of the non-governing parties, almost all of which condemned it. Longo was in Moscow when the invasion happened but was told nothing in advance while Spanish objections were brushed aside by the Soviet leader Suslov with the cold observation: 'You're only a little party'. Moscow subsequently gave overt support to pro-Soviet dissident groups within the Spanish, Greek and Austrian parties (the latter eventually withdrew its condemnation of the invasion) and gave tacit backing to the pro-Soviet criticism made by internal opponents of the Italian and French leaderships. This was offensive enough to those leaderships. Yet the real objection to the crushing of Dubcek lies not in this Soviet interference in domestic party affairs, nor indeed in the destruction of a form of socialist rule very acceptable to Western communists; it lies rather in the Soviet contempt for the theoretical equality of socialist states. The Dubcek government did not threaten to withdraw Czechoslovakia from the Warsaw Pact, nor did it propose to dismantle the socialist state, either of which would have justified in the name of proletarian internationalism the use of armed force to defend the socialist world.[28] By nevertheless invading a socialist state, the Soviets showed the unacceptable face of proletarian internationalism.

All faces of proletarian internationalism will be unacceptable to most policy-makers in the West – we are back at the beginning. Nevertheless there is a further shift that has taken place within some at least of the Western parties and which may suggest a continuing evolution of their political assumptions. It is very obvious that, as has already been suggested, the 'humanizing' of Western communism depended on détente but that détente, with its assumption of the international division of labour and its echoes of Yalta, could be seen to make more difficult communist aspirations of achieving national political power in the Western democracies. Already in 1967 Brezhnev was complaining to his fellow communist leaders Gomulka and Ulbricht about the intransigence of the PCF: 'Le P.C.F., étroit dans ses conceptions et qui ne voit que ses propres intérêts, a cherché à nous monter contre de Gaulle. . . . Qu'ils aillent au diable, tous ces partis qui veulent nous donner des leçons.' In the 1970s the cautious Soviet response to the Portuguese revolution further irritated radical communist opinion and at the 1976 conference of European communist parties, Western leaders – notably Marchais – rejected the equation of détente and status quo. What is interesting about the most recent evolution of some Western parties is their response to the darkening international climate of the late 1970s and to the apparent end of détente, symbolized by the Soviet invasion of Afghanistan, the crisis in Poland and the renewed arms race. As is well known, the PCF appeared to retreat into a position of total pre-Sovietism; the reports of its journalists from Kabul bore a chilling similarity to the descriptions of Budapest in 1956. Once again the world was divided absolutely between the forces of war (US-led imperialism) and the forces of peace (USSR-led socialism). The significance of Afghanistan for Western communism is the extent to which other parties – and, again, notably the PCI and PCE – refused to accept this Manichean view and instead saw the USSR as being as responsible as the USA for threatening world, and expecially European, peace. A worsening of international tension is due not to imperialism but to the behaviour of a superpower – in this case the Soviet Union – and thus the Soviet

Union is equated with the United States. It is a view of international politics quite at variance with that traditionally held by Western parties, and still held by the French and Portuguese communists. The contacts which the PCI and PCE have been nurturing with social democratic parties – in 1980 Berlinguer met Brandt and the year before the PCI Congress was attended by delegations from socialist parties in France, Belgium, Holland, Britain, Denmark, Switzerland, Norway, Sweden and Greece. These contacts are, of course, interesting for what they say about the 'alliance strategies' which were so fashionable during the Eurocommunist period and which posed the question of the extent to which vanguard parties can tolerate the sharing, and therefore the limiting, of political power. Yet their primary significance is that, at a time when the international détente on which Eurocommunism depended has weakened, some communist parties are continuing to seek agreement with parties who assert that Europe's safety is threatened at least as much by Russian as by American 'imperialism'. Thus European security and détente are seen as prior to – and separate from – the strategic interests of the Soviet Union.

Of course, the USSR seeks to use social democratic leaders like Foot and Brandt to weaken the influence of the Pentagon in Western Europe and thus is not hostile to agreements between members of the 2nd and 3rd International; while the fact that the most intransigent of the Western parties, the PCF, participates in the overtly Atlanticist Mitterrand administration tells us more about changes in French politics than about any 'change' in French communism. Yet it remains the case that some Western communist parties are no longer prepared to accept the foreign policy assumptions and practices of the Soviet Union. Between a Western communist leader like Togliatti who once said, 'Beware of criticising Soviet tanks; we may need them ourselves one day,' and his successor Berlinguer who has argued that European security requires the presence of an American nuclear shield, the difference of analysis is profound.

The international state system is still central to an understanding of the political assumptions of all Western communist parties; what has changed is the perception which some of them have of that system. We cannot deduce from this what would be the behaviour of even the most 'independent' parties in the case of a conflict between the two European alliances. Politicians and analysts will continue to urge that communists be excluded from the national governments of the West, and, failing that, that the French Minister of State and Transport

Minister, who is also comrade Charles Fiterman, Number 2 in the PCF, be kept away from military transport plans. Yet the fact that we may reasonably be uncertain about the relationship between some Western communist parties and the USSR is actually evidence of how that relationship has altered. In the old days, there neither would, nor could, have been any uncertainty at all.

Notes

1 E. Mandel, *From Stalinism to Eurocommunism* (London, 1978); S. Haseler and R. Godson, *Eurocommunism : Implications for East and West* (London, 1978); J.F. Revel, 'The Myths of Euro-Communism', *Foreign Affairs*, January 1978.

2 L. Kolakowski, *Main Currents of Marxism* (3 vols, Oxford, 1978), vol. 3, pp. 106-7.

3 M. Waller, *The Language of Communism* (1972), p. 144.

4 Kolakowski, op. cit. vol. 3, p. 108.

5 J. Stalin, *Sochinania*, vol. x (1949), p. 61. Quoted in C. Gatt, 'The Europeanisation of Communism', *Foreign Affairs*, April 1977, p. 539.

6 Mandel, op. cit., pp. 42-3.

7 *Marxism Today*, September 1979. D. Desanti, *L'Internationale Communiste* (Paris, 1970), p. 242.

8 Carrillo made the comparison at the conference of European communist parties held in East Germany in June 1976.

9 Quoted in C. Tillon, *Un procès de Moscou à Paris* (Paris, 1970), p. 76.

10 G. Ceretti, *A l'ombre des deux T* (Paris, 1973); D. Desanti, *Les Staliniens* (Paris, 1975).

11 Quoted in *Marxism Today*, August 1979, p. 233.

12 Waller, op. cit., p. 150.

13 J. Saville, 'The Twentieth Congress and the British Communist Party', *Socialist Register*, 1976, p. 3.

14 Desanti, *Les Staliniens*, p. 317; A. Kriegel, *Les grands procès dans les systèmes communistes* (Paris, 1972), pp. 30-1.

15 K. Middlemas, *Power and the Party* (London, 1980), p. 249 note.

16 D. Blackmer, *Unity in Diversity: Italian Communism and the Communist World* (Cambridge, Mass., 1968), p. 137.

17 P. Elliott and P. Schlesinger, *Eurocommunism: Their Word or Ours*, in D.H. Childs (ed.), *The Changing Face of Western Communism* (London, 1980).

18 ibid., p. 41.

19 S. Carrillo, *Eurocommunism and the State* (London, 1977).

20 The insistence on the importance of *national* conditions and traditions is found in all the bilateral communiqués of the Eurocommunist parties.

21 Blackmer, op. cit., p. 347.

22 F. Fëjto, *The French Communist Party and the Crisis of International Communism* (Cambridge, Mass., 1967), p. 159.
23 Radio Free Europe background report 17 March 1975 and 2 March 1979. The Gramsci Institute is properly called the Centre for Studies of the Socialist Countries; *Marxism Today* (October 1978) has details of the CPGB's Committee for the Study of European Socialist Countries.
24 Parti Communiste Francais, *La lutte contre l'antisovietisme* (Paris, n.d.).
25 A. Adler, F. Cohen, M. Décoillot, C. Frioux and L. Robel, *L'U.R.S.S. et Nous* (Paris, 1978).
26 I am grateful to Dr J. Howarth of the University of Aston for this information. Cf. too *Le Monde*, 20 June 1979.
27 The Moscow *New Times* published a bitter attack on Carrillo's *Eurocommunism and the State* on 23 June 1977, and the theoretical journal *Kommunist* in 1978 strongly criticized *L'URSS et nous* in a review entitled 'Against Distortion of the Experience of Real Socialism'. See also R. Lowenthal, 'Moscow and the "Eurocommunists"', *Problems of Communism*, July–August 1978, pp. 47–8. As early as December 1976, the Bulgarian leader, Zhivkov, called Eurocommunism a new form of anti-Sovietism.
28 Waller, op. cit., pp. 151–2.

4

Soviet attitudes to national communism in Western Europe*

Leonard Schapiro

Nationalism is, in theory, incompatible with Marxism since, in the words of the Communist Manifesto, 'the workers have no fatherland'. Some followers of Marx – Rosa Luxemburg, for example – tried to follow this precept dogmatically, to its extreme logical conclusion. The founding fathers of Marxism were more flexible in their approach, and their inconsistency of attitude on current political problems involving the national issue showed that they were more concerned with tactics than with principles. Lenin also understood the potential value of nationalism as a disruptive force which could be harnessed in the interests of revolution – to help in the disintegration of the Russian empire, for example.

There is a long history of the failure of the Comintern to understand the importance of nationalism as a force, and its ineffective leadership of the communist movement in the colonial world as a result. This was only altered after Stalin's death. But this chapter is only concerned with nationalism in the sense of the conflict between the national interests of a communist party and the policy of the Soviet Union.

It was precisely because of its disruptive nature that any manifestations of nationalism have been sternly discouraged in the national branches of the highly centralized Soviet Communist Party by all its leaders – in the Ukrainian Communist Party, or in the Georgian Communist Party, in the early years of the Soviet state. Stalin was ruthless in combating signs of nationalism in any segment of the communist party, and was prepared to go to greater lengths in this respect than Lenin. Thus, when the Tatar communist leader, Mirza Sultan-

* Part of this chapter appeared in *West European Politics*, 2 (2) (May 1979) and is reprinted by kind permission of the Editors.

Galiev, demanded the re-establishment of the former autonomous Moslem Communist Party, disbanded by the Soviet central committee in 1918, Stalin, with the aid of faked evidence, persuaded the other members of the Politburo to have him arrested – a dangerous precedent. He eventually perished, presumably in one of the camps. There were thousands of victims of charges of nationalism during the years of Stalin's mass terror, but it is impossible to judge what element of truth there was in the charges.

The central authorities of the Communist Party of the Soviet Union (CPSU) have never at any time relaxed their vigilance against the emergence of nationalist tendencies in the ranks of the party, even if they have not prevented it with the brutal savagery which characterized Stalin's method of rule. While fourteen of the fifteen union republics of the USSR (the Russian Republic, the RSFSR, has no separate party) and the various autonomous republics and regions have their own, nominally independent, party organizations, they are in practice as rigidly controlled from the centre as any regional or district Russian party organization, with the same central decision on all appointments and direction of policy. In the case of the union republics the normal practice is to allow the republic a first secretary of the local nationality, but to appoint a Russian as second secretary, with effective power of real control.

The fact that disciplinary action, such as expulsion or demotion, on charges of nationalism (usually described as 'bourgeois nationalism') occurs fairly frequently demonstrates that national feelings are far from extinct among Soviet communists. In some cases the nationalist motive is economic in origin – where a union republican leader, for example, tries to secure an economic advantage for his own republic, to the detriment of, or in conflict with, the central economic plan, which is no respecter of the frontiers of union republics. As in the case of the use of the Russian language, such economic centralism is dictated more by practical than by chauvinistic motives, though no doubt this is scarcely likely to placate nationalist resentment.

From the start, the Soviet Communist Party began to extend its principle of centralized control, which inevitably meant Soviet control, to the international scene. It enjoyed the enormous prestige and advantage over the nascent communist parties who composed the new Third (Communist) International in that Soviet Russia was the first country in which the capture of power by a revolutionary party had succeeded. The aim of ensuring the survival of the new Soviet state was readily acknowledged as paramount. The twenty-one conditions of membership of the Communist International adopted in 1920 virtually imposed on all parties the model of centralized control devised by Lenin for the Russian party, as well as the duty of rendering unrestricted support and help to Soviet Russia. In the course of the three decades of the existence of the Comintern, Stalin succeeded in imposing on the non-Russian communist parties iron discipline and conformity which made them into blind instruments of Soviet policy. They were expected to, and did, subordinate the demands of their own revolutionary policies to the interests of the USSR.

The dissolution of the Comintern in 1943 made no difference, since the rigid control by Moscow was taken over by an appropriate department of the Soviet central committee. But the first real assertion of national independence by a communist party came with the defection of the League of Communists of Yugoslavia after the Second World War, culminating in defiance of the Soviet Union in 1948, and expulsion from the Cominform (a short-lived Soviet-dominated international organization of some communist parties). Although for the time being the USSR could secure condemnation of Yugoslavia by other communist parties, it never succeeded in its undoubted intention of bringing Yugoslavia forcibly back into the fold, and, after the death of Stalin, was forced to patch up a reluctant accommodation with these communist rebels. The defection of Yugoslavia caused a major break in the communist world movement, since Yugoslavia offered an alternative model of communism to that provided by the Soviet Union, hitherto regarded as the only possible one.

But much more serious than the rebellion of Yugoslavia was the rebellion of Communist China. The Chinese Communist Party, led by Mao Tse-tung, had in fact achieved victory by ignoring Stalin's advice, rather than by following it. Theoretical disagreements between the Chinese and Soviet parties came into the open after Stalin's death at the end of the 1950s, and before many years culminated in a hostile breach. This was much more damaging for Soviet prestige than the defiance of Yugoslavia. The Chinese model offered alternatives to nascent communist parties in the underdeveloped parts of the world where the Soviet example was often seen as less relevant to their conditions. Moreover, the Soviet Union proved incapable in the two decades after the open breach in the early 1960s of rallying the world communist movement to condemn China.

The most significant national challenge to Soviet leadership of recent years is the so-called 'Eurocommunist' movement, to which the bulk of this chapter is devoted. But it is necessary first to glance at the significance of nationalist communism among the dominant parties of the countries of the Soviet bloc. There is not one country of the Central and East European Soviet-dominated bloc of 'People's Republics' which has not been affected by nationalist leanings which usually take the form of resistance to Soviet control, and an attempt to follow domestic policies which are inconsistent with the rigid pattern laid down by Moscow. The Albanian Communist Party (which alone among the bloc parties came to power without the aid of the Soviet army, and which operates in an area geographically separated from the Soviet bloc by Yugoslavia) broke with the CPSU in 1961, and with the Warsaw Pact in 1968. The Soviet Union proved powerless to do anything about it. Military force was used to subjugate Eastern Germany, Hungary and Czechoslovakia, and the threat of it to keep Poland nominally loyal to the USSR. Romania has to date (1982) successfully asserted national independence both within the Warsaw Pact (by refusing to allow Soviet troops on its soil, for example) and in its foreign policy. However, the Soviet Union is prepared to tolerate this measure of independence because it does not have to fear (as in the case of Czechoslovakia) that the infection of dangerous liberalism will spread to the Soviet Union, since the Romanian Communist Party maintains an iron tyranny within its own borders. The differentiating characteristics on national lines within the bloc probably causes little concern to the CPSU since the several parties are held together by the strong ties of economic dependence and organizational integration, and above all by the realization that in the event of an attempt to break away from Soviet control they would be left at the mercy of the powerful Soviet army.

The term 'Eurocommunism', which was given currency by an Italian journalist to describe the assertion of their independence from Moscow by some Western communist parties, is rejected both by social democrats and by the CPSU, and for not dissimilar reasons. For social democrats the acceptance of the term as a correct description of an actuality would be to recognize the position of the French, Italian, Spanish and other parties as a new and distinct form of communism, less objectionable than the Soviet form, and therefore perhaps likely to pave the way for an alliance which could prove fatal to social democrats. For the CPSU the very suggestion that there can be some form of communism in the contemporary world which differs from Leninism is unacceptable. There are other good reasons for rejecting the term. The Japanese Communist Party, for example, which can scarcely be subsumed under any term prefixed by 'Euro', has maintained its independence from Moscow in similar terms to the French (PCF), Italian (PCI) or Spanish (PCE) parties for many years before any of these three. Besides, there are considerable differences which become even more accentuated if one includes the Belgian (CPB) and the British (CPGB) parties in the category as well. There are, for example, marked differences of the extent to which each party is prepared to criticize the Soviet Union – and criticism of the Soviet Union has become the acid test of Eurocommunism. There are also important differences on major issues of policy. For example, the PCI is in favour of greater integration of the European Community, of direct election to and greater power for the European Parliament, and of the extension of its membership to include Spain, Portugal and Greece; and it is vigorously opposed on every one of these issues by the PCF.

Already in the 1960s it became apparent that several of the Western communist parties were finding it necessary to dissociate themselves from some of the more discreditable Soviet actions – no doubt having in mind the effect that unqualified support of such policies would have on their standing with their electorates. Most West European parties, for example, criticized the undemocratic way in which Khrushchev was ousted in 1964, and some sent delegations to Moscow to seek an explanation. The trial in 1966 of Andrei Siniavski and Julii Daniel (which signalled the end of the Khrushchev era of relative 'liberalism') evoked a storm of criticism from Western parties. The Prague 'Spring' in 1968 had the most dramatic effect. The PCI expressed support for the reforms from the very first and by March the British, French, Austrian, Swedish and Finnish parties had joined in. This enthusiastic support for the Czechoslovak reforms has persisted since then, as the reactions of the various parties to the tenth anniversary of the invasion in 1978 showed. (The only party which has changed its stand since 1968 is the now solidly pro-Moscow Austrian Communist Party, bludgeoned into submission and retraction in March 1971.) By July 1968, when armed intervention by the Warsaw Pact forces appeared likely, a joint delegation of the PCI and PCF flew to Moscow to warn the CPSU that the use of force against the Czech reforms would be unacceptable. The PCE conveyed a similar warning around the same time. It was therefore in full knowledge of the effect their action would have on communism in Europe that the Soviet Union and its allies invaded Czechoslovakia in August 1968, and evoked a storm of protest. Open criticism of the Soviet Union by some of the parties of Western Europe really dates from then.

The Soviet Union must have anticipated this development, and presumably felt confident that it could deal with the situation. A number of parties did indicate that they would find it impossible to attend a long-planned international conference of communist parties, scheduled to meet in Moscow on 25 November. But when the conference, postponed until July 1969, did meet, the CPSU did secure the acceptance by the majority (five parties did not sign) of the principle of 'proletarian internationalism', the long-accepted phrase in communist jargon for the supremacy of the Soviet Union within the international communist movement. There was, however, open criticism of the invasion of Czechoslovakia, and other signs of the erosion of Soviet authority, such as the refusal of all the participants, in advance of the conference, to condemn the Chinese Communist Party. The extent of this erosion became more evident as time went on. After the inauguration of the policy of 'détente' in 1972 even more serious disagreements between the Soviet Union and some of the Western communist parties began to come into the open. A spate of assurances by Soviet leaders and propagandists that détente did not preclude the ideological or class struggle, and indeed provided better opportunities for it, began immediately after the USA/USSR agreements were signed. These were evidently designed to allay suspicions that the Soviet Union was a satisfied power, and no longer interested in promoting revolution in Europe. Much of Soviet propaganda was certainly intended for internal consumption – conflict on the issue of détente among Soviet party leaders was only resolved by March 1973, at a central committee plenum. But that the propaganda was also directed at foreign communist parties was made evident, for example, by the publication in *Problems of Peace and Socialism* of an article by B.N. Ponomarev (who is the main architect of Soviet policy on Eurocommunism), which stressed that detente, so far from being inconsistent with the advancement of revolution, was in fact advantageous to it. For example, it had the effect of neutralizing anti-communism within the social democratic parties, of undermining the militaristic preparations of the imperialist powers and of strengthening the 'realistically minded elements within the bourgeoisie'. The main duty of communist parties, the article stressed, was to combat anti-Soviet criticism and to show complete loyalty to proletarian internationalism.[1] Ponomarev's deputy, V.V. Zagladin, made the same points in another article around the same time.

But the real barrage of Soviet agitation, both overt and private, opened up in connection with a proposed further international communist conference. A world-wide conference was first proposed by János Kádár at the end of 1973, and the proposal was endorsed by *Pravda* on 5 June 1974. The proposal met with opposition – apparently one of the fears of some of the parties was that the Soviet Union would once again try to use the conference in order to secure condemnation of China, and the recognition of Moscow as the sole centre of communist authority. So a counter-proposal was made by Poland that a conference of the European parties only should be held – the suggestion was endorsed by Leonid Brezhnev. There followed eighteen months of heated discussions and working parties in which attempts were repeatedly made to work out the text of a communiqué and the procedure of the final conference. Issues both old and new emerged as the main stumbling blocks in the course of these lengthy discussions. There was the perennial question of 'proletarian internationalism'. This was fiercely rejected at the outset by Yugoslavia, and thereafter by a number of the West European parties – and with particular vehemence by the Spanish party. The main obstacle to agreement in the case of France was the resentment by the French communists of Soviet insistence on the priority of state relations over revolutionary tactics. Several factors emerged clearly. One was Soviet opposition to the PCF's electoral alliance with the socialists. It was reported in France that Brezhnev had said in a communist conclave in Warsaw that the tactic of alliance with non-communist parties was not suitable for a time of capitalist economic crisis.[2] And a leading French communist, Jean Kanapa, in an interview in April 1976, criticized the Soviet Union for praising President Giscard d'Estaing's policy at a time when the PCF was fighting it because it would have the effect of bringing France back into the orbit of American strategy.[3] This complaint was not new. A year before, in *L'Humanité* of 14 May 1975, the PCF stated that the real point at issue with the Soviet Union was whether imperialism should be treated delicately for diplomatic reasons and international considerations, or whether, as the PCF advocated, détente should be 'consolidated by a more resolute struggle against imperialism'. Even earlier, in 1974, the Soviet party journal had attacked the leading ideologist of the PCE, Manuel Azcárate, for alleging that there was a contradiction between the state interests of the socialist countries (*scilicet* the USSR) and the revolutionary movement.[4] A further point of disagreement which emerged, and which was to loom large later in

Soviet polemics with the PCE in 1977, was over Soviet insistence (eventually abandoned) in meetings in December 1975 and January 1976 that the parties should denounce NATO as aggressive, and support the Warsaw Pact as defensive. This was opposed, reputedly, by the Yugoslav, Romanian, Italian, French and Spanish parties, who expressed objection to all military blocs. As events would show, one of the later Soviet criticisms of the Eurocommunists was their advocacy, especially by the PCE and the PCI, of a socialist Europe which would maintain a neutral position between the opposing military powers of the USA and USSR.

Another aspect of the Soviet position was made plain in a number of articles published in 1975. This was to the effect that tactical alliances with socialist parties were only permissible so long as the communist parties retained their complete independence and their dominance over the socialists – a Soviet principle well established in Comintern 'popular front' tactics in the late 1930s, and by the communist parties of the countries of the Soviet bloc after World War II. In an article in *Pravda* on 6 August 1975 (which attracted much attention because Brezhnev went out of his way ostentatiously to honour the author), Dr K. Zarodov, the editor of *Problems of Peace and Socialism*, in an historical article on the seventieth anniversary of Lenin's *Two Tactics of Social Democracy in the Democratic Revolution*, stressed several lessons for the modern scene. The revolutionary democratic dictatorship of the proletariat and peasantry, proposed by Lenin in 1905, is created by the masses from below, but this dictatorship ensures their leadership from above. Reliance on the majority is the first commandment of Leninism, but this majority is 'not an arithmetical but a political concept'. The modern compromisers (meaning the PCI and the PCF, though without naming them) do not even pay lip-service to the independence of the 'proletarian party', but are prepared to dissolve it in an ideologically amorphous organization. This article was, it would seem, mainly directed at the PCF and its deal with the socialists – at any rate it was so understood by the PCF which, of the three parties which replied to it (the PCI, the PCF and the CPGB), denounced the Soviet article in the most forthright terms. This theme of communist leadership was repeatedly stressed in a number of other articles, notably in one by Zagladin, who also indirectly attacked the Eurocommunists (without naming them) by claiming that Western allegations about violations of human rights were 'the ultimate in hypocrisy and cant',[5] though such allegations had for some time past been repeatedly made by a number of the West European parties.

That the CPSU had failed to persuade or browbeat the dissident West European parties into abandoning their 'heretical' course was already evident at the 25th Congress of the CPSU in March 1976. Georges Marchais, the secretary-general of the PCF, declined to attend as 'fraternal delegate', explaining his decision by divergence of views on socialist democracy and evaluation of French foreign policy. His substitute, Gaston Plissonnier, was unprovocative at the Congress, but proceeded to attack 'proletarian internationalism' and the Soviet assessment of French foreign policy at a press conference. Santiago Carrillo, the secretary-general of the PCE, also did not attend, but made an even more outspoken statement at a press conference in Rome. The secretary-general of the PCI, Enrico Berlinguer, was, characteristically, more tactful, though expressing clearly 'unorthodox' views. Soviet critics were also muted. Brezhnev gave a veiled warning against concession to opportunism, though another Politburo member was rather more abrasive. The decencies were observed. The rumbling dispute was there for all to see, but the CPSU evidently had no wish to emphasize it – perhaps it still hoped that the coming long-delayed conference of the European communist parties would result in agreement.

If this was so, disappointment was in store. Ponomarev, at a number of the preliminary meetings, had laid down the line which he considered the conference should adopt. It should stress, he told one of the many preparatory meetings (in Warsaw on 17 October 1974), that the progress of socialism in Europe was due to Soviet foreign policy, and especially to the policy of détente; emphasize the need to fight against the main instrument of imperialism, anti-Sovietism; and actively resist Chinese propaganda attacking proletarian internationalism, 'our unique weapon in the struggle against imperialism'.[6] On 20 December 1975, at a further preparatory meeting in Budapest, he emphasized that economic relations between the Soviet Union and the capitalist powers do not have the effect of strengthening the latter – a particularly sore point with the PCF; that there is no incompatibility whatever between détente and the class struggle; and that proletarian internationalism had grown even more important when so many divergent international situations had come into existence in the different countries of the Western world.[7]

But it was all to no avail. The conference when it met rejected virtually all the Soviet formulations. There is no mention in the communiqué of the sacred Soviet formula, 'proletarian internationalism'. The communiqué uses such phrases as 'mutual solidarity among working people of all countries', coupled with stress on the independence of each party, equality of rights and non-interference in the internal affairs of any one party by another. It contains none of the usual ritual praise of the Soviet Union, nor any phrase which could be interpreted as acceptance of the Soviet demand for the hegemony of communist parties in alliances concluded with socialist parties. The only reference to 'anti-Sovietism' is a passage deploring the harm done by 'militant anti-communism'. While communist parties do not regard everyone who criticizes them as anti-communist, they object to 'campaigns against communist countries, beginning with the Soviet Union'. In their speeches the Italian and Spanish delegates stressed the independence of their parties, their rejection of any form of inter-national centre, and the right to criticize such actions as the invasion of Czechoslovakia, and stressed the need for democratic freedoms. The French delegate, Marchais, as usual stressed the incompatibility of Soviet state policy with the revolutionary policy of the PCF. After ritual praise for peaceful coexistence, he said 'however we cannot accept any measure which, claiming to be taken in the name of peace-ful coexistence, would run counter to the interests of the struggle which we are waging against the might of big business for democracy and socialism'. For the CPSU, Brezhnev stressed the Soviet positions, but avoided polemics.[8]

While it would be quite inaccurate to discern a uniform, let alone co-ordinated policy among the parties mainly concerned (the PCI, the PCF, the PCE and the CPGB), there were certain aspects of their atti-tude to the Soviet Union which they shared. There is no evidence that any party has any intention of breaking off relations with the CPSU. Equally, no party is any longer prepared to accept, so far as its domestic tactics are concerned, direction from the CPSU, let alone to acknowledge Moscow as the international centre of the world com-munist movement, with the right to 'excommunicate' a disobedient party. Each party claims the right to criticize Soviet internal policies, especially in the sphere of civil rights or suppression of opinion – though the tone and the severity of the criticisms vary from party to party. (On the positive side, the Soviet Union can rely on the Eurocommunists to support its foreign policy.) It is also characteristic of every so-called 'Eurocommunist' party to profess respect in greater or lesser degree for liberal–democratic principles – how sincerely it is not in this context necessary to enquire.

Soviet reactions are examined below, but it may be useful to list what appear to be the main apprehensions of the CPSU about these developments in communist parties which until recently had in the main accepted Moscow's leadership without explicit demur – however reluctantly. Outraged vanity must not be underestimated in the case of a party which has for so long arrogantly taken its own pre-eminence for granted. But vanity apart, the CPSU considers criticism of its own internal policy as a very real cause for alarm, since so much of Soviet policy, both internal and external, is dependent for its success on deception about the reality of the conditions of Soviet life. And there is the added fact that criticism of these conditions from communists who had hitherto been fulsome in their admiration of all things Soviet is considerably more telling than adverse comment from those who are opposed to communism. The Soviet Union may well have legitimate cause for apprehension that the Eurocommunist championship of the civil rights movement within the USSR could bolster the case presented by their own internal dissidents, or, even more plausibly, a natural fear that the policy of the Western communist parties could strengthen the opposition to Soviet domination which is latent in all the countries of the Soviet bloc. Again, apart from natural resentment at the blow dealt to the authority of Lenin, the CPSU may well fear that the kind of alliances advocated by the PCF or PCI with socialists for tactical reasons may endanger the survival of the identity, let alone the supremacy of the communist party – Lenin's formula for communist alliances with other parties is, of course, one which guarantees complete communist domination (or, to quote the late Hilaire Belloc in another context, the union of the stockbroker with the sandwich). There may also be legitimate fears that a premature communist electoral victory in France or Italy would wreck the economies of those countries, or frighten the USA, or both; and in either case endanger the economic and technological benefits which the USSR hopes to derive from its relations with the capitalist world and on which the USSR is becoming increasingly dependent. More recently two other causes for apprehension have appeared. One is the spectre of China as a rival communist centre for both the control of the Soviet bloc and for the Western communist parties. The peril may, as yet, be remote. But if it materialized, it could both endanger the cohesion of the Soviet empire, and make it harder for the USSR to rely on the communist parties for support for its foreign policy as it has invariably been able hitherto. The other development which is causing alarm to the Soviet Union is a view which became apparent in the PCI in 1982: that a true disarmament policy should include dismantling of weapons by the Warsaw Pact as well as by the NATO powers. This argument runs totally contrary to established communist propaganda, which always maintains that only NATO weapons are aggressive, while Warsaw Pact armament is designed solely for the preservation of peace.

There is, however, another aspect of Eurocommunism which does not seem to have troubled the Soviet leaders excessively and is comparatively seldom referred to in their polemics with the parties concerned: this is the claim by the PCI, the PCE, the PCF and the CPGB to be the real champions of democracy in government, and of civil rights, which forms a vital part of their tactics. The PCI and the PCF have, for the time being, opted for a victory through the ballot box. The PCE, until recently concerned to secure legalization, is anxious to build itself up as a party of mass support, liberated from its past links with Moscow. The CPGB, with no hope of any kind of electoral success, has staked its future on its ability to influence ('penetrate' would be a more accurate description) the Labour party, and therefore has a similar need for a respectable image. The conversion to democracy was proclaimed by the parties concerned in a series of documents in the course of 1975 and 1976. For example, in mid-November 1975 the PCI and PCF, after talks in Rome, issued a statement which committed the two parties to give support 'for the plurality of political parties, for the right to existence and activity of opposition parties and for democratic alternation between the majority and the minority'. There would be continued 'democratization' of economic, social and political life, guarantee of bourgeois liberties, freedom of thought, press, assembly, association, religion, etc. At its subsequent 22nd Congress the PCF, which by then had followed the PCI and PCE in voicing criticism of Soviet violations of human rights, removed the commitment to the 'dictatorship of the proletariat' from its programme. Similar joint statements were issued by the PCI-PCE and by the PCF-PCE. (The CPGB made comparable declarations in separate documents.) All this seems to have passed with little comment from Soviet ideologists and publicists, yet a more fundamental inroad into the principles of Leninism can hardly be imagined. It is probable that the CPSU did not take the statements very seriously – Lenin made very similar promises before the Bolshevik victory in 1917, and so did the communist leaders on their road to power in the countries of what became the Soviet bloc. Support for this view of the Soviet interpretation of the Eurocommunists' protestations of democracy is to be found in a speech in February 1976 by one of the CPSU's leading experts on Italian affairs, S.I. Dorofeev. Dorofeev justified the PCI tactics of advocating certain specific freedoms on the grounds that this was intended solely as a means of winning over the Italian petty bourgeoisie. He explained that in reality the proletariat interpreted freedom quite differently from its temporary allies. Consequently there was no need to be alarmed by changes of this kind in the programmes of CPs which maintained a consistently revolutionary position.[9]

Before considering Soviet reactions to the appearance of Eurocommunism, it is necessary to discount allegations frequently made by both academics and politicians that Soviet policy in this respect is in disarray, that there are dissensions between the party and the government, or between the armed forces and both. As regards the latter suggestion, the evidence is overwhelming that the Soviet armed forces do not intervene in political directives and accept without question the leading role in policy formulation of the CPSU.[10] The formulation of foreign policy within the CPSU is strictly co-ordinated by the international department of the central committee of the CPSU.

The emergence of this department after the dissolution of the Comintern had the effect of bringing the control of foreign policy into line with all other issues of policy, which follow the pattern whereby one of the twenty or more departments of the central committee prepares the issue for Politburo decision. But a mere glance at the international department shows it to be of much greater prestige and influence than any of the others. Its head, B.N. Ponomarev – a high official of the defunct Comintern – has been a secretary of the CPSU since 1961, a full member of the Academy of Sciences since 1962, and since 1972 (the year of the inauguration of the policy of détente) a candidate member of the Politburo. He has several deputies who are considerable experts in their own right – one of them, V.V. Zagladin, a specialist on West European affairs, has played a prominent part in the controversy with the Eurocommunists. The international department has well-developed research staffs, and can call on panels of experts and on appropriate Institutes of the Academy of Sciences, such as the influential Institute for the USA. It is responsible for *Problems of Peace and Socialism* (or *World Marxist Review*), which has been one of the main organs in elaborating the Soviet view on Eurocommunism, especially through its editor, Dr K. Zarodov. But that is not all. The international department also plays an intelligence role, probably in co-operation with the KGB, and for this purpose maintains in several embassies – notably in France, but also elsewhere – representatives who enjoy a virtually independent status in the embassy concerned in their clandestine pursuits. The Ministry of Foreign Affairs cannot be compared with the international department either in expertise or status, and indeed the latter is responsible for all appointments and promotions in the former.

Soviet reaction to the emergence of Eurocommunism has, on the whole, been cautious and relatively restrained. It has, in the main, taken three forms: open propaganda attacks, serious ideological argument aimed at persuasion rather than abuse, and covert activity. The only known seriously critical outburst before 1976 was the one directed at Azcárate in 1974, which has already been referred to.

Moscow's immediate reaction to its defeat at the Berlin conference in 1976 was to pretend that it had not happened. For example, an analysis by Ponomarev of the international significance of the conference published in July pretended that the result had followed the Soviet line by means of considerable distortion of what in fact had been agreed about 'anti-Sovietism'; and by the completely untrue statement that the communiqué had followed the Soviet directives as laid down at the preparatory conference in Warsaw in 1974. He also, by means of a loose paraphrase, attempted to convey the impression that there had been greater agreement than there in fact was on the subject of international solidarity. A very similar line was taken in an article by a group of pro-Soviet communists a few months later.[11] The nearest that Moscow got in 1976 to a direct attack on Eurocommunism (before a diatribe by the then leader of the Bulgarian Communist Party, Todor Zhivkov, appeared in December) was the publication in the September issue of *Problems of Peace and Socialism* of the report of a conference which had taken place in May 1976. There was no mention of Eurocommunism at this conference, nor was any party attacked or criticized by name. But the purpose of the conference, which was held in Tihany in Hungary, was plain: to demonstrate that the Eurocommunist view, which was defended at this conference by the Spanish delegate alone, would find no favour with the overwhelming majority of communist parties, and thus serve as a warning for the Berlin conference due to meet in a month's time. Communists from forty-five countries attended: France sent no delegate, Italy did, but the Italian representatives were very cautious and tentative in what they said, and obviously anxious not to provoke controversy.[12]

Many of the speeches were devoted to emphasizing the value of détente: particular stress was laid on its role in creating improved conditions for enhanced class struggle and revolution. There was also general agreement on the need to draw all democratic forces into the struggle. One of the Italian delegates, Gensini, advocated broader unity encompassing a wide range of social forces, including social democrats, Christian Democrats and Catholics. This idea, which in Italian communist tradition derives from Gramsci, was not seriously challenged by the Soviet delegate Timofeev (who is head of the important Institute of the International Workers' Movement). In general, the Soviet Union seems much less worried about Italian theories on the need for a communist party to win allies and adherents over a wider spectrum of worker and intellectual strata than by the practical policy of the PCF (after 1977 in ruins, but in 1976 still in full force) of electoral alliance with the socialists.

There was much vigorous condemnation of anti-Sovietism – in other words, of the tactics of the Eurocommunists to seek electoral support by criticism of the repression of human rights in the USSR and the countries of Eastern Europe. There were tart remarks from some representatives about abandoning long-term principles for the sake of the tactical advantages of votes; and the Portuguese delegate aptly drew a truly Leninist distinction between real political strength and mere 'electoral' strength.

The dominant theme of the conference was undoubtedly 'proletarian internationalism', and the refutation of the suspicion in the minds of the Eurocommunists that the Soviet Union puts its state interest in reaping the fruits of détente above the revolutionary ambitions of parties like the PCF, the PCE, the PCI and the CPGB; and that therefore these parties, if they are to advance the cause of revolution in their countries, must go it alone if they cannot rely on support from the CPSU. But only one delegate, the Spaniard Pretel, even got near to saying so directly. The closing speech by Zarodov, reprinted in full, was mainly concerned to refute a charge which he attributed, tactfully, to 'bourgeois ideologists' – that on winning power the working class abandoned its class interests in favour of 'great power' interests; and he argued at length on the strength which derives from unity and co-ordination of revolutionary action, a view with which the overwhelming majority of the parties represented agreed. Zarodov also complained – ostensibly still attributing the tactic to 'bourgeois ideologists' – that one deduction made from the mistaken view that the working class becomes unrevolutionary when it comes to power is that the revolutionary movement in capitalist countries can be made more effective by dissociating it from the socialist countries – and that this explains why some communist parties in capitalist countries join in ideological attacks on the Soviet Union. The lines along which the future debate in the communist movement would develop became clear at this conference as never before. Zhivkov's attack a few months later (though it said nothing new) was even more robust, and echoed the hardest Soviet line. He attacked Eurocommunism as something put into circulation by bourgeois propaganda, and deplored deviations from proletarian internationalism – solidarity with the Soviet Union was the touchstone of internationalism, and indeed the best recipe for revolution.[13] But it was noteworthy that the most unrestrained attacks came in response to criticism of the Soviet Union, and there is no doubt at all that this remains the most sensitive of all the issues so far as the CPSU is concerned. In January 1977 an article in *New Times* was very critical of the French communist historian, Jean Elleinstein, for his outspoken strictures not only on the Stalin period but on contemporary USSR. But the sharpest attack of all was reserved for Santiago Carrillo, the general secretary of the PCE, whose best-seller, *'Eurocomunismo' y Estado*, was published early in the year.

The article criticizing Carrillo, which received wide publicity and is familiar, was beyond doubt the sharpest in tone, and the most personal, that the CPSU had ever made in this particular dispute. It was widely interpreted as a general attack on Eurocommunism: its very exceptional character suggests that there may have been some truth in subsequent Soviet statements that it was not directed at a communist party, or parties, but at an individual. Carrillo did indeed go further in his criticism of the Soviet Union than even Jean Elleinstein, and besides, Carrillo was general secretary of the party and not just a historian and research director. It was not, as often before in other contests, Carrillo's advocacy of democracy and freedoms that worried the CPSU – as Carrillo says (p.168), the revolutionary path to power has by no means been discounted, and no doubt the CPSU may have been sceptical about Carrillo's assurances that the PCE has no intention of becoming the 'dominant force' in the country or to 'impose its ideology' but only to 'contribute to the conquest of political-social hegemony by the forces of labour and culture' – whatever that may mean (p.129). Carrillo also refers to the need for socialist forces to gain control of the communications media, which does not seem compatible with his professions of democracy. But his main offence in Soviet eyes was his sharp attack on the Soviet regime: he refers several times to the USSR as 'totalitarian'; criticizes Lenin's mistakes; and in effect suggests that the Soviet Union is not socialist.

It was scarcely surprising that an onslaught of this kind should have drawn a violent Soviet riposte: Carrillo's aim is to divide Western parties from the Soviet Union; he has abused the Soviet Union in terms which even the most reactionary writers would not venture to use; he is deliberately anti-Soviet and plays into the hands of the class enemy, etc.[14] Both this article and the subsequent attempt to counteract the bad impression produced by such violent polemics among the Western parties[15] (a denial that any attack on Western parties was intended, but merely a defence against crude anti-Soviet abuse) contain what appear to be hints of an invitation to the Spanish rank and file communists to disown their secretary-general. This was certainly suggested by an article in *Pravda* (by A. Krasikov) which was distributed by TASS on the same day as the article in *New Times* was given publicity by TASS. (Krasikov criticized Carrillo's domestic policies, and blamed him for the disappointing results in the recent elections.) If such was the Soviet intention it was the result of a bad miscalculation, or of misjudging the Spanish character; the central committee of the PCE at an enlarged plenum which included eight communists who had recently returned from the USSR unanimously rejected Soviet criticism, condemned the method of 'anathema and excommunication', and enthusiastically supported Eurocommunism as the only way of moving towards socialism in advanced Western countries. What is more, the resolution was proposed by Dolores Ibárruri, the old Stalinist war-horse who had only recently returned from Moscow, and who had been wooed by Soviet propaganda in the obvious hopes that she would become the focal point of a revolt against Carrillo. It is indeed the case that there are still many critics of Eurocommunism within the PCE – Ibárruri herself is on record, according to the Italian press, of describing Eurocommunism as 'nonsense'. Evidently solidarity in face of attack and insult proved stronger than ideological disagreement.

But while the sharpest attacks were (understandably) reserved for the more outspoken communist critics of Soviet reality, more theoretical criticism of Eurocommunism continued throughout 1977 and 1978. The most familiar theme, played with many variations, was that in criticizing the Soviet Union the Eurocommunists were allowing themselves to be deceived by capitalist propaganda and falling victims to the imperialists' attempts to split the world socialist movement. This was the line adopted by two of the main articles of the year – the later one added for full measure the moral homily that 'sacrificing principles for the sake of tactical advantages has never given anyone anything except defeat'.[16] Particular indignation was expressed in *Pravda* in April 1978 in response to the decision of the PCE at its 9th Congress to describe itself as a 'Marxist, democratic and revolutionary party' and reject the proposition that 'Leninism is the Marxism of our epoch' – a familiar Soviet formulation.[17] The most important recent statement on the subject of Eurocommunism took place at a theoretical conference in Sofia early in December 1978 on 'Socialist and Communist Construction and World Developments'. Over seventy communist parties were said to be represented, though only thirty were listed, none of the Eurocommunists being among them. B.N. Ponomarev, the architect of Soviet policy on Eurocommunism, delivered the key speech, in which the main emphasis was on 'realistic socialism' as the key to world peace. ('Realistic socialism' is the latest euphemism for the Soviet regime.) The communist parties, which are the main defenders of peace, must never for a moment forget that imperialism is preparing for aggressive war at an enforced pace. The imperialists are now playing the Chinese card. Realistic socialism is the main defence against these aggressive intentions. 'Regrettably, the slanderous campaign by imperialism on the question of socialist democracy and its relation to human rights has led some of our friends astray.' While the socialist countries do not claim to have reached the utmost limit of perfection in the matter of human rights, nevertheless, as the great Bernard Shaw said several decades ago, the Soviet Union has already overtaken the capitalist countries by 'at least a century'. In the interests of peace, the Western communist parties must repudiate the imperialist slanders about the Soviet Union. Ponomarev went on to say that the Soviet experience remained a model for revolutionary progress everywhere. Of course, the CPSU has always maintained that every party must take account of the specific conditions of the country in which it operates, but this search for an individual course should not become an excuse for counter-opposing that course to existing socialism, 'let alone for vilifying it'. It is extremely harmful to 'attempt to cast a shadow on Leninism, to contrast it with Marxism, to narrow its role to a purely "Russian" doctrine'.[18]

It was not for nothing that Ponomarev chose foreign policy as the pivot of his appeal to the Eurocommunists since these Western parties, however critical of Soviet internal policies, have in the main stoutly supported the USSR's foreign policy. Some of the Italian leaders, no doubt with US reactions in mind, have given some sort of qualified or ambiguous support to NATO, but there could be little doubt where, in the event of a head-on collision with the USSR, their sympathies would lie.[19] The PCE and the PCI have both made occasional references to a 'neutral' Europe, in which neither the USA nor the USSR would have any influence, as a desirable objective. But this is so unrealistic an idea that the USSR, while very critical of it, can scarcely regard it as a serious threat to its policy. There is no doubt that in terms of foreign policy the Soviet Union derives benefit from all the Western communist parties, which is one of the reasons why an open break between the CPSU and any of the Eurocommunist parties remains extremely improbable in the foreseeable future. It also explains both the relative patience which the CPSU has shown in the face of very humiliating criticism from these parties, and the occasional moves towards what looks like compromise that some-times occur. For example, in October 1978, Enrico Berlinguer, the general secretary of the PCI, went on what appears to have been a peace-making mission which took him to Paris, Belgrade and Moscow. A TASS communiqué issued on 9 October contained what at the time looked very much like an agreement to disagree, since it enunciated the view that 'some differences' between the various parties 'must not be allowed to interfere with the strengthening and expansion of co-operation and international solidarity among communist and workers' parties of all countries.' However, the compromise – if compromise it was – did not last long. On 6 November, in an article in *Pravda* on the subject of the anniversary of the October revolution, V. Zagladin, Ponomarev's deputy, stressed the familiar Soviet theme that there are no new solutions for the attainment of socialism, and that the so-called 'Eurocommunists' are merely the dupes of bourgeois propaganda – a view which was indignantly repudiated next day by the PCI in *Unitá*. The speech by Ponomarev in Sofia in December (quoted above) also does not suggest that the CPSU has abandoned any of its basic positions.

So far as Soviet covert operations for combating Eurocommunism are concerned, little is naturally known about them. In view of Soviet predilection for subversive activity, and bearing in mind that the International Department maintains secret sections in some foreign embassies, this kind of activity may be assumed to exist. Its only visible result has been the setting up of splinter groups loyal to Moscow within certain communist parties – for example the PCE, the CPI and the CPGB. They have not achieved any considerable success so far. But they serve to remind party members of the presence of Moscow. Moreover, as the CPSU is well aware, there exists within all communist parties in Europe a widespread sentimental attachment for the CPSU, the mother party. In the event of an actual showdown between Moscow and a Western party a splinter group could provide a rallying point for those who lack the resolution to support a break with the CPSU. There is also the question of finance since it is possible that some communist parties are still in some degree dependent on Soviet subsidies. According to a recent study[20] even the PCF, which derives a huge income from enterprises of all sorts, could be indirectly subject to control by Soviet agents in the matter of the disposition of its monies.

To return to Soviet apprehensions about the influence of Eurocommunism. So far as its effect on dissenters is concerned, Western support for individuals is particularly effective when it comes from the left, and to that extent the Eurocommunist backing for dissenters is an embarrassment to the Soviet authorities and has in a number of cases been successful in helping individuals. But it is unlikely that Eurocommunist ideas could influence the democratic movement within the USSR, since its adherents have little time for any form of communist doctrine.

There can be no doubt that the possible repercussions of Eurocommunism on the bloc countries is a matter which seriously worries the CPSU. There have been repeated meetings of Soviet and Warsaw Pact ideologists and propagandists at which, reportedly, Eurocommunist criticism of the Soviet Union was condemned and a strategy of concerted action evolved. The latest such conference was held in Budapest in October 1978. Again, leading Eurocommunists pay visits to Warsaw Pact countries from time to time, and the visits are returned by the Warsaw Pact party leaders. Nicolae Ceausescu recently visited Rome and Madrid, Berlinguer has repeatedly visited Hungary, and there are other frequent contacts between the parties. Relations appear to be cordial, with constant emphasis on 'voluntary co-operation' and mutual respect for independence. Even more demonstrative, perhaps, was Carrillo's visit to Romania at the end of July 1977 for discussions with Ceausescu at a time when most of the other Warsaw Pact communist leaders were basking in the Black Sea in the company of Brezhnev. There is no doubt some cause for Soviet alarm that the inflection of Eurocommunism could endanger the cohesion of the bloc. Yugoslavia, for one thing, has been a consistent and enthusiastic supporter of the rebel parties up to a point – the point where Tito's support came to an abrupt end being the issue of championing Soviet and East European dissidents. No doubt Moscow was grateful enough for this to offer Tito decorations and junketings when he visited Moscow in August 1978, but, as the Yugoslavs quickly noted, the gratitude stopped short of the more practical economic aid that Tito was hoping to obtain.

Reactions to Eurocommunism, and in particular to the Soviet attack on Carrillo's book in June 1977, have shown a certain variation of approval. At one extreme, the Czech communists have been stalwart in their denunciations – many of the Eurocommunist theses are too uncomfortably like 'socialism with a human face' and 'Charter 77' for a government with virtually no popular support to risk antagonizing the Soviet Union. At the other extreme, Romania has been most forthright in the defence of the right of communist parties to independence, while at the same time being careful to draw a distinction between conditions applicable to a Western European country and those which exist in the Eastern European countries so far as civil rights are concerned[21] – which is not a surprising position if one bears in mind the repressive regime which Ceausescu maintains at home. Of the other bloc countries, Bulgaria was the first to attack Eurocommunism at the end of 1976, presumably on Soviet orders. But since then it has been rather reticent on the subject – even the *New Times* attack on Carrillo took ten days to reach the Bulgarian press, and then one presumes as a result of Soviet prodding. Poland and Hungary have both revealed guarded sympathy for Eurocommunism in their propaganda, though observers noted that criticism became markedly sharper in the party press of both countries after the visit of the general secretaries of their parties to Brezhnev in the Crimea in 1977. For the realities of the situation are that the bond between the bloc countries and the Soviet Union has little to do with sympathy or ideology: it consists of a high degree of economic dependence, close links between the bloc security services and the KGB, and the ultimate threat of military action if a situation in a bloc country should get out of hand. The varying degrees of support which the Western communist parties expressed for Solidarity in Poland after 1980 were no doubt of comfort to the leaders of that movement. But there is little evidence that such declarations of sympathy played any part in events.

The emergence of China as a power on the European scene is a further matter of concern to the Soviet Union. China has, so far, shown little interest in the Eurocommunists, though some of them, notably in the PCI, have hinted at their desire for closer relations with China – and it will be recalled that as far back as 1969 all of them rejected a

Soviet demand for condemnation of China. The Soviet Union reacted with the greatest suspicion and apprehension to the visit of Hua Kuo-feng to Romania in August 1978, and may indeed have grounds to fear that China might try to subvert the bloc and that in so doing might seek the support of the Eurocommunists. China was accused by TASS of 'undermining the unity of the Socialist states'.

During 1979 the familiar pattern of Eurocommunism continued, followed by a startling event in 1980. The PCE continued its familiar unbridled criticism of Soviet policy. Manuel Azcárate, in an article published in January in the journal of the dissident Austrian communists (the official Austrian party line being pro-Soviet), attacked both Soviet internal repressive policy and the CPSU's refusal to debate ideas either with its own dissident critics or with the Eurocommunists. On the other hand Berlinguer, with characteristically cautious fence-sitting, paid two visits to Moscow, one in early September and one a month later, when he was received by Brezhnev. The communiqué issued after this meeting expressed complete solidarity on all the issues of foreign policy supported by the Soviet Union, such as détente or the struggle of the people of Asia, Africa and Latin America for national liberation. The communiqué also referred to the value of co-operation between communists, social democrats 'and other democratic, including Christian' organizations for the development of social progress and international democracy; and said that 'certain differences in the position of both parties' need not prevent co-operation and international solidarity. In general the CPSU does not favour such co-operation with social democrats, but it is a measure of the confidence which it feels in the ultimate reliability of the PCI that the CPSU is prepared to tolerate certain eccentricities from Italian communists that it would strongly criticize in others.[22]

However, eight days after Berlinguer left Moscow, on 17 October 1979, TASS published a stinging attack by B.N. Ponomarev on 'so-called Eurocommunism'. This was in a report of a speech by this leading Soviet theorist at a two-day all-Union meeting devoted to ideology. Without mentioning any party by name, Ponomarev attacked 'the pitting of one particular model of socialism which has been directly influenced by social democratic and bourgeois concepts against that of real socialism, and in the attempt to deny the universal and historical significance of our achievement'. According to Radio Prague, Ponomarev called for a determined struggle by the CPSU against all attempts to revise Marxist–Leninist doctrine. All three

Eurocommunist parties repudiated Ponomarev's attack. The PCI even pointed to differences in the reporting of Ponomarev's speech in various Soviet news media and drew the inference (rightly or wrongly) that 'not even in Moscow is everything so "monolithic"'. The PCF and PCE were more outspoken still in their criticism of Ponomarev.[23] It may be that the CPSU's attack was provoked by the discovery that immediately before his visit to Moscow, Berlinguer had met Carrillo in Madrid as a preliminary to consulting with other West European communist parties, as well as with social democratic parties, with a view to finding a solution for the social and economic crisis of Western Europe.[24] Relations between the PCI and the CPSU have remained strained. They are likely to be exacerbated by the PCI's unorthodox views on disarmament referred to above.

But the CPSU scored a definite triumph at the beginning of January 1980 when the political bureau of the PCF, alone among all the West European parties, issued a statement justifying the Soviet military action in Afghanistan on the grounds that the Afghan people had called for help against a rebellion supported by American imperialism. (There were objections voiced by some party intellectuals.) This was shortly followed by a visit to Moscow of Marchais, the general secretary of the PCF, to be warmly greeted by leaders of the CPSU and to sign a communique in which the Soviet line was fully endorsed without qualification. The rapidity with which this volte-face was acomplished by the CPSU confirmed long-held suspicions that Moscow has some clandestine hold over the PCF, or over Marchais. For the time being, at any rate, Eurocommunism was dead so far as France was concerned.

To conclude, it is, of course, the case that the CPSU has had to accept a certain degree of independence asserted by the European communist parties concerned – mainly the PCF, the PCI, the PCE and the CPGB. How far it is reconciled to accepting this is another matter. There is no reason to suppose that the CPSU will abandon its traditional policy of using all available clandestine means to keep the unruly parties as much under control as it can – though the success of such means is impossible to predict. Secondly, it is clear beyond doubt that the main aspect of Eurocommunism which worries the Soviet leaders is criticism of the Soviet regime for its undemocratic and illiberal practices, though PCI views on disarmament may yet present a threat to Soviet anti-nuclear and peace propaganda. This is the only aspect of Eurocommunism which has shown itself capable of leading to an explosion on the Soviet side. The other aspects of

Eurocommunism – pluralism or acceptance of democratic principles, for example – have never given rise to serious conflict. It may be that the CPSU does not take the Western parties' conversion to democracy very seriously. But criticism of the Soviet Union is another matter. Western communist support has, for example, in certain instances been of help to dissenters, and a hindrance to the Soviet leaders in their constant efforts to minimize dissent, and to browbeat Western governments into abandoning their support for it. Even if the Soviet authorities can, by manipulation of the information media, reduce the impact of Western communist criticism on the home audience, they can do little about the effect of these strictures on public opinion in the West. There is also, from the Soviet point of view, the ever-present danger that Eurocommunist criticism could endanger the cohesion of the communist bloc. However, in the case of the bloc, the Soviet Union does not have to rely merely on propaganda, but has available – economic stranglehold, co-operation of KGB and bloc security services, and the ultimate sanction of the Soviet army.

So serious a factor in Soviet eyes does Eurocommunist criticism of Soviet malpractices appear to be, that if ever a break were to come about between the CPSU and a Western communist party this would be its most likely cause. However, everything points to the fact that contrary to the view expressed by some authors such a break is unlikely in any foreseeable circumstances. So far as the Soviet Union is concerned, its traditional tactics have always been to pursue several policies at once, looking for advantage to fall wherever it may. Whatever the disadvantages of Eurocommunism may be to the Soviet Union – and they should not be exaggerated – the Soviet leaders are not likely to forget two things: that in the longer perspective, the advance of communist allies in Western Europe can only work to their advantage; and that even if they are unruly at times, there are still many clandestine shots in the locker which can help in the exercise of control over them. However, from the Eurocommunists' point of view as well, a break with the CPSU might well leave them isolated and a prey to a left-wing revolt inside their own countries; or it might even, as Suslov is once reported to have suggested, drive them into the Western sphere of influence. Be that as it may, all indications to date suggest that no Eurocommunist party has any intention of allowing a break with the CPSU to come about, if it can help it.

Notes

1 B.N. Ponomarev, 'The World Situation and the Revolutionary Process', *Problems of Peace and Socialism*, no. 6 (1974).
2 Neil McInnes, *Eurocommunism*, Washington Papers no. 37.
3 *Keesing's Contemporary Archives*, 30 April 1976.
4 *Partiinaia zhizn'*, no. 4 (1974), pp. 54-63.
5 *Novoe vremia*, no. 9 (1974).
6 *Pravda*, 18 October 1974.
7 *Pravda*, 21 December 1975.
8 The communiqué is printed in *Kommunist*, no. 10 (July 1976); the debate is reported in *Summary of World Broadcasts* (BBC) of 2 July 1976.
9 In *Rabochii klass i sovremennyi mir*, no. 4 (1976).
10 See my contribution to *The Strategic Intentions of the Soviet Union*, Report of a Study Group of the Institute for the Study of Conflict, March 1978, pp. 12-22.
11 'The Common Cause of Europe's Communists', *Problems of Peace and Socialism*, no. 9 (September 1976).
12 See *Problems of Peace and Socialism*, no. 9 (September 1976).
13 *Problems of Peace and Socialism* (*World Marxist Review*), no. 12 (December 1976).
14 *New Times*, no. 26 (June 1977).
15 *New Times*, no. 28 (July 1977).
16 *New Times*, no. 38 (September 1977); *Kommunist*, no. 24 (December 1977).
17 Radio Free Europe, RAD Background Report, no. 80, 25 April 1978.
18 *Pravda*, 13 December 1978.
19 See, for example, the somewhat naive hedging on this question by Lombardo Radice in G.R. Urban (ed.), *Eurocommunism* (London, 1978), pp. 41-2.
20 Jean Montaldo, *Les Finances du PCF* (Paris, 1977).
21 See, for example, an interview with Ceausescu in the *Washington Post*, 8 July 1977.
22 *Pravda*, 10 October 1979.
23 Radio Free Europe RAD Background Report, no. 232, 23 October 1979.
24 Ibid., no. 220, 11 October 1979.

5

Foreign politics, Eurocommunism and national communist strategies

Annette Morgan

On 5 January 1980 (Georges Marchais having just returned from a semi-private, semi-political visit to Cuba and Nicaragua), the political bureau of the PCF issued a public statement justifying the Russian intervention in Afghanistan on the grounds that any country is entitled to call for help by an ally if it has to face unwarrantable interference by foreign agents. On the same day, a declaration from the Italian Communist Party leadership officially confirmed the PCI's uncompromising disapproval of an intervention 'which violates the principles of independence and national sovereignty', while a few hours earlier, the Spanish communist daily, *Mundo Obrero*, had adopted an intermediate stance, deploring the Soviet intervention but assuming that it had resulted from the Afghans' inability to free themselves from 'imperialism'.[1] Thus did the Soviet tanks that set off waves of fear and indignation round the world also cruelly tear through the already threadbare cloak of 'Eurocommunist' solidarity.

Historically, the Third International was the agency through which West European communist parties constitutionally came into existence, and the model of the Soviet Revolution crystallized all the hopes and secured all the loyalties of generations of their members: therefore the degree of differentiation now established *vis-à-vis* Moscow inevitably constitutes the acid test of the authenticity of an autonomous European communism, and this is true in terms not just of ideology but also of its operational capabilities in national and international politics. Other major foreign policy issues such as the normalization of relations with China, or the acceptance or rejection of NATO, are inextricably enmeshed with that of loosening the ties with the Soviet Union, and so is – if to a lesser degree – the form of the commitment to facilitate the liberation of emergent nations from the appetites of Western imperialism. Finally, the ideologically most original and concrete step of some Eurocommunist parties has been to locate the 'third way' between Soviet communism and Western capitalism in Europe, with the aim of recruiting all the socialist and socially progressive forces willing to use the available European communist institutional structures in order to build up a truly social-ist European polity.

The outcome of the debates generated by these issues will contribute in a crucial manner to the eventual self-definition of Euro-communism and will determine the future not just of the communist parties concerned, but also of the overall party alignments of their respective countries, and eventually of the viability of Eurocommu-nism as an international force. The stand taken by individual communist parties on specific issues of foreign policy is a good indicator of the reality and strength of the Eurocommunist pheno-menon precisely because of the very breadth and complexity of the linkages which it involves. First of all, communist party attitudes, like those of other political parties, must be evaluated in the context of national politics and historical legacies. It is not just a matter of a party's readjusting its political platform when its situation alters from a tradition of total opposition to the prospect of limited participation in government, as was the case for France and Italy in the mid-1970s, when one saw the PCF reconsidering the foundations of its defence policy and the PCI reassuringly advocating the maintenance of Italian membership of NATO. It is also a matter of a party's operating within a certain national political culture: the PCF's opposition to NATO does not, for the French electorate, have the same subversive overtone it might have for an Italian electorate because the Gaullist myth of national independence is popular with the whole mass of French public opinion. Similarly, the acceptance or indeed the advocacy of a supranational Europe by the PCI finds favourable echoes in the Italian electorate, which has long recognized the economic benefits accruing from the EEC and the safeguard for Italian democracy which an institutionally stable European Community provides. Divergences between various Western European communist parties must therefore be analysed with particular sensitivity to the con-straints and biases of national politics.

Secondly, once it is accepted that Eurocommunist parties have adopted the rules of pluralism, that is competition with other political parties with the overriding sanction of universal and secret suffrage, the shaping of their foreign policy programme is bound to be affected by their location on the political spectrum, and vice versa. The Italian communists have not, until very recently, had to contend with a strong Italian Socialist Party, and can with relative ease nurture amicable relations with other socialist parties without endangering their status at home. The notoriously thorny relationship between French communists and socialists and the threat posed by the dynamism of the Socialist Party (PS), far from encouraging a comparable flexibility, forced the PCF to emphasize and perhaps to exaggerate its anti-Western (i.e. anti-capitalist) programme, for instance in its very strident 1979 campaign against what it proclaimed as the threat of powerful supra-national European institutions slavishly serving the interests of multinational companies.

Thirdly, it must be recognized that ever since their foundation West European communist parties have been subjected to the stresses of conflicting loyalties to the Soviet model and to their own national personalities. The Italians are prompt to emphasize the Western and Italian founts of their ideological development, and their detachment from Moscow has been gradual and relatively free of traumas. The Spaniards, having experienced the cruelty of their dependence on Moscow during the Spanish Civil War, and most of their leaders having spent the bulk of their years of exile in the relative comfort of Western democracies, have gone furthest in proclaiming the irrelevance of the Leninist model. Conversely, the French Communist Party, which from its years of early Bolshevization to the era of Thorezian filial behaviour towards Stalin (including the painful endorsement of the Soviet–Nazi Pact of August 1939) and which up to its 22nd Congress of 1976 drew its strength from its recognized status as the 'eldest daughter of the Moscow Church', finds weaning from the maternal milk (however sour that milk) extremely upsetting, and has therefore undergone periods of sulking and even tantrums against Moscow, while being manifestly uncertain about its independent status. Hence, for instance, the recent spate of books by communist party members or sympathizers trying to undertake a critical analysis of Soviet society, or the insistence in communiqués that Moscow and Paris do not see eye to eye on a number of issues and are respectful of their mutual differences. This means that one cannot use a single gauge to measure recent advances or setbacks of Western communist parties in terms of autonomy from Moscow, and that the degree of convergence between those parties must be judged in a dynamic perspective.

Finally, there is no escaping the conundrum of the vacuity of Euro-communism as a concept unless it is shown to possess a minimum corpus of ideological and strategic cohesion, even though one accepts the national, political and historical brakes which limit the development of a Eurocommunist entity. After all, when they met in Madrid in March 1977, the leaders of the three major Western communist parties accepted the label 'Eurocommunism', and Georges Marchais in 1980 actually claimed that the PCF was the most truly Eurocommunist party of all! In reality, the picture in the early 1980s is one of fragmentation of the Eurocommunist front on all major foreign policy issues, or more precisely of a cleavage between the Italian and Spanish parties on the one hand, with their leadership concerned to build up a new foreign policy doctrine, notwithstanding misgivings among the rank and file; and the French party on the other hand, with the leadership veering back towards a conservative line which does little to alleviate the malaise pervading the PCF since the fiasco of the quarrels on the common programme. Reactions to martial law in Poland illustrate this diversity. After the crest of the mid-1970s which excited the curiosity and then the hopes of those who believed in the possible humanization and rejuvenation of communism in Western Europe, the hardening of East–West relations and the receding prospect of communist participation in Western governments have exposed the fragile nature of Eurocommunism. In the hostile environment of the early 1980s, Eurocommunism appears to many observers at best as an obsolete tactical move which allowed the parties to adjust their rhetoric to contemporary moods; at worst as a sham which temporarily masked their basic inability to match their policies with their rhetoric. But Eurocommunism was not an instantaneous artefact, and the policies which it advocated, on foreign as on domestic issues, resulted from a combination of changes in the international and specially European environment, and in the ideological and political systems of the parties involved. A recapitulation of these changes should help to determine what is fundamental and what is merely expedient in the character of Eurocommunism. It should also be noted that, as it now seems unlikely that these parties will be put to the test of government participation in the near future, the degree of cohesion and consistency of Eurocommunist doctrine will perforce be assessed on the basis of the programmatic output of the three parties and the nature of their expressed responses to international crises.

Recent historical foundations of Eurocommunist foreign policy

Even though some commentators like to trace the origins of Eurocommunism to the times of Gramsci or even Rosa Luxemburg, the main agent which made its development possible was actually the dramatic alteration of power relationships which led to a reopening and proliferation of communication networks between East and West after the arid years of the Cold War and of Stalinist intransigence. Three main areas of changed power relationships can easily be identified: relations between the CPSU and other communist parties (and regimes where applicable); relations between the Soviet Union and the USA; and relations between Western European states.

When at the end of May 1955, at Belgrade Airport, Tito received Khrushchev's apologies for past Soviet mistakes and then went on to receive assurances from the Soviet leaders that 'questions of internal reorganization or differences of social systems and different forms of socialist development are solely the concern of the individual countries',[2] he won a famous victory for all communist parties and all communist states. While this is not the place for retelling the chequered history of the parties which attempted with varying degrees of success to loosen their ties with Moscow, it should be noted that a succession of events have shaken the supremacy of the Soviet Union in its own ideological sphere of influence. The most damaging of those has been the growing enmity between Moscow and Peking, so that any third communist party's rapprochement with Peking is necessarily treated with great apprehension by Moscow. At the same time, the Soviet Union cannot recant on the doctrine of the legitimacy of 'national paths' to socialism which was solemnly endorsed at the CPSU's 20th Congress – even though it was greatly threatened by the Brezhnev doctrine of 1968 – and which has allowed certain communist regimes either to remain proudly independent of the Soviet Union like Yugoslavia, or to engage in a fairly independent foreign policy like Romania (which even disapproved of the Soviet intervention of Afghanistan).[3] It has also allowed the Italians tenaciously to uphold and apply the doctrine of 'polycentrism' in a climate of singular tolerance on the part of the Soviet leadership.

This relative decline of Soviet power within the communist world has to a certain extent been compensated by a perceivable lessening of tension between the superpowers. Not only did the 20th CPSU Congress adopt the concept of 'peaceful coexistence' which defused the issue of competition between communism and capitalism by transferring it from a military–territorial conflict (stabilized by the NATO-Warsaw Pact equilibrium) to a struggle for politico-economic influence, but it greatly facilitated the resumption of communications between the two blocs, and even produced agreements such as the

Test Ban Treaty and the Non-Proliferation Treaty, SALT I, and the CSCE agreement. Furthermore, the fissiparousness of the Soviet bloc was matched by that of the Western bloc, in which various tensions have laid open serious differences between the USA and their European partners, from the Vietnam war to the regulation of international trade competition, to relations with the Middle East, and to the conduct of the North–South Dialogue, to name but a few issues. These various assaults on the bipolar system of the first two post-war decades have enabled West European states to distance themselves diplomatically and economically from the Washington nerve centre, so that the two superpowers appear to have lessened their grip (albeit in very different styles and to a very different extent) on their allied subsystems, thus allowing for a good deal more flexibility in diplomatic postures and the consolidation of channels of communication by-passing Moscow and Washington.

The European Community has been the most notable new terminal for these channels of communication. The institutional development, economic performance and international status of the Community could not be disregarded by the Soviet bloc, which reacted with a predictable mixture of conservatism and pragmatism. It demonstrated its official hostility to the EEC by refusing to open official diplomatic relations, but, subjected to a combination of external East European and internal economic pressures, it has accommodated an increasing if limited number of advantageous trade negotiations to the extent that some of the ensuing transactions have generated some degree of political irritation in the West. However tainted with liberal economic policies and subjection to capitalist interests, the European Community, from a communist point of view, offers at the very least a negative potential of setting limits to American hegemony in the West. As a dense and now well-established network of administrative co-ordination and political communication, it could even provide the backbone of a new progressive society, should Western European electorates respond to appeals for a 'left-wing democratic front' and should governments thus elected generate a strong enough political will to revitalize and radicalize the existing institutions.

To those who consider these views as utopian, it might be retorted that communist parties of Western Europe have already gone a very long way towards accepting that the new international order requires a new set of political goals and a new code of behaviour. Having recognized not only the permanent character of post-industrial democracies for Western Europe but the strong attachment of their citizens to the political freedoms inherent in these regimes, Eurocommunists have worked the respect of those freedoms into one of their most pressing motivations for rejecting the Soviet model of socialism and for disengaging themselves from the Soviet bloc in international politics. Protest against the violation of the right of self-determination triggered off a reaction of defiance against the Soviet Union after the 1968 intervention in Czechoslovakia, and a growing aversion for Soviet disregard and repression of basic individual rights effectively undermined the emotional attachment which Western communists had traditionally demonstrated for the regime which had liberated its people from tsarist slavery. Despite its partial failure to convince some non-communists of its genuine character and some communists of its validity, this well-publicized process of conversion which took place in the post-1968 decade decisively increased the credibility of communist parties as partners in coalition governments. This in turn forced Eurocommunists to revise their foreign policy programmes to make them at least reconcilable with those of their potential partners in government, all of which required, notwithstanding certain historical differences in the respective national outlooks, an avoidance of any policies likely to modify the *status quo* of East–West equilibrium. The now receding prospect of communist participation in government has tended to sharpen mercilessly the differences both between and within communist parties of the West, which can no longer let their postures be explained away by the constraints either of unquestioning endorsement of Soviet command or of submitting to democratic accountability. Having evaded the test of governmental responsibility, they now stand to be judged on the consistency and sincerity of their foreign policy programmes taken at their face value, and this exposure has so far revealed a widening gap between on the one hand the Spanish and Italian parties, which have gone furthest in the same direction, and on the other hand the French party, which seems to be pulled in opposite directions at the same time.

There are three areas of major sensitivity for Eurocommunists located in the West but ideologically committed in the East: relations with the Soviet Union and the communist political systems; relations with the USA and the Atlantic defence system; and relations with the European Community. Whereas the geographical and strategic boundaries of these areas are sharply defined, their ideological, political and economic implications, while subject to question within these boundaries, extend well beyond them, and it is precisely this phenomenon of non-coincidence which gives Eurocommunism its developmental potential but renders it vulnerable to different and even conflicting points of view.

Implications of a changed relationship
with the Soviet Union

In practice, Eurocommunist parties reveal the state of their relationship with the Soviet Union by the frequency and publicity of their contacts with Soviet leaders, by the degree of approval of Soviet foreign policy initiatives, and by the degree of similarity of their own networks of international relationships with that of the Soviet Union.

On these three counts, the French Communist Party is undoubtedly the least estranged from the Soviet Union, particularly since the general election of March 1978. After the débâcle of the common programme and the ensuing electoral defeat, the PCF compensated for its political isolation in the country by activating its historical reflex of tightening up its links with its ideological fatherland.[4] Since March 1978, the PCF has shown its concern to demonstrate its loyalty to the Soviet Union on three main occasions. First of all, the 23rd Congress in May 1979, in sharp contrast to the momentous 22nd Congress, was a very perfunctory affair which satisfied nobody. While confirming the Eurocommunist vocation of the party, Georges Marchais maintained that the balance-sheet of East European socialist regimes was 'globally positive' and that on a world scale socialism was gaining ground to the detriment of capitalism: he thus endorsed the Soviet concept of socialism. The organizers of the Congress noticeably failed to take advantage of the presence of an official Czech delegation to mention, let alone to protest against, the trial of the Charter 77 militants in spite of previous repeated requests by French militants that the PCF should do so. The Chinese invasion of Vietnam of the previous February was naturally condemned – an opposite judgement to that passed on Vietnamese intervention in Kampuchea – and Chinese leaders were also warned against pointing to the Soviet Union as the principal enemy.

The mood of sorrow with which the French communists greeted the Chinese aggression in Vietnam was not transferred to Afghanistan some seven months later. A fortnight after the Russian intervention a French delegation visited Moscow, and even though Georges Marchais met Brezhnev three times, and must have at least alluded to recent events, the official communiqué made absolutely no mention of Afghanistan. The French party leadership's approval of Soviet foreign policy, first muted then explicit, was not easily accepted by some militants, and their dismay is well illustrated in an article by a communist intellectual, Yvonne Quilès, writing: 'We are told ... that Kabul and Prague are not the same thing. In reality, what is not the same is the attitude of the PCF. On Prague, it had refused to believe the Soviets, on Kabul it believed them, that is all there is to it!'[5] This attitude was all the more indicative of the isolation of the PCF, as not only 'Western' parties such as the PCI and PCE condemned the Soviet Union, but also Yugoslavia and Romania. Unrepentant, Georges Marchais carried his enthusiasm for Soviet dynamism into the sports arena by his conspicuous presence at the Moscow Olympic Games where he out-Frenched the French in his devotion to national colours.

Meanwhile, the French and Polish Communist Parties jointly organized a conference of European communist parties which was held in Paris at the end of April 1980. The theme of the conference was deliberately limited to 'peace and disarmament', and the conference predictably turned into a paean of praise for the 'peace-loving' communist movements of the world, devoid of any critical analysis of recent international developments. None of the British, Dutch, Italian, Spanish or Swedish Communist Parties sent delegates, and Belgium and Switzerland only had observers. From beyond the Iron Curtain, there were no representatives from Àlbania, Romania or Yugoslavia. Whether through deliberate planning or not, the star of the show was the leader of the Soviet delegation, Ponomarev, who reminded his docile audience that there could not be any third path between those of the Warsaw Pact and NATO. Everyone kept cannily silent over Afghanistan, thus negating any force of conviction which might have inspired the appeal of 'Letter of Peace', the only official document to come out of the conference. The French political scientist, Lilly Marcou, rightly remarked on the Zhdanovian character of the whole performance.[6]

It is all very well for official communiqués like that of January 1980 to underline that the PCF and the CPSU do not see eye to eye on numerous issues and are anxious to preserve and respect their mutual differences, or for Marchais to insist at public meetings or elsewhere that 'the PCF is indefectibly attached to Eurocommunism', but then he immediately redefines Eurocommunism as 'the struggle against capital, for political, economic and social transformations',[7] which empties the concept of any meaning. Only by such rhetorical contortions can the PCF maintain a claim to some Eurocommunist autonomy from Moscow, but in fact the April 1980 conference blatantly located the PCF as the westernmost island (together with the Portuguese Communist Party) of the Soviet archipelago. The French inconsistency stands in sharp contrast to the Italian determination to formulate and develop an original Eurocommunist foreign policy doctrine distinct from, and if necessary opposed to, a Soviet-dominated outlook. The electoral setback of 1979, which must be attributed at least in part to some communists' distress at Berlinguer's overt lack of loyalty to the Soviet Union, did not deter the Italian party leadership from pursuing an independent course and *de facto* heading and encouraging a movement towards the regrouping of all 'progressive' European forces genuinely concerned to find the 'third path' which was specifically denounced by Ponomarev.

Like all Western communist parties, the PCI is subjected to a combination of contrary forces extending from those 'Stalinist' members who even deplored the condemnation of Soviet intervention in Czechoslovakia to the uncompromising critics who consider Soviet foreign policy not just as suspect, but as downright imperialistic with no mitigating circumstances. This may explain the zig-zag path of the PCI's behaviour towards the Soviet Union, sympathetic and friendly in 1979, uncompromisingly and almost provocatively critical and aloof in 1980.

Even before the election of June 1979, which confirmed a worrying disaffection of the younger and poorer electorate from the PCI, Berlinguer's speech at the 15th Party Congress in March was characterized by an attempt to sound conciliatory. Worried by the 'crisis of détente', he roundly condemned any foreign interference in the affairs of any state, and called for a new internationalism based on recognition of diversity and on respect for the autonomy of each communist party, and rallying all revolutionary and progressive forces. When it came to specific statements, he expressed concern at Chinese foreign policy which had patently violated the principle of non-interference against Vietnam, and which upheld the view that the Soviet Union was China's worst enemy. This statement was all the more significant as it was delivered in the presence of the Chinese ambassador, attending an Italian Communist Party Congress for the first time ever. It was clear that Berlinguer wanted at the same time to start a process of normalizing relations with China without offending and worrying the Soviet Union.

In the summer of 1979, Berlinguer spent a holiday in the Soviet

Union (East European resorts are traditionally great favourites with Western European communist leaders) and met Brezhnev in early September. The published communiqué emphasized Berlinguer's appreciation of the achievements of the Soviet people in the fields of economy, science, culture and society and totally ignored any contentious issues which might have clouded the friendly atmosphere of the meeting (whereas on a similar occasion in 1978 the communiqué had been explicit on divergences between the two parties). Berlinguer returned home having once more secured the friendliness and tolerance of Moscow towards his commitment to an independent line. Or so it seemed.

The Soviets having shown no regard at all for Berlinguer's sacrosanct principle of non-interference in the affairs of other countries, the leadership of the PCI was prompted to express its clear and unequivocal condemnation of the Soviet invasion of Afghanistan as an 'unacceptable violation of the principles of sovereignty, of independence and of non-interference in internal affairs which must form the basis of relations between states and must be adhered to in all circumstances'.[8] This proved to be the watershed in the relationship between the Soviet Union and the PCI. As the latter saw it, not only had the Soviet Union comtemptibly disregarded and destroyed Afghan independence, but she had also irresponsibly endangered détente between East and West.

Italian disapproval of the Soviet Union has hardened the PCI's posture in two major ways. It refused to take part in the European communist parties' meeting in Paris in April 1980 as contrary to the PCI's policy of non-alignment with any bloc and it completed the normalization of relations with China. Not only had the Italians and Chinese extended mutual invitations to each other's social functions, but Italian journalists and delegations started visiting China in the 1979–80 winter, culminating with Berlinguer's own official visit to Peking in mid-April. On this occasion again, Berlinguer argued that the new friendship between the two parties, far from being an act of enmity towards any other, was a positive contribution to a better understanding and increased co-operation between all parties. For all these protestations of good will, nobody could fail to notice that all of a sudden Peking had become closer to Rome than Paris at the very time when the distance between Paris and Moscow had considerably shrunk. The myth of a unified Eurocommunist policy was thus exploded, but so was that of the automatic primacy of Moscow over Peking for West European communist parties.

The denunciation of the Soviet Union as a valid model and trend-setter for Western parties was first and most exhaustively publicized by the Spanish leader, Santiago Carrillo, in 1977. Whereas, with a share of rather less than 10 per cent of the Spanish vote, the PCE is even less likely to become a party of government than the PCI or the PCF in the foreseeable future, Carrillo has acquired considerable international stature not just as a theoretician of Eurocommunism but as a very sanguine advocate of an independent foreign policy. In this context, the PCI and the PCE follow parallel or even convergent paths. Going even further than Berlinguer, Carrillo in February 1979 roundly condemned both the Vietnamese invasion of Kampuchea and the Chinese invasion of Vietnam as identical in essence to the Russian invasion of Czechoslovakia in 1968: nothing could ever justify the invasion of a socialist country by another socialist country.

Even before, but still more so since its legalization in April 1977, the PCE's foreign policy could without exaggeration be characterized as aggressively moderate, except at the level of personal relations between Carrillo and the Soviet leaders which have been, quite simply, aggressively inimical. Mutual recriminations are carried over by the respective organs *Mundo Obrero* and *Novoye Vremya*, perhaps in a curious attempt literally to hammer out the differences between the two parties, since relations have not been severed but on the contrary an intermittent stream of delegations keep open the channel between Moscow and Madrid. Not unlike the Italian leadership in Italy, the Spanish leadership in Spain has failed to quash the nostalgia of some militants for Soviet communism, and a total break with Moscow would certainly be considered as dangerously compromising Eurocommunist (Spanish-style) autonomy between East and West. That is why the first condemnation by Madrid of the Afghan invasion was tempered by a negative reference to Afghanistan's inability to free itself from the clutches of imperialism. The tactical justification for Carrillo's reiteration of his condemnation in much more forthright terms a month later was the potential threat to the *status quo* by the Soviet Union, accused of 'hegemonism' and 'expansionism'.

The logical consequence of the Carrillo analysis was the PCE's refusal to attend the European communists' Paris meeting of April 1980. Again, like Berlinguer, Carrillo estimated that the very membership of that meeting would preclude it from holding independent views and would tilt the balance of forces towards the Warsaw Pact constellation, thus contributing to a further deterioration of East–West détente and undermining the communist goal of preserving peace.

The Spanish and Italian positions, though not totally identical, are very close, and getting even closer now that Berlinguer's defiance of Moscow could be the signal of a new departure for Eurocommunism. This negative element cannot on its own nurture a new doctrine, but it is a pre-condition for the acceptance by the West of a Eurocommunist partner which might eventually play a governmental role in a parliamentary regime. Nor does autonomy from the Soviet bloc necessarily mean automatic disapproval of policies initiated in Moscow: all three Western parties considered here have supported Cuban intervention in Angola, for instance, and on the whole they would tend to adopt a pro-Soviet stance on African matters. But this is of course due to their anti-capitalist convictions which remain the cornerstone of a doctrine fostering the development of non-capitalist regimes within a Western industrial society.

Survival in a hostile environment: relations with the USA and the Atlantic Alliance

It has been widely argued that a climate of détente between East and West would be essential to Eurocommunist chances of getting off the ground. Does then the heightening of international tension in the recent months totally jeopardize the future of Eurocommunism? In reality, if perceptions of East–West relations have altered as a result of the relative deterioration of NATO's position, of the invasion of Afghanistan, of the non-ratification of SALT II and of the greater instability of the Middle East, the basic structures of the rival security systems remain the same, and the strategic thinking of Eurocommunist parties assumes the maintenance of this *status quo* at least as a point of departure.

All three parties are very critical of the USA as a matter of course. Even the PCE had recourse to the rather worn argument that 'imperialist' (i.e. American) interference in Afghan affairs explained if not justified the Soviet invasion. The USA easily fitted into the role of the villain that supported the Shah's repressive regime for a considerable period after it should have collapsed through its own deficiencies. Similarly, the survival of Israel, long branded as an outpost of capitalist exploitation and suppression of legitimate Arab national aspirations, is attributed to American ambition to maintain political and economic control of the Middle East.

It was predictable that a PCF Congress would hail the progress of socialist forces in the world to the detriment of the capitalist camp, and would maintain a crudely Manichean outlook on American foreign policy. But even Enrico Berlinguer cannot have been converted to the view of American innocence after the American ambassador in Rome had given a less than discreet warning to the Italian Government that Washington would watch the setting up of a communist coalition government with the greatest displeasure.

The outright condemnation of the USA as the *locus* of capitalist imperialism does not extend to the Atlantic Alliance, where ideological considerations play a minimal role, and which is seen as essential to the maintenance of peace. In this respect, the attitudes of the Western communist parties are inevitably conditioned by the respective statuses of their countries *vis-à-vis* NATO.

Foreign and defence policy was one of the areas of the French left's common programme where the drafters had kept to generalities and a prudently vague style. French communist thinking in these matters is above all French, with communist rhetoric coming in for packaging rather than substance. Since Marchais radically altered the PCF defence doctrine by coming out in favour of 'maintaining' the *force de frappe* in May 1977, that doctrine has come to resemble closely that of orthodox Gaullism. The official stand of the PCF is that it would not call for the withdrawal of France from the Atlantic Alliance, but that France must maintain exclusive control of her own nuclear weapons. While accepting that NATO could not be dismantled under the present conditions of East–West equilibrium, the PCF is opposed to any reinforcement of NATO. It therefore denounced in very vigorous terms the decision taken in December 1979 by the Atlantic Council to include cruise missiles and Pershing rockets in its European-based arsenal. The arguments used by the PCF were twofold: that it altered the East–West military balance (Marchais claimed that since the SS20s had been introduced by the Soviet Union in 1975, i.e. before the SALT II negotiations, they were part of the assessed parity between the two blocs), and that it was a barely disguised manner of providing the West German Republic with the most advanced form of nuclear weapons in violation of international treaties. However genuine the PCF alarm may have been (and it is shared by some non-communists in Europe), the strident tone was uncomfortably reminiscent of the Cold War rhetoric of 'capitalist warmongering', and crude anti-Germanism. The programme of the PCF includes the reduction of military budgets and the creation of a nuclear-free zone around the Mediterranean. The strong unilaterally directed protest against the introduction of new weapons is of course of little practical relevance, since France is not a member of the military organization. But France's peculiar position in the European security system entitles her, in the opinion of the PCF leadership, to be considered as a partner with peculiar entitlement to participate in international negotiations for strategic arms limitations. Marchais therefore claimed in his report to the 23rd Congress that France should take part in future SALT negotiations.

Overall, the PCF doctrine is that in the present circumstances the present institutional *status quo* should be maintained, but that the gradual withering away of the two main blocs should be encouraged, partly through the increased recognition of national defence interests, and partly through the development of alliances of non-aligned states.

The Italian communists, while having broadly similar preoccupations as the French on the maintenance of security in Europe, hold much more sophisticated and internationalist views on the matter. Under Berlinguer's leadership, the PCI has consistently proclaimed its commitment to Italian membership of NATO, not just for the sake of Italian security but as an additional safeguard of political stability. Like the French, they are worried by the prospect of installing cruise missiles and Pershings in Europe, but unlike them, they hold the Soviet decision to set up a network of SS20s responsible for contributing to the atmosphere of mutual suspicion. The most pressing issue for them is to avoid an escalation of the armaments race and to preserve what is left of détente. They therefore feel that the bipolar concept of rigorous respect of spheres of influence is obsolete and should be modified. This could include a more active role for Western Europe within the Atlantic Alliance, support for the non-aligned position of Yugoslavia, and full recognition of the needs and rights of China.[9] These various initiatives should of course be convincingly presented as defusing East-West tensions and not threatening the position of the Warsaw Pact Alliance. In order to reassure the Warsaw Pact countries, and to lower the tension between East and West, the PCI actually suggested in October 1979 that a NATO-Warsaw Pact conference should be convened in order to assess the state of nuclear weapons in Europe and to consider jointly the problems of conventional and nuclear armaments.

While the PCI insists that Italian international commitments and alliances are not open to question, its overriding concern is that the preservation of détente is the most crucial contributor to Italian national security. In practice, it can only mean keeping open and perhaps diversifying channels of communication between East and West, and checking the arms race. In the present inchoate state of Eurocommunism, which has neither a clearly defined territorial entity nor an autonomous military doctrine, it is obvious that Berlinguer is neither qualified nor prepared to advance any specifically Eurocommunist point of view.

As Spain is not a member of NATO the PCE has not addressed itself to problems of international security with the same degree of urgency as the PCF or the PCI, but Carrillo's support for the maintenance of American bases in Europe is a good enough indication that he considers Spain must be included in the Atlantic system of security, and there is no evidence that Carrillo would want to differ substantially from Berlinguer on matters of détente and arms control. If only the Italian and Spanish leaders could work out a joint political structure (however loosely defined), they could carry considerable weight in promoting a programme of multilateral détente based on the Italian agenda in a world again sensitized to the dangers of a military East-West conflict.

A new internationalism? Is Europe a suitable territorial base?

It is not by mere coincidence in time that the setting up of the Atlantic security system was paralleled by the setting up of European Community institutions in the decade following the division of Europe by the Iron Curtain. It should not be forgotten that the Schuman Plan was born from a desire to ensure peace through Franco-German reconciliation and the political unification of Europe. Western communist parties could not remain indifferent to the evolution of that Europe, and their policies have been greatly affected by its own vagaries. Even when denouncing the EEC as an agency of capitalist trusts and an anti-Soviet device, communists had to recognize its economic vitality and international status. The Italian communists were first in coming to terms with the European Community, and the French communists eventually followed suit.

The common programme of 1972 officially recognized the European Community, and at no time has the PCF asked for French withdrawal from the EEC institutions. Nevertheless, the PCF has remained extremely critical of the EEC on two major counts: that it encroaches dangerously on French national sovereignty, and that it is detrimental to the interests of French workers. The PCF position is unashamedly nationalistic (and in that respect close to the Gaullist–RPR position), and has led to extremely negative attitudes on the issues of direct election to the European Parliament and of enlargement of the European Community. The communist–Gaullist parliamentary coalition forced the French Government to pass legislation which would render impossible an extension of the powers of the European Assembly without French parliamentary assent, and the PCF then conducted a chauvinistic campaign in which the EEC was presented as a device to ensure the domination of Europe (*viz.* France) by the capitalist-imperialist-militarist government of Bonn, inevitably leading to the economic ruin of France. This process would be completed by the enlargement of the EEC. Spanish membership would have the following consequences: it would lower the standard of living of French workers and bring ruin, in particular to the small farmers of southern France; it would create enmity between French and Spanish workers; it would eventually be detrimental to the economic interests of the Spanish workers themselves. These arguments are still advanced by the PCF even though Carrillo himself strongly supports Spanish membership of the European Community. Marchais's brand of Eurocommunism has justifiably been labelled not just as 'Gallo-communism' but as 'Gaullo-communism', and is clearly autonomous like that of the PCI or the PCE.

Considerations of national economic interest were undoubtedly instrumental to the PCI's conversion towards support of the Community in the 1960s. Since then, the PCI has gone very far indeed not only in accepting the limitations on national sovereignty inherent in the running of the Community, but in promoting even the supra-national character of the EEC and in particular in restoring the jaded political muscle of the Commission. This is not just in order to solve the economic problems of Italy, but increasingly to consolidate a new and still malleable polity based on 'freedom, democracy and pluralism'. Not only does the PCI support the development of an authentic European Parliament and the enlargement of the EEC which would in any case dramatically enhance the Mediterranean outlook of the Community, but it considers the Community as a suitable territorial base for a radical political realignment. By far the most original, imaginative and in certain ways controversial démarche of Berlinguer in the recent months has been the series of soundings he took in the spring of 1980 among European socialist and social democratic leaders. Having explained at the 15th Party Congress in March 1979 that the time had come for a rally of all communist, socialist, lay- and Christian Democratic forces to a new internationalism, Berlinguer actually used the facilities of the European Parliament to meet Willy Brandt and François Mitterrand to try and lay the foundations of a new international alliance based on the building up of a truly West European socialism. This is what is sometimes referred to as the third path, and the scheme is still at the stage of gestation rather than infancy.

In this attempt Berlinguer has the support of Carrillo who not only approves of the European Community and supports his country's own candidature for membership, but feels, like Berlinguer, the urgency of giving Western Europe the institutional and political means to play the international role to which it is entitled, and indeed duty-bound, to help revivify détente and guide the North–South dialogue.

Needless to say, this initiative has provoked the indignation of the PCF which considers it as a mere conversion to class collaboration, an unforgivable betrayal of basic Marxist principles, the crime being compounded by involvement with the *German* social democrats. The *de facto* breach between Paris and Rome does not necessarily make Berlinguer's task any easier. Numerous PCI (and PCE) militants will find it very difficult, and certainly heart-breaking, to have to accept social democrats as partners in preference to communists. But they should be reminded that the French communists have now gone too far in the direction of unconditional subservience to Moscow (in terms of foreign policy) to allow for any true rallying to an Italian concept of Eurocommunism as long as the present PCF leadership remains in power. Only an effective revolt from the French militants could alter the situation, and the permanence of democratic centralism makes this prospect unrealistic.

Conclusion

The comet-like passage of Eurocommunism through the political stage of the 1970s has left political actors and observers equally bewildered. Is Eurocommunism a reality or an illusion? Is it going to come again or has it gone for good? What is its shape? What is its size? Has it generated divisive or unifying forces? The answers to all these questions depend on the observation sites, and are therefore varied.

Assuming a certain degree of adhesion to the opinion that Euro-communism primarily concerns West European communist parties, the first preoccupation must be to identify the territorial and ideological boundaries of a European political space. It is now largely accepted that the tripartite form of Eurocommunism of the 1970s is now defunct. The preferences of the Spanish Communist Party would probably go to a Mediterranean alliance of non-aligned countries whose nucleus would be Spain, Italy, Yugoslavia and Romania. But this is unrealistic for the time being as it would deprive NATO of Italy and the Warsaw Pact of Romania, and neither of the two security systems would be likely to accept such a strategic weakening of their southern flanks. The alternative seems to be the territorial basis of the enlarged Community within which Berlinguer is attempting to give substance to a Euroleft movement which might be converted into a Eurosocialism rather than a Eurocommunism Mark II. If both territorial integrity and ideological purity are to be preserved, then only the Italo-Spanish rump Eurocommunism would remain. With the receding prospects of communist participation in governments, and without the unanimous support of its rank and file, this limited informal structure would quickly lose its credibility.

In this context, foreign policy issues become crucial to the survival of Eurocommunism. If Eurocommunist leaders can handle these issues with consistency and independence of mind, the greater specificity of a 'Eurocommunist policy' which would not be merely the rejection of the Soviet model is bound to attract the favourable attention of political groups in search of original solutions. It is widely recognized that the political malaise of the Western world is due not to the presence of political parties, but to their failure to convince their electorates that they can adapt their programmes and behaviour to contemporary political issues instead of refurbishing tired slogans and fighting out-of-date wars. In terms of international politics, if Berlinguer, Giancarlo Pajetta and their European colleagues can give some substance to their concept of 'new internationalism' by proposing a programme which would mobilize popular support and thus reassure other parties' leaders that their ranks won't be depleted if they depart from conventional rhetoric, then some form of Euro-socialism has a good chance of development between the Eastern bloc undermined by the intolerable burden of its military budgets and the Western bloc grappling with its ill-disciplined economies. If the 'new internationalism' can generate coherent policies as substitutes for the increasingly unconvincing balance of terror, or for the timid approach of the Western governments to the unbalance between North and South, if it can persuade public opinion that some form of mutually agreed international discipline within a democratic framework can effectively bring about the control of unemployment, then it has a good chance not just of survival but overwhelming success. It is a risk that Berlinguer is trying to take in order to extricate himself from the present stalemate. He may be defeated by the aggravation of international conflicts and the force of nationalist reflexes.

One of the major handicaps of Eurocommunism is that under the guise of internationalism it has nevertheless, like all other communist parties (and indeed all political parties), been subjected to the constraints of national habits and narrowly perceived national interests. Those nationalist reflexes are aggravated by the censure of national electorates. Under those circumstances, the chances of a rapid and lasting revival of Eurocommunism remain extremely slender.

Notes

1 See various articles in *Le Monde*, 4–8 January 1980.
2 Phyllis Auty, *Tito, A Biography* (London, 1974), p. 302.
3 Clearly, the Polish *Solidarity* Union constituted too great a threat to the power structure in Poland and the risk of contagion seemed considerable.
4 The temptation to return to the well-trodden if somewhat arid path of *de facto* alignment with the Soviet Union's foreign policy was probably also strengthened by the death at the end of 1978 of Jean Kanapa who, as the Politburo member in charge of international affairs, had contributed a considerable impetus and a clear orientation to French Eurocommunist policies.
5 Yvonne Quilès, 'Un plaidoyer de trop', *Le Monde*, 17 January 1980. *Le Monde* has now become the main platform for dissenters from official PCF policies who are barred from publication in the communist press.
6 Lilly Marcou, 'La recontre à Paris des PC d'Europe. Comment, avec de l'ancien, faire du nouveau . . .', *Le Monde Diplomatique*, June 1980, p. 3.
7 Meeting at Pantin. Speech by Georges Marchais reported in *Le Monde*, 29 March 1980.
8 *L'Unitá*, 4 April 1979.
9 Programme outlined by a prominent PCI leader at a private meeting in June 1980.

6

The French Communist Party during the Fifth Republic: the troubled path

Vincent Wright

The purpose of this chapter is not to demonstrate in what ways and to what extent the French Communist Party (PCF) is or is not Eurocommunist by contrasting it with the Italian and Spanish Communist Parties. Nor is it to examine the nature of the relationship of the PCF with the PCI and the PCE (which has been done elsewhere in this book). Rather it is to analyse how far the PCF appears committed to the three major policies which are normally associated with Eurocommunism: de-Sovietization or de-Russification, liberalization, and national political integration.

A number of main arguments will emerge from the analysis:

1 The commitment of the party to each of the three policies may clearly be discerned by the early 1970s, but it was belated (compared with the PCI and the PCE), sometimes begrudged and always limited.

2 The party's flirtation with Eurocommunism was always basically tactical in motivation, but it had strategical implications which were not quickly perceived by the leadership.

3 The roots of each policy may be traced to the earlier acts and writings of the party. Of course, the PCF entertains a calculated ambiguity on many issues and this enables it both to shift tactics and to justify such a shift by quoting precedent. Nevertheless, the break with the past was never radical and it should not be exaggerated.

4 The acceptance of the three policies unfolded at somewhat different times.

5 The three policies were eventually perceived as closely interre-

lated, contradictory and, more significantly, dangerous because of that interrelationship and those contradictions.

6 The Eurocommunist experiment was ended in the autumn of 1977 because the pursuit of each policy posed too many intractable problems for the party.

7 The abandonment of the Eurocommunist experiment in favour of the more traditional strategy proved equally unrewarding, and was unceremoniously abandoned after the disastrous election results of April and June 1981.

8 The present state of disorientation and division of the party may be explained by its incapacity to elaborate a strategy which avoids the pitfalls of both the traditional Stalinist and the Eurocommunist ones.

The PCF and the pressures for change 1960–74[1]

At the beginning of the Fifth Republic the outlook of the party was decidedly bleak: it was isolated, marginalized, mistrusted and in decline. It was the most Stalinist communist party of Western Europe – *la fille aînée de l'Eglise communiste* – and its servility to Moscow was legendary: it was the 'party of foreign patriotism' according to the unkind, but not unfair, jibe of the time. Its doctrines and policies were largely unmodified since the Bolshevization of the party in the 1920s. Its isolation from the mainstream of French politics, which was the consequence of its attitudes during the Cold War, was confirmed by the support it gave for the Russian invasion of Hungary and its unfavourable reactions towards the Anglo-French invasion of the Suez Canal area in the autumn of 1956. Its isolation also became clear when it proved to be the only major party unanimously to oppose General de Gaulle's assumption of power towards the constitutional referendum of October 1958. The position of the party recalled early periods of its history: 1928–34 during its 'class against class' phase; 1939–40 between the signature of the Molotov–Ribbentrop Pact and the German invasion of the Soviet Union; 1947–52, the Cold War years.

The process of de-Sovietization, liberalization and national political integration was not an easy one; the ghetto, like the womb, can be comforting and undemanding. The party's position in 1958 was founded on a reassuring logic: it was the guardian of an orthodoxy which justified the decision-making structure, whilst the structure was 'the tabernacle' of that orthodoxy.[2] It was difficult to touch one without endangering the other. It was scarcely surprising, therefore, that there were powerful forces within the party urging the maintenance of the *status quo*. Yet the 1960s and early 1970s saw the emergence of pressures for change. Those pressures emanated from the international environment, the French political system and within the party itself. They are too familiar to require detailed elaboration.

Outside France, the pressures were multiple: the policy of de-Stalinization in the Soviet Union following the Khrushchev Report; the emergence of the policy of détente; the Sino-Soviet schism which called into question the primacy of the Soviet Union in the communist world; the example of Cuba which seemingly achieved and consolidated a revolution without recourse to classic Leninist means; the Italian Communist Party's apparently inexorable growth and its popularity based on a policy of polycentrism and liberalization; the events in Allende's Chile which underlined the need for a Marxist party in power to build a wide consensus; the inability of the Portuguese Communist Party to seize power after the April 1974 revolution by classic Leninist means. Inside France, the pressures were no less important: the effect of President de Gaulle's foreign policy, with its anti-European and anti-American tone and with its greater sensitivity towards the USSR, which had the effect of rendering the party's own foreign policy less peculiar; the emergence of a strong presidency elected by a system which placed a premium upon unity with the other parties of the left; the demise of Parliament (where the party had been destructively powerful during the Fourth Republic) which deprived the party of an effective political power base; the first parliamentary elections which indicated that with a reasonably disciplined right-wing coalition a dislocated left suffered disproportionately badly (the PCF in 1958, for example, won 19 per cent of the votes but only 2 per cent of the seats in the Assembly); the changes in the socialist party which entered into early opposition to General de Gaulle and which, especially under the leadership of Francois Mitterrand, radicalized its policies and pursued a strategy of left-wing unity; the unprecedented social and economic changes which characterized the period and which rendered even more obsolete some of the party's policies. Within the party change was facilitated by a different leadership (the apparently indestructible Thorez, general secretary of the party for thirty years, died in 1964 and was replaced by Waldeck Rochet), and by the arrival of 'les nouveaux communistes' who were less marked by the battles of yesteryear and, finally, by the restlessness of a new generation of communist intellectuals.

There was, therefore, a complex of pressures both forcing and facilitating the process of change. With the transformation of the international and domestic environment the party was obliged to rethink its position. Marxists, noted Jacques Julliard, 'needed not only to change the world: they needed, too, accurately to interpret it'. This need was all the greater since the party was in slow and apparently ineluctable decline: the state of its electorate, its membership, its militancy, its satellite organizations, its press, bore witness to this phenomenon. The 1960s presented both the need and the conditions for change.

The process of change – de-Russification

The history of the PCF has been closely moulded by the twenty-one conditions adopted at the Congress of Tours (December 1920) and by the later edicts of the Third International. More than any other West European communist party it voluntarily subordinated itself to the imperatives of Soviet policy. The occasional private protest by Thorez was accompanied by massive and unrelenting assent in public.[3] The party was badly shaken by the Molotov–Ribbentrop pact and the early policies of the party after the German occupation in 1940 but internal dissenters such as Paul Nizan were branded as traitors and expelled from the party. The party's policies in the 1950s merely underlined its total subservience to a Stalinist Moscow; its vituperative attacks on Tito; its attitude during the East Berlin uprising of 1952; its reluctance to accept the Khrushchev Report and Thorez's personal request to the Soviet leader not to rehabilitate Bukharin; the party's denunciation of the Anglo-French invasion of Suez in 1956 and its approval of the Soviet invasion of Hungary in the same year.

The party's apparently slavish acceptance of the dictates of Soviet policy always posed a dilemma for the party, and occasional purges of 'nationalist elements' (those demanding greater independence) brought to the surface the divisions within the party on the issue. The party has always been proud of its revolutionary Jacobin heritage, and 1793 looms as large in the ritualistic historiography of the party as 1871, 1917 or 1920. Furthermore, its sporadic yearning for national integration, the sentiment of its own social and political marginality and its intense dislike of the accusation of being 'the party of foreign nationalism' combined to push the party into highly nationalistic stances and posturing. The tension between the national requirements of the party and the exigencies arising out of its membership of the communist world was not, therefore, merely a phenomenon of the 1960s and 1970s.

There were, of course, periods when domestic and Soviet interests coincided, when it was possible to reconcile the apparently irreconcilable. Between 1934 and 1938 and 1940 and 1945 the party could be both patriotic and pro-Soviet. But such periods were rare and the dilemma remained. The tentative process of de-Sovietization, undertaken by the party from mid-1960 to mid-1970, must be seen not only as an attempt to reduce obligations that constrained the party's freedom of manoeuvre at home but also a means of solving this painful dilemma.

The process of de-Sovietization during the period[4] involved three interconnected, yet distinct, strands, and it is important in judging the record to disentangle them. They are

1 the party's attitude towards the foreign policy of the USSR,
2 the party's views on the internal policies of the USSR,
3 the party's acceptance of the universal applicability of the Soviet model.

Until the mid-1970s it appeared that the PCF was taking its distance *vis-à-vis* of the Soviet Union on all three fronts. Louis Aragon's attack in *L'Humanité*, on 16 February 1966, on the Daniel–Siniavski trial was the first open attack on the Soviet Union's policy on civil rights whilst the hostile reaction to the Soviet invasion of Czechoslovakia in August 1968 constituted the first public demonstration of the party's attitude towards Eastern Europe. By this time the party's campaign in favour of *Socialisme aux couleurs de la France* was well advanced. Since this latter aspect – the rejection of the universal applicability of the Soviet model – is discussed at length below, this section will concentrate on the first two aspects.

The early 1970s were punctuated by constant reminders of French independence: in December 1970, *L'Humanité* carried a series of critical articles by Etienne Fajon (reputed to be an arch-Stalinist) on the handling of the workers' demonstrations in the Baltic ports; from early 1973 it openly appealed on behalf of the Soviet Jews; in May 1974 it protested strongly against Soviet interference in the presidential elections (the Soviet ambassador visited Giscard d'Estaing in the middle of the campaign); in 1974 it allowed *Gulag Archipelago* to go on sale at the *Fête de l'Humanité*; in October of that year it appealed on behalf of Leonid Plyusch, the Soviet mathematician and dissident. From the autumn of 1975 protests about specific acts or features of the

Soviet Union intensified. For instance, in October 1976, Juquin, a member of the party's *bureau politique* joined a public demonstration against repression in Latin America, Czechoslovakia and the Soviet Union, and in December of that year Jean Kanapa, the party's foreign affairs spokesman, denounced Soviet concentration camps on *Dossiers de l'Ecran*, a popular French television programme. More significantly, a more general revision of the party's relationship with Moscow began to emerge from the winter of 1975 (perhaps under the impact of the November 1975 Rome meeting with Berlinguer). At the November 1975 preparatory meeting of the Pan-European Conference of Communist Parties the party, whilst taking a tough line on civil rights in the Soviet Union, was still defending the principle of 'proletarian internationalism' against the PCI which advocated 'internationalist solidarity'. But by the time of the 22nd Congress in February 1976 Kanapa was arguing for a looser and more flexible relationship with Moscow. In the following month he told the central committee of the party in a severely critical report that 'la notion de patrie du socialisme n'a plus aucun sens aujourd'hui.[5] By mid-1977 'internationalist solidarity' had become the official doctrine of the party.[6]

The existence of a much looser, more flexible, less aligned and increasingly critical party *vis-a-vis* Moscow was dramatically illustrated by a number of events: the absence of Soviet observers at the PCF Congress of February 1976 and the refusal of Marchais to attend the 25th Congress of the CPSU in the same month: the Marchais visit to the Japanese Communist Party (which had notoriously bad relations with the CPSU) in April 1976; the party's highly critical line at the East Berlin conference of June 1976 (at which it rejected the idea of any future conferences on the same lines); the absence of any meeting between Marchais and Leonid Brezhnev when the latter visited Paris in June 1977; the withdrawal from the *bureau* of the Moscow-orientated *Fédération Syndicale Mondiale* by the PCF-dominated CGT. September 1978 marks the culmination of this radically critical phase, with the appearance of *L'URSS et Nous* by five leading intellectuals of the party.[7] The book, which was recommended by *L'Humanité* (4 September) and was bitterly criticized by *Kommunist* (the theoretical review of the central committee of the CPSU),[8] purported to analyse 'the errors, deviations and distortions' of the Soviet system, and raised (but did not answer) the vital question: could the USSR be considered as a Marxist–Leninist state?

The policy of de-Sovietization was never a smooth one: it was always hesitant and generally half-hearted: 'two steps forward, one step back' seemed to characterize the party's position. For instance, the party gave its blessings to Alexander Dubcek ('socialism with a human face' was precisely what the party was seeking) in the famous spring of 1968, and the *bureau politique* roundly and immediately condemned, 21 August 1968, the Soviet invasion of Czechoslovakia. However, the following day, the central committee softened the condemnation. Moreover, the PCF was quick to accept the 'normalization' process in Czechoslovakia. A delegation of the PCF visited the USSR in November 1968 (the first West European communist party to do so after the Czechoslovakian invasion), and, unlike, the PCI, the PCF signed the Resolution, adopted at the Third World Conference of Communist Parties in 1969, which enunciated the principle of the 'limited sovereignty' of the East European states. Furthermore, the bilateral *communiqué*, signed by the PCF and the CPSU on 5 July 1971, served further to underline the French Communist Party's acceptance of 'normalization'. When Roger Garaudy began to argue that the invasion was not an error but a crime rooted in the logic of the Soviet system he was given no credit for his acerbic observations. Yet the party in the 1970s became increasingly critical of 'normalization' in Czechoslovakia, and by January 1978 Kanapa, under pressure from party intellectuals, openly condemned (in a television programme) Prague's treatment of its dissidents.

The party's critical policy was not only hesitant and sporadic. It was also limited and often contradictory.

Even at the height of the party's de-Sovietization phase, effective links between it and 'the fatherland of socialism' remained strong: the weight of the past remained heavy, 'the protectors of palaeo-orthodoxy' (to use Annie Kriegel's expression) remained powerful, and the historical references too anchored in the collective consciousness of the *militants*. The basic instinct of the party was always one of defence of the Soviet Union. It was revealing that the 'bourgeois' press was always taken to task for 'anti-Sovietism' when it criticized the Soviet Union – sometimes for condemning the things that were denounced in *L'Humanité*. A reading of the party newspaper during the Yuri Orlov trial in Moscow in the spring of 1978 makes instructive reading in that respect. More significantly, the PCF continued to support the Soviet Union's position *vis-à-vis* China, its doctrine of the limited sovereignty of the East European states, and its foreign policy initiatives in Africa and the Far East.

Even more significantly, the PCF always refused fully to explore the

Soviet reality. As Roger Garaudy frequently pointed out, the 'crimes' of the Soviet Union were always ascribed to the 'excesses' or 'errors' of the system, to its 'Stalinist distortions' and never to its inherent logic.[9] In spite of the Soviet repression in Prague (1948 and 1968), in Berlin (1952), in Budapest (1956) and in Stettin (1970); in spite of banning the right to strike; and in spite of the Gulag, the Soviet experiment was consistently portrayed as representing enormous progress for the workers, and the Soviet Union was projected as 'the fatherland of socialism'. Thus, the 1976 PCF Congress could denounce the infringement of human rights but still claim that 'great historical progress' had been accomplished in the Soviet Union, and that co-operation with it was vital in the struggle against imperialism.

In spite of the experiment in de-Russification (in the sense of criticizing certain policies and practices) the PCF remained wedded to the historical centrality of the Soviet model. It rejected many aspects of the Soviet version of the transitional phase to socialism, but it shared throughout the Eurocommunist experiment a theoretical belief in the ultimate Marxist millennium and a practice of the Soviet model of party organization and functioning. These points form the basis of the following section.

The process of change – liberalization

Liberalization of the PCF was often referred to as the 'Italianization' of the French party. In essence it involved the rejection of the Soviet model of the transitional phase to socialism and the adoption of a policy of 'socialism in French colours'. This policy had many facets. The concept of revolution being rooted in a violent and sudden overthrow of the bourgeois state was rejected, although in practice, the party was probably never (with the possible exception of the very early period of its history) really committed to the concept.[10] During two key periods – at the time of the Liberation[11] and during the 'events' of May 1968[12] – the party demonstrated its attachment to 'Republican order', although the motives varied greatly.

The policy of a 'peaceful transition to socialism' was officially adopted by the 17th Congress in 1964 and the commitment was reiterated at frequent intervals in party policy documents, reports and resolutions throughout the late 1960s and early 1970s, notably in the December 1968 Manifesto of Champigny, in the *Programme pour un gouvernement démocratique populaire* (adopted by the central committee in October 1971), in the joint programme of government which it signed with the socialists in June 1972, and in the *Charte des Libertés* of early 1975.

Party spokesmen multiplied their reassurances about the party's dedication to the parliamentary path to socialism, its respect for the verdict of the electorate, and its acceptance of the principle of 'alternation' (a left-wing government would give way to a right-wing one, if elected). They also accepted the principle of multi-partism and proclaimed their attachment to traditional 'bourgeois' freedoms, especially in the *Charte des Libertés* promulgated on 16 May 1975. The 22nd Congress, 4–8 February 1976 – the most liberal in the party's history – gave its blessing to the liberalization process and also to the party's decision (announced by Georges Marchais on television on 7 January of that year) to abandon the concept of the dictatorship of the proletariat. Thus, by the mid-1970s the party was firmly committed to 'a peaceful, democratic, majoritarian and pluralistic' path to socialism. 'Construire le Socialisme dans la liberté' was its rallying cry.

The process of liberalization was, however, limited in nature.[13] In the first place, if the party adopted the parliamentary road to socialism, 'the struggle of the masses' outside Parliament – *à la base* – remained imperative. Deradicalization was never viewed as mere electoralism.[14] The electoral battle was always coupled with another battle, based on a policy of *encadrement*, and organized through the party cells, through the CGT and through its other satellite organizations. It is in this context that the controversy with the socialist party over the need radically to extend the public sector takes on its full significance. Concessions to the socialists in the political domain demanded compensations in the economic field. It has frequently been argued that even Maurice Thorez never really conceived the party as an agent of violent revolution, or as a 'reformist' party, but rather as an instrument for extending a bureaucratic state system (gradually superseding the bourgeois state) which would be penetrated by the party.

The second limitation on the party's liberalization process relates to its view of multi-partism. Sceptics were confirmed on this issue when Marchais, in his *Défi Démocratique* (1975), informed his readers that multi-party systems could be found in Eastern Europe. The party, it was claimed, always confused East and West European notions of pluralism.[15] The sceptics also rightly pointed out that the dominant role of the party remained intact, in spite of pluralism. The hegemonic pretensions of the PCF as the sole representative of the organized working class, its insistent claim to be the repository of scientific truth and the carrier of a historic mission merely underlined the party's conception of its role in a multi-party system.

The Manifesto of Champigny, elaborated after the May 1968 'events', anchored the strategy of the party in a theory of state monopoly capitalism, a stage of capitalism seen by several as 'the ante-chamber of socialism'. The strategy had basically three require-ments: a political one which involved left-wing joint action based on a programme for 'advanced democracy'; the extension of the public domain through nationalization (which breaks the link between private monopoly power and the state, thus commencing the transformation of society); and a guiding or vanguard role for the party – *the* party of the working class, the only class which escapes the contradictions of capitalism.

The third major limitation on the liberalization process of the 1960s and early 1970s related to internal party democracy, since the Stalinist practice, rather than the Leninist principle, of democratic centralism remained unshaken.[16] The party's process of decision-making remained shaped and legitimized by the seventh of the twenty-one conditions imposed by the Third International and by the Bolshevization of the party in the early 1920s when factions and ten-dencies were purged and a disciplined hierarchical command structure was created.

Several examples taken from the party's Eurocommunist period illustrate its willingness to impose decisions on a base which was fre-quently ill-prepared or even totally unprepared: its intention of abandoning the concept of the dictatorship of the proletariat was announced by Marchais on television; its volte-face on the European elections which had previously been condemned as 'a crime against the people of France'; its decision to accept the French *force de frappe* (which involved a major shift in its defence policy), announced on 11 May 1977; and its decision to break with the socialists in September 1977, which left many party militants bewildered and even stupefied.

Factionalism is still anti-party and still susceptible to purge, although it should be noted that since the departure of Roger Garaudy in 1970 there has been little resort to this classic Stalinist device.[17] Indeed, party critics such as Jean Elleinstein and Henri Fizbin were allowed a degree of freedom which would have been intolerable to the leadership in the 1960s. Nevertheless, the party press was totally closed to self-criticism throughout the period. Other tenets of democratic centralism also remain intact: the primacy of the cell in the party base; the careful control in the selection of cadres and the election of delegates; the banning of discussion of a 'horizontal' (anti-hierarchical) nature; the binding nature of decisions on all party members. For a party given to the occasional volte-face the organizational structure of the party is clearly a great help.[18]

The final major limitation of the party's liberalization process lies in its retention of its traditional goals. Its position over the transitional phase to socialism (the stage of 'advanced democracy') may have changed, but at no stage did the party renounce its millenarian vision of the shape of future socialist and communist society.

There was, therefore, some liberalization of the PCF's thinking but the limits to this process were clear and important. Furthermore, even its conversion to a non-violent revolutionary strategy was called into question by its public support (in private, it counselled prudence)[19] for Alvaro Cunhal's actions in 1975.

The process of change – national political integration

The policy of national political integration was clearly linked with the policies of de-Sovietization and liberalization, since they were seen as the essential prerequisites for its accomplishment. The integrative urge had always been present in the party and the wish to be an integral part of the national community had been a recurrent feature of the party's history. As already noted, the party at the beginning of the Fifth Republic was in a political ghetto – a ghetto which the leadership seemed determined to leave. The party's strategy involved two major drives, both of which may be traced to earlier party history. The first was the construction of a wide alliance, embracing 'all the victims of monopoly capitalism'. In the 1970s this alliance took embarrassingly wide contours: the *Union du Peuple de France* (elaborated in June 1974) was all-encompassing, designed to attract not only Catholics (the dialogue had started with the Catholics in the 1960s) but also improbable groups such as the Gaullists . . . Of course, these anti-monopolist groups were not perceived as revolutionary, but were the objective allies of the working class which was led by the party. This vague alliance strategy, reaffirmed as recently as the May 1979 Party Congress, never materialized, and was never vigorously pursued except in the rhetoric of the party. Much more central to the party's political integration plans was the alliance with the socialists – the second drive.

The relationship between the communists and the socialists in France had always been turbulent.[20] As recently as 1955 Auguste Lecoeur had been expelled from the party for advocating an alliance with the French Socialist Party; he was not the first in the party's history to illustrate the dictum that in the PCF one must never be right too early.

The relationship between the communists and socialists during the 1960s and early 1970s was a sporadic and fitful affair punctuated by genuine and historically significant steps on the road to left-wing unity: the presidential elections of December 1965 and May 1974 when François Mitterrand – 'cher François' in the words of Marchais – alone carried the standard of the left, and in 1974 came within an ace of giving the left its first national election victory; the 1967 and 1973 legislative elections when the left negotiated a harmonious second ballot electoral agreement (only the best-placed candidate of the left at the first ballot was allowed to stand at the second); the June 1972 joint programme of government which was not merely a catalogue of points on which the socialists and communists agreed, not merely an imprecise minimum programme, but a binding negotiated governmental package applicable for the duration of a legislature. It required compromises, concessions and a very real unitary will from both sides.

By mid-1977 the left had a programme, a parliamentary co-ordinating committee, an electoral agreement, a unitary spirit at the base of each party. It had lost the presidential elections by a very small margin, but had swept to victory in the local elections (particularly those of 1977 when it captured most of the major towns of France) and its standing in the opinion polls suggested victory in the 1978 legislative elections.

Yet throughout the period October 1962 (when the drive to unity was really commenced) to September 1977 (when it was effectively brought to an end) there were constant reminders of the vulnerability of the left-wing alliance. The May 1968 'events' brought to the surface all the latent fears and suspicions of the non-communist left about the possible intentions of the PCF. Left-wing unity virtually collapsed and the left faced the 1969 presidential elections in divided and dispirited shape. On the other hand, sweeping socialist gains in the autumn 1974 by-elections crystallized growing communist fears about the socialist party's pretensions to electoral hegemony, and they were quickly followed by a prolonged and bitter communist campaign against the socialists.

For the communists, the stability and durability of the alliance with the socialists hinged upon the interaction of a number of complex factors: the prevailing political situation in France; the international environment (détente was conducive to unity); the political radicalization of the socialists (which occurred under Mitterrand's leadership); the relative strengths of the two parties; and the advantages derived from the alliance by the party. Throughout the period 1962–77, in spite of the occasional moments of euphoria, the alliance was a wary, suspicion-wracked affair, based (at least for the leadership) on a fine calculation of political self-interest. And for the PCF, 'l' union est un combat',[21] a constant struggle to keep the socialists from backsliding into their traditional reformism. In truth, national political integration based on a left-wing coalition strategy faced the party with a number of dilemmas. For the left to achieve victory or even attract wide electoral support the socialists had to be seen as the dominant partner. And if an over-dominant socialist party was unacceptable to the party, a weak one was too afraid to negotiate an alliance. The success of the alliance depended, therefore, on a relatively even balance between the two parties, with the socialists being the somewhat, but not too, dominant partner. Its success depended, too, on the party's capacity and willingness to project an image of moderation, responsibility and respectability, of discretion and self-effacement. Such was the case in the 1974 presidential elections. But not only did this blurring of its own image endanger its very identity, it also generally enhanced the status and prestige of the socialists. As François Mitterrand was to point out with telling cruelty, 'the key to [left-wing] victory is with the socialist party, the key to defeat with them' (the communists).

The left-wing alliance of 1962–77 was not only fragile and turbulent, it was also limited in nature. The joint programme of government, the binding second ballot electoral agreements at national and local level and the common experience of running most of France's major cities represented considerable progress on the road to left-wing unity. But the divisions of the left remained numerous and significant. There remained too many battlefields on which each party of the left vied for supremacy – in numerous pressure groups, within the trades union movement, at the factory level (where the socialists began to build a base). There were too many policy differences – for example, over the desirable extent of nationalization, over *autogestion*, over Europe, over the distribution of income, over NATO and over defence in general. And although the gap between the parties had lessened on these issues, serious differences

remained. Finally, there were insurmountable ideological differences between the two parties, for although they had narrowed their
differences on the transitional phase to socialism they were in disagreement about the nature of the future socialist society and in total
disagreement about the ultimate ideal society. Indeed, it might be
argued that the gulf between the two parties on these fundamental
issues was so great that they could never be discussed, only ignored.
The effect of not wishing to advertise basic differences, for the sake of
the stability of the alliance, was to block any genuine debate within
the party on the nature of the ideal socialist society. Paradoxically,
therefore, the policy of national integration through alliance may
have placed a premium upon liberalizing and de-Sovietizing but it
also imposed limits upon the party's capacity to do so.

National political integration based on an alliance strategy was,
therefore, limited in nature, and, as such, it resembled both the
process of de-Russification and liberalization. The changes in the
strategies of the party after 1977 may have been dramatic but they
were not as radical as many have supposed.

The party's changes of strategy 1977–1981

From the breakdown in the negotiations to update the joint
programme of government in September 1977 until the presidential
elections of May 1981, the party appeared to revise its strategy on all
three fronts – either by reversing or by freezing the various processes
of change in which it had been engaged.

Relations with the USSR were greatly strengthened, atavistic pro-
Soviet loyalties were reactivated, and fidelity to 'the fatherland of
socialism' constantly proclaimed. The foreign policy initiatives of the
Soviet Union continued to be applauded and approved[22] whether they
were in South-East Asia, in Africa, the Middle East or Nicaragua.
The PCF's attitude to the Soviet invasion of Afghanistan – 'a lesson
inflicted on imperialism in the interests of détente'[23] – starkly
confirmed the party's total acceptance of the Soviet Union's foreign
policy. So, too, did the party's nervous initial reaction to the events in
Poland (the PCI and the PCE supported the strikers from the
outset),[24] and its (abortive) attempt to mobilize a mass campaign of
protest against the NATO decision of 12 December 1979 to renew its
nuclear arsenal in Europe.[25] It appeared that the PCF had a somewhat
different conception of 'internationalist solidarity' than the PCI.

Relations with the Soviet Union were vastly improved. Bilateral meetings were resumed from the beginning of 1979, and Marchais visited the Soviet Union in provocative style during the Olympic Games and in January 1981.[26] It was the French party which was to sponsor, together with the Polish party, the European communist parties' meeting in Paris, 28–9 April 1980 (which the PCI and the PCE refused to attend) on peace and disarmament – a meeting which condoned the foreign policies of the USSR and which avoided all reference to Afghanistan. Maxime Gremetz (Kanapa's successor as the party's foreign affairs spokesman) rejected the accusation that the meeting was comparable with that held in East Berlin in 1976, since no attempt was made to elaborate a common strategy, and no attempt was made to bind all the parties to decisions determined by the 'centre'.[27] But the impression of French alignment with Moscow was nonetheless reinforced by the meeting.

Perhaps most significant of all, a systematic attempt was made by the party leadership to re-establish the place and prestige of the USSR in the rhetoric and mythology of the party. The 23rd Congress of the PCF in May 1979 accepted that the balance-sheet of the Soviet bloc was *globalement positif* – a claim already made by Marchais in his December 1978 meeting with the party's intellectuals. A carefully orchestrated campaign began. It was now claimed that the socialist countries (for they remain unquestionably socialist for the PCF) had created the conditions for real democracy,[28] that there was growing evidence that they were sensitive to the problems of democracy,[29] and even that workers' rights were being extended there.[30] By June 1980, the *bilan globalement positif* had been transformed into a *formidable bilan de réalisations positives*.[31] Moreover, a more Manichean vision of the world also resurfaced in the political discourse of the party: there were two camps, one destined by history to succeed, the other collapsing under the weight of its own contradictions.[32]

Why this clear move back into the Soviet orbit? A victory of the pro-Soviets in the secretariat or *bureau politique*, particularly after the death of Jean Kanapa in September 1978? Finding friendship outside to compensate for its increasing loneliness at home? A desire to re-assert its political distinctiveness when it was seen to be losing its identity? A wish to rally the activists who were disgruntled with the anti-Sovietism of the 1968–78 period? A rereading of the international situation which the full impact of the post-1974 oil crisis had rendered unstable and vulnerable to revolution? There is no way of knowing, for the decision was taken without discussion within the party.

Whilst the party clearly moved back into the Soviet orbit, the Euro-communist phase left its traces. The 23rd Congress of May 1979 recognized that the Soviet Union was not a model to be emulated, and criticized Moscow for the violation of human rights. The party still reminded its activists that the invasion of Czechoslovakia in 1968 was reprehensible,[33] and continued to condemn individual acts of the Soviet Union, such as its decision to deprive Rostropovich of his Soviet nationality and its measures taken against Anatolii Shcharan-ski and Sakharov.[34] Furthermore, the problem of the party's relations with the USSR was clearly highlighted – notably by the party's increasingly querulous intellectuals. If, they asked, the party clearly linked democracy with socialism in France, why should this not be the case in the Soviet Union? Logically, if the Soviet Union is condemned as undemocratic why is it not denounced as unsocialist? For party critics such as Jean Elleinstein, Jean Kahayan and Jacques Frémontier, the Soviet Union had to be considered as an anti-model, the very antithesis of socialism. This will never be conceded by the leadership: the identification with the USSR constitutes one of the distinguishing characteristics of the party, defines part of its personality and provides its activists with historical references and myths. The result will be continuing tension between the party and its disgruntled intellectuals.

The party was once again acquiring the reputation of being *le parti de l'étranger*, and, as if to compensate, had resorted to its traditional tactic – a reassertion of its nationalist identity.[35] The resurgence of nationalism in the party could be seen in its increasingly hostile attitude towards the 'German-dominated' European Community[36] and in its virulent attacks on the Federal Republic during the steel crisis in Lorraine and during the elections to the European Parliament. It could also be seen in its defence of Concorde, its attempt to organize a mass protest against the siting of Pershing II missiles in Western Europe, and its intensive opposition to the entry into the EEC of Spain, Portugal and Greece (a policy supported by the PCE and the PCI). Its renewed anti-Europeanism, anti-Germanism and anti-Americanism led observers to suggest that Eurocommunism had been replaced by a primitive Gallo-communism. The result was to increase the already considerable rift with the socialists, to increase its political isolation and further to hinder national integration.

On the liberalization front there was no dramatic reversal of policy. In his meeting with Berlinguer, 5 October 1978, and at the May 1979 Congress Marchais asserted the party's continuing commitment to a 'peaceful, democratic, majoritarian, pluralistic' passage to socialism. But all the limitations noted above remain. Hints were dropped that some changes in the practice of democratic centralism were not inconceivable,[37] but the final concessions left nothing of substance in danger.[38] The party's method of approving the Soviet invasion of Afghanistan and of selecting Georges Marchais as its candidate for the presidential elections demonstrated that important decisions continued – and continue – to be made amongst the small élite at the top without prior discussion in the party – the traditional practice of democratic centralism. Indeed, the party responded to the criticisms of its intellectuals by reasserting the necessity for democratic centralism. In terms reminiscent of those employed by Thorez at the 4th Congress in July 1956, Marchais reminded his party (in his report to the central committee in April 1978) that 'permanent discussion is, in the final analysis, the paralysis of decisions and actions. We are a democratic party, not a debating club.'[39] Party reviews such as *France Nouvelle* and *Nouvelle Critique* which attempted to open a debate on the party's options were suppressed, and the party press was closed to the critics.

The practice of democratic centralism is unlikely to change, for its *raison d'être* is linked with the revolutionary finality of the party, with its historic mission. It is also embedded in the party's declared relationship with the working class – *its* working class – for the party remains the self-conscious spokesman of that class, its vanguard, ensuring not only its guidance but also, through democratic centralism, its unity of action.

The path to internal liberalization is fraught with danger and replete with destabilizing implications.[40] Perhaps, as Pierre Daix has argued in his *La crise du PCF* (1978), the party is incapable of real de-Stalinization, because it does not perceive itself as Stalinist.

It was on the third front – national political integration – that the change in the party's direction was most dramatic. First, the anti-monopolist grouping of the *Union du Peuple de France* was discreetly buried.[41] Second, the left-wing alliance was also buried – but much less discreetly.

It was clear from the virulence of its attacks on the socialist party, its maximalist interpretation of the joint programme of government during the September 1977 negotiations, its demand for a full share of ministerial posts in 1978 and its demagogic *ouvriérisme* – in short, its eschewal of a moderate, reassuring and relatively self-effacing role – that the party was determined to break with the socialists and, by so doing, sabotage the electoral chances of the left. After the *rupture* of September 1977 the party intensified its violent campaign against Mitterrand, the socialist party leadership and even its electorate. It was a campaign based on an old Stalinist tactic: establish a hypothesis, and then prove it by declamation and assertive axioms. The hypothesis was that the socialists had taken 'a turn to the right' (*un virage à droite*) in order to construct an eventual alliance with President Giscard d'Estaing and/or Jacques Chirac. More specifically, the socialist party was accused of wishing to *gérer la crise du capitalisme*, of refusing to honour its commitments contained in the 1972 joint programme of government, of being willing to sacrifice Europe to the Germans, of being intrinsically Atlanticist, of lacking interest in the poor, of practising opportunistic electoralism.[42] It was also consistently asserted that the socialist party was inherently reformist – its very nature led it to class collaboration, and to an unwillingness to transform capitalism.[43]

Several reasons have been advanced to explain the party's change of strategy *vis-à-vis* the socialists:

1 The strategy benefited the left, but within the left the socialists did disproportionately well. Indeed, the electoral position of the PCF had not improved at all, and all the signs[44] suggested that the socialists were poised to replace the communists as the biggest party of the left. The 1978 legislative elections and the 1979 European Parliament elections were to confirm the signs. But it is revealing that when the socialists failed to do as well as expected in those two elections the relief in the communist leadership was almost palpable. It was eventually admitted within the party that the alliance was scrapped because the socialists derived too much gain from it.[45]

2 The party's necessary moderation and self-effacement had disorientated the membership and certain key elements in the leadership. The party, it was argued, was in danger of losing its revolutionary identity – and this at a time when the socialists had radicalized theirs and when the party was under pressure from the various varieties of *gauchistes*.

3 The alliance had legitimized the socialists in the opinion of the working class over which the party kept an obsessively possessive eye.[46]

4 A new assessment of the international situation (the failure of Allende's peaceful experiment in Chile, the success of armed re-

volution in South Vietnam and the partial success of the PC in Portugal) suggested that the potential for revolutionary activity was growing.[47] Moreover, the growing economic crisis in the capitalist world increased this potential in the long run. In the short run, it might entail a left-wing government demanding sacrifices from the working class – the party's working class.

5 The party was pressurized by Moscow to prevent the expected left-wing victory of 1978, since a left-wing government under Mitterrand might jeopardize Gaullist foreign policy, have a destabilizing effect in Western Europe and endanger détente. This view was widely held by socialist leaders.[48]

6 The price of national integration was too great: the alliance involved not only a loosening of the ties with Moscow and a revision of some of the party's doctrines and policies but also a liberalization process which, if carried to its logical extreme, would threaten the ultimate ends of the party and, more immediately, its decision-making structure.

Whatever the reason or reasons, the party clearly embarked upon a policy of dismantling the bases of an alliance which it had striven to construct in the 1960s and early 1970s. By the time of the May 1981 presidential election, the party was still officially committed to left-wing unity – which was claimed to be essential and *irrévocable*.[49] But the policy of reaching an agreement amongst the leaders (*au sommet*), of a negotiated electoral and programmatic compromise, was abandoned in favour of a policy of *unité d'action à la base* – an imprecise and unrealizable objective (and the policy adopted by the party in its previous ghetto periods).[50] Meetings between the leaders of the two parties of the left ceased completely, and parliamentary co-operation was coincidental rather than planned.

At the electoral level, the PCF had warned the socialists that automatic second ballot withdrawal for a better placed socialist was no longer the case,[51] and in the 1980 senatorial elections, the party, by failing to withdraw its candidates in certain *départements*, ensured the defeat of very well-placed socialists. However, in the 1978 legislative elections and 1979 departmental elections the parties of the left respected the automatic withdrawal rule. What was surprising was that the *esprit unitaire* of the electors had, to a large extent, survived the bitter confrontation between the two parties. The gulf between the two parties was fully revealed in the European Parliament elections of June 1979 when each party presented its own list and in the April 1981 presidential elections when each had its own candidate. There were still left-wing coalitions in power in most of the major towns of France, but relations between the parties in many of them are either non-existent, strained or even poisonous.

The left was also *déprogrammée*: the joint programme of government, considered to be one of the great milestones on the road back to left-wing unity, was totally discarded by both parties, and was openly criticized by party spokesmen. On most of the important issues of the day, but especially on defence[53] and European and foreign policy, the gulf between the parties was unbridgeable. In the nature of their electoral support, in their policies, their internal organization, their historical references, and in their conceptions of the ideal society the two major parties of the left differed profoundly. And, unlike the euphoric years of the early 1970s, there was very little desire on either side to eradicate or even attenuate the differences. Indeed, the prolonged campaign of mutual recriminations merely exacerbated them.

National integration based on a wide coalition of anti-monopolistic forces and, more specifically, a direct alliance with the socialists gave way to a policy of withdrawal and introspection – a *stratégie de repli*, with the party falling back to its traditional positions, particularly to its working class. *Ouvriérisme* became the order of the day. This emerged in the electoral themes of the party, in its dramatic defence of the steel workers of Lorraine, in its backing for the nuclear energy policy of the right-wing government and in its attacks on immigrant workers. It emerged, too, in the party's reiterated references to the working class as the only revolutionary class, as the bearer of a great historic mission. This *ouvriérisme* profoundly irritated the party's intellectuals, and was one of the major criticisms levelled against the party leadership by Henri Fizbin, then first secretary of the Paris federation (see below).

The electoral trauma of 1981

At the first ballot of the presidential elections of April 1981 and in the June 1981 legislative elections the PCF suffered its worst electoral defeats since the war. The defeats were brutal and humiliating and led, almost inevitably, to a total reversal of previous policy. In the presidential elections Georges Marchais received only 15.3 per cent of the votes cast. He was deserted by a quarter of traditional communist voters, most of whom switched to Mitterrand who, with 26.2 per cent of the votes, largely outdistanced his communist rival. The defeat at the legislative elections was perhaps even more significant. The party won only 16.1 per cent of the votes cast at the first ballot (compared with 37.5 per cent for the socialists and their left-wing radical allies) and its parliamentary representation was decimated, falling from 86 to 44 Deputies. Of those Deputies who belonged to the party secretariat only Marchais saved his seat, whilst six of the eleven Deputies who were members of the 21-man *bureau politique* lost their seats. The electoral landslide which swept the rival socialists to their historic victory (with 269 Deputies the socialist group enjoys an overall majority in the new National Assembly) eloquently confirmed the verdict of the presidential elections. In some areas the communist defeat was overwhelming: in Paris, for example, the party lost two-fifths of its vote and has become a marginal electoral force.

The PCF contributed to the victory of Mitterrand on 10 May and his socialist party a month later in two ways. First and most obviously, it mobilized its voters in their favour at the second ballot. It really had no choice, since climbing onto the Mitterrand bandwagon was the only way of saving what little remained from the débâcle. Secondly, the very scale of the party's defeat and its manifest weakness within the left reassured wavering centrist voters who wanted to vote for the socialist left but who were afraid that a future left-wing government would be communist dominated.

The 1981 presidential elections saw not only the crushing of the party, it also led to the formation of the first left-wing government of the Fifth Republic – from which the party was pointedly excluded, in spite of its second ballot support for Mitterrand and its persistent clamour for communist ministers. It was not until after the legislative elections that Mitterrand consented to the appointment of four PCF ministers in a reshuffled government. It was the first time since May 1947 that the communists entered a French government. But they did so on conditions rigorously imposed by their socialist partners. Those conditions, which involved the party in a sharp reversal of policy on several fronts, are contained in the 4 June document in which the two parties of the left merely alluded to their disagreements and specified areas of agreement, and in the 23 June 'remarriage contract' (in Raymond Barrillon's ironic phrase) – a joint document in which the party made further concessions to the socialists.[54] The communists were obliged to accept Mitterrand's presidential programme as the 'charter for governmental action' (and that programme made no concessions to the communists and very few to the left of his own party). The 131 presidential propositions of Georges Marchais, the demands made by the PCF in September 1977 together with its biting criticisms of Mitterrand, were swiftly shelved. The PCF was also forced to promise solidarity not only at governmental level but also in the left-wing local councils and at factory level. The socialists were intent on preventing the communists from speaking with two voices, one within the government, the other outside - and critical of that government. Finally, the party was forced into a series of policy changes. On domestic issues such as nationalization (the extent, the rate, the type of managing board and the scale of compensation) - one of the major sticking points in September 1977 - the PCF has had to accept Mitterrand's policies. It has also had to swallow concessions on French participation in the Atlantic Alliance and on a future active role for France in the European Community. Most significantly, the party has had to accept the socialists' line on Afghanistan (a line which requires the withdrawal of Soviet troops) and on Poland (which welcomes the process of democratic renewal in that country). The 4 June document also advocates international negotiations for the reduction of armaments in Europe - negotiations which would encompass the Pershing and SS20 missiles.[55]

The electoral defeats and concessions to the socialists have exacerbated the divisions within the party. Critics, led by Henri Fizbin and François Hincker, have created *Rencontres Communistes* in order to push the party along a more coherent and liberal line, although they, together with nine other members of this 'parallel structure', were expelled from the Paris Federal Committee at the end of June 1981 for their activities.[56] There is also evidence that a small pro-Stalinist, pro-Soviet minority is beginning to marshall its forces.[57] Even the leadership is clearly divided, and rumours and leaks are legion. Marchais's declaration after the first ballot of the presidential elections was approved by the *bureau politique* by only one vote, and the decision to accept the socialist party demands in order to enter government was taken by the central committee only after 'une très riche discussion' - a revealing phrase. More significantly, the central committee meeting of 25-6 June was unable to choose a successor to Charles Fiterman (who had become a minister in the Mauroy government) to the secretariat of the party. The leadership readily admitted certain 'errors' (notably over its anti-immigrants campaign and its *ouvriérisme*);[58] it also promised that the next Congress - the 24th - which took place at the end of January 1982 - would be preceded by 'wide-reaching and deep debate'.

With the PCF once again practising left-wing unity 'at the summit', its major concessions over Poland, Afghanistan and the Middle East (the Camp David agreements are no longer denounced), its recognition of and its reaffirmation of the need to follow 'the French road to socialism', it may be that the party had been jolted back into involuntary Eurocommunism. If this is so it merely confirms that the Eurocommunist option is a tactical response to immediate difficulties rather than a genuine strategical conversion.

Some concluding remarks

The PCF, like any other powerfully entrenched party of self-declared revolutionary intent locked into a non-revolutionary system, faces intrinsic problems relating not only to its self-declared functions but also to the objective roles it assumes. As Georges Lavau, Kriegel and Ronald Tiersky have shown, the PCF has multiple roles which not only do not further but may actually hinder the achievement of its proclaimed revolutionary ends. The party has learnt to live with its conflicting roles, striking an uneasy and ever-changing balance between them. At the moment, however, the party is confronted with a series of pressing and serious problems which require attention. First, it seems incapable of preventing its electoral decline, in spite of the arrival of the 18–21-year-old voters on the register, the general increase in the left-wing vote since the beginning of the 1970s, and the dramatically worsened economic situation in France.[59] It has clearly losts its dominant electoral position within the left to the socialists. But the real situation is worse than the national figures suggest. For example, even by 1978 the PCF was the biggest party of the left in only 36 per cent of the constituencies, and was in danger of becoming a regional phenomenon, whilst the socialists were rapidly becoming a national party. The 1981 presidential and legislative elections as already noted were a traumatic experience for the party since it was reduced to its pre-war dimensions, and gained fewer than half the votes of its socialist rival.

Second, party membership has grown rapidly in recent years, particularly since the post-war lowest point of 225,000 in 1960, and the success has been much vaunted in the party press. By the beginning of 1981, official membership stood at 709,000, which makes the party the biggest in France in membership terms.[60] Of course, some caution is warranted in discussing membership figures (for any party),[61] yet it would be churlish to deny the success of the party's efforts in this field. Nevertheless, part of the success must be attributed to the loosening of the requirements for membership in the 1960s.[62] Moreover, the discipline, militancy and general commitment of this rapidly expanded membership has been reported – even by party leaders – as unsatisfactory.[63] Other facets of the party's general activities are equally unsatisfactory. For instance, organizations linked with or sympathetic to the party, such as the CGT, are in decline, whilst its press is in a lamentable state.[64] (*L'Humanité* has an average daily circulation of only 140,000 and lost four million francs in 1980.)

The third pressing problem is the party's relationship with the declining, increasingly divided and recalcitrant CGT – its main leverage on the industrial scene.[65] There is recent evidence to suggest that not only are the socialists of the CGT more forthright in condemning interference from the party, but communists, too, are growing restless with some of the party's policies.[66]

The fourth major problem confronting the party is the generalized revolt of its intellectuals. Whilst the party was able to mobilize *patriotisme du parti* (a very powerful adhesive in the PCF) to re-establish control over a base which was initially totally disorientated by the break with the socialists,[67] it has been unable to stem the revolt of its intellectuals. The importance of the present revolt lies in its duration, its extent and its nature. The revolt has lasted since the break with the socialists in the autumn of 1977, and shows no signs of waning. It embraces not only the customary faint-hearts of the university and artistic world, but, more important from the viewpoint of the party, it has also contaminated the cadres of the party[68] and a number of intellectual activists directly associated with the work of the party – the historians of the Institut Maurice Thorez or the journalists of *L'Humanité* (eight left the paper between 1978 and 1980[69]), *Révolution* (which lost two of its four deputy editors[70]) or *Action*, the publication of the important *secteur d'entreprise* of the party, which was shaken by the resignation of Jacques Frémontier, its editor-in-chief. The staff of *Editions Sociales*, the party's publishing house, was also affected, since two of its leading figures, Lucien Séve and Antoine Spire, were to resign. Even certain *élus* have joined the intellectuals' protest – a sure sign of its extent.[71] The most celebrated dissident is Henri Fizbin, ex-first secretary of the Paris federation, ex-Deputy of Paris, the party's candidate for mayor in the last Paris elections and ex-member of the party's central committee. His account of his revolt in 1979 is contained in his *Les bouches s'ouvrent*, one of the most remarkable books ever to appear on the internal functioning of the PCF.[72] The *Affaire Fizbin* has completely shaken the Paris federation which is in a state of sullen obstreperousness (five Paris councillors publicly announced their intention not to vote for Marchais in the presidential elections).[73]

The dissidents have organized or signed petitions,[74] written countless books (published generally by Le Seuil or Maspéro[75]), or have written articles in *Le Monde, Nouvel Observateur, Libération, Le Matin* or, in the case of Althusser, in *Paese Sera*, or even organized a protest group – *Rencontres Communistes* – within the party. Some have left the party in disgust[76] whilst others such as Elleinstein and Fizbin initially stayed on to continue the fight and urged others to do so.[77]

The result of this flood of protest is *la crise la plus grave* of the party.[78] All previous post-war crises – the Marty–Tillon crisis of 1952, that following the Soviet invasion of Hungary in 1956, the Servin–Casanova crisis of 1961 or that after the Soviet intervention in Czechoslovakia in 1968 – related to parts of the party's strategy or were reactions to a particular event. The present crisis is more fundamental because the critique of the intellectuals is more global: relations with the USSR, the relationship with the rest of the left, the general role and aims of the party, and internal party democracy.

The party's response to the revolt has been mixed. In some cases it has resorted to the classic Stalinist tactic: *marginaliser, isoler et culpabiliser*. It has purged several of its leading intellectual organs (often through 'reorganization'), has censured several publications (notably a brochure entitled *Vivre* which had on the cover an earlier photograph of Pierre Juquin, member of the *bureau politique*, shaking hands with Plyusch, the Soviet dissident)[79] and suppressed the somewhat critical *La Nouvelle Critique, France Nouvelle* and *Paris-Hebdo*. It opened *L'Humanité* to the dissidents during the 23rd Congress, but ensured that they did not intervene in the Congress debates.[80] It has expelled leading dissidents. On the other hand, the party has not expelled from its ranks men such as Jean Elleinstein whose constant stream of articles (some in the bitterly disliked *Le Figaro*) has been bitingly critical. And it has also organized several meetings with its intellectuals.[81] This relative sensitivity may be motivated by an awareness that the intellectuals are merely articulating sentiments which are widespread in the party.

The fifth problem facing the party is its intellectual sclerosis. Critics such as Alain Touraine and Jean-Marie Domenach write about the discordance of the PCF with French society, about its total incapacity to analyse the present problems of France,[82] whilst Pierre Daix claims that there is 'a divorce between history and communism' in France, and Jacques Brière notes that the party's vision of the world is exclusively economic; the social crisis is either ignored or misunderstood.[83] The critics exaggerate: during the Fifth Republic the party has begun to look more critically at the Soviet bloc; it is beginning to analyse objectively its own history (although history remains judged in terms of its contemporary utility, as a source of legitimacy for the prevailing party line); it has revised its thinking on the nature of capitalism and the state; it has engaged in a debate with Catholic intellectuals on whether Marxism is a humanistic ideology or a science; it has abandoned some of its early dogmas such as the dictatorship of the proletariat and dialectical materialism; it has rethought its position on the transitional phase to socialism; finally, since the 23rd Congress of May 1979, Marxist–Leninism (the institutional ideology of the Eastern bloc) has been replaced as the guiding principle of the party by 'scientific socialism' 'founded by Marx and Engels, then developed by Lenin and other leaders and theoreticians of the workers' movement'.

Nevertheless, intellectual sclerosis may be perceived in two directions. First, the party seems incapable of reinterpreting some of its traditional stances in the light of dramatically changing circumstances. Its policies of *ouvriérisme* and pro-Sovietism have an anachronistic air about them, especially when couched in the arcane revolutionary rhetoric that characterizes the party's propaganda. The increasing complexity and diversification of French society, the fragmentation of the working class and its questionable revolutionary zeal have had little impact on party thinking. The divisions and confusion of the communist world (and the occasional ambivalence of Soviet foreign policy), of the Third World and of the capitalist world, whilst appreciated in the early and mid-1970s, have not prevented a recurrent Manicheism. Second, the party appears insensitive to new social and economic problems and forces: the student, ecologist, consumer, anti-nuclear and feminist movements, for example, the racial problem in the major French cities, the question of urban decay, the demands for greater participation at work and local level, the impact of the Europeanization and internationalization of the economy, the fiscal revolt. These problems have been either ignored or treated in belated and half-hearted fashion. In some cases, the party has dealt with these new problems in a way designed to produce inconsistencies, ambiguities or even contradictions.[84]

Inconsistencies, ambiguities and contradictions also characterize its theories, practices, strategy or strategies. And this is the sixth major problem of the party. How to square its new commitment to *socialisme autogestionnaire* (now written into the statutes of the party since the 23rd Congress) with democratic centralism, with a national planning system, with its statist and heavily bureaucratic *Weltanschauung*, and with the vanguard role of the party? How does this latter concept fit with the enthusiastically pursued goal of constructing an (ideologically immature) *parti de masse*? How to proclaim, as it did at the 23rd Congress, both its revolutionary mission (*parti de lutte*) and fulfil its present governmental commitments (*parti de gouvernement*)? How to marry a belief in democratic pluralism with its own decision-making system and with the *bilan globalement positif* of the Soviet bloc countries? How, in practice, to harmonize a policy of widening its base with a militant *ouvriérisme*? How to reconcile its previously virulent denunciations of the socialists as inherently unreliable and reformist with its present sharing of govermental office with them? How to harmonize its belief that an irreversible break within capitalism is possible within the nation-state with its acceptance of the inherently internationalist doctrine of state monopoly capitalism?

Perhaps these contradictions are inevitable. The party has always had difficulty in keeping some sort of balance between its desire to be integrated into an increasingly complex society and its wish to retain autonomy based on a self-perceived exclusive relationship with *its* working class.[85] It is constantly cross-pressured by the exigencies of its various 'dimensions', for it is, at once, a working-class party, a party of the left, a national party and an international party.[86] As Ronald Tiersky has noted, the contradications of the party are due to 'the burden of finding a workable and politically advantageous strategy within a triangle of Soviet power, Gallo-communism and Eurocommunism'.[87] Even at the domestic level, the party is caught between the conflicting demands that arise out of its self-declared and 'objective roles'.[88] Finally, the party is no monolithic structure; it is constantly torn by the conflicting aspirations of the *courants* and *tendances* which proliferate within the party.[89]

It may be that the contradictions and qualifications which abound in each policy statement and the ambiguities which permeate the activity of the party are, in some measure, functional. Since the seeds of a perfectly contradictory policy are contained in each policy it is always possible to indulge in the occasional volte-face (one of the characteristics of the party's history), and to justify it by invoking previous texts which demonstrate consistency and continuity.

The PCF is in a curious position at the moment. At the time of its worst electoral performance since the war it has entered government. It has made major concessions to President Mitterrand and his socialist party and yet is accused of *Rétro-communisme, Gallo-communisme and Archéo-communisme*. It is in a state of intellectual turmoil yet suffers from ideological sclerosis, incapable of defining a coherent strategy or mobilizing any hopes. It is accused of both intransigence and opportunism, of following a *stratégie de repli* and the tactics of survival based on *ouverture*, of indulging in introversion and introspection and also in a thoughtless embracing of outside influences, of adopting the mentality of the fortress under siege[90] and of too readily opening the fortress gates to the socialist enemy.

Some commentators have discerned a strategy or series of strategies. The party is presented as some kind of Soviet fifth column intent simply on furthering the foreign policy aims of the 'fatherland of socialism'. Or it is perceived as obsessed by the need to break the electoral power of the socialist party in order to reassert its lost hegemony within the French left. Others point to a strategy based on *encadrement*, a policy of consolidating and reinforcing its traditional bastions.

Other critics, however, claim that the party is totally devoid of strategy. It can no longer harbour pretensions to hegemony within French society; it is afraid of governmental power yet embraces it; it is apprehensive about any alliance with the socialists yet is forced into one; it is nervous about the implications of any shift in direction yet constant pressures demand such a shift. For a brief period (from the early 1960s until 1977) the French Communist Party voluntarily flirted with the different elements of the Eurocommunist syndrome. That break with the past should not, of course, be exaggerated, for the seeds of each had been present in earlier periods of the party's history. The peculiar feature of the Eurocommunist experiment of the PCF was that all three aims - de-Sovietization, liberalization and national integration - were attempted. But not to the same extent and not at precisely the same time - a discordance which may have been one of the major causes of its failure.[91] None was ever fully pursued, and although interrelated the aims were kept distinct. Yet the interrelationship was too manifest; the pursuit of each was pregnant with implications for the others. Each was a Pandora's box. Together they threatened the structures, methods, traditional strategies and ultimate ends of the party. Small wonder that the experiment was brief.

Eurocommunism for the PCF was buried in September 1977[92] and its death was probably facilitated by the fact that it had few affective roots in the party: characteristically it was imposed by the leadership and never really emerged as the result of informed discussion at the base. The problem for the party leadership was that the only viable alternative appeared to be its traditional pro-Soviet, nationalistic *ouvriériste* line, pursued between 1977 and 1981. During this period the party entrenched itself in its slowly declining or stagnant bastions, offering religion rather than the prospects of power to its activists, providing succour for the poor and an infinite source of irritated fascination for the intellectuals (especially its own). Yet the non-government line presented as many acute problems as the Eurocommunist one. The elections of 1981 represented a resounding repudiation of its change of direction. The party is, therefore, apparently faced with two unpalatable choices. Tracing a third and profitable one presents the party with its major challenge for the 1980s.

Notes

1 On the general background of the party during this period see Jean Elleinstein, *Le PC* (Paris 1976); Jacques Fauvet, *Histoire du Parti communiste français* (Paris 1978); Annie Kriegel, *Les Communistes francais* (Paris 1970); Ronald Tiersky, *French Communism 1920-1972* (New York, 1972); Olivier Duhamel and Henri Weber, *Changer le PC?* (Paris 1979); Donald L.M. Blackmer and Sidney Tarrow (eds), *Communism in Italy and France* (Princeton, N.J., 1975); Kenneth R. Libbey, 'The French Communist Party in the 1960s: An Ideological Profile', *Journal of Contemporary History*, 1976, pp. 145-65; Jean Burles, *Le Parti Communiste dans la Société française* (Paris, 1979); F. Bon *et al.*, *Le Communisme en France* (Paris, 1968).

2 An expression taken from Michel Winock, 'Table Ronde', in 'L' Enigme Communiste', *Esprit*, February 1975, p. 174.

3 A point made frequently by Philippe Robrieux in his excellent biography of Thorez - *Maurice Thorez - vie secrète et vie publique* (Paris, 1975).

4 See A. Eisenberg Stiefbold, *The French Communist Party in Transition: PCF-CPSU Relations and the Challenge to Soviet Authority* (New York, 1977), and Ronald Tiersky, 'Le PCF et la Détente', *Esprit*, February 1975, pp. 218-41; Kevin Devlin, 'The Challenge of Eurocommunism', *Problems of Communism*, January 1977, pp. 1-20.

5 Quoted in Michèle Cotta, 'PCF: le Rétro-communisme', *Le Point*, 14

January 1980. A version of the report was later published in *Luttes et Combats* in April 1979. Cf. *Le Monde*, 3 May 1979 and *Le Matin*, 2 May 1979.

6 See especially the article by Jean Kanapa, 'Le Mouvement Communiste International hier et aujourd'hui', *France Nouvelle*, 12 December 1977, and *L'Humanité*, 30 June 1977.

7 Alexandre Adler, Francis Cohen, Maurice Decaillot, Claude Frious, Léon Robel.

8 *Le Monde*, 24–5 December 1978.

9 It is revealing that *L'USSR et Nous* left almost all the important questions it raised unanswered. Cf. Jolyon Howorth, 'Four Lessons in Communist Introspection', *Bulletin of the Society for the Study of Labour History*, Spring 1980, no. 1640, pp. 69–70.

10 Edward Mortimer, 'Un Socialisme aux couleurs de la France: the French Communist Party', in Paolo Filo della Torre *et al.*, *Eurocommunism: Myth or Reality* (London, 1979).

11 The subject of a number of recent books: cf. Jean-Pierre Rious, 'La double Stratégie des Communistes à la Libération', *Le Monde de Dimanche*, 21 November 1979 which reviews them.

12 The theme of Richard Johnson's book, *The French Communist Party versus the Students*, New Haven, 1972.

13 There is a brief, trenchant and acute analysis of the limits in Roy C. Macridis, 'The French Communist Party's Many Faces', *Problems of Communism*, May–June 1976, pp. 59–64.

14 Sue Ellen M. Charlton, 'Deradicalisation and the French Communist Party', *The Review of Politics*, 41 (1), 38–60.

15 See, for example, Maurice Duverger, 'L'Autre Pluralisme', *Le Monde*, 2 February 1978.

16 Jolyon Howorth, 'The French Communist Party: Return to the Ghetto', *The World Today*, 36 (4), 141–2. Jack Hayward, 'Submerged Factionalism in the French Communist Party', Paper ECPR workshop, Florence, March 1980.

17 The last important purges date from 1959 (the Servin-Casanova and Kriegel-Valrimont purge) and 1966 when the PC cell of the Sorbonne Arts Faculty was purged for 'sectarian deviationism'.

18 Charlton, op. cit, pp. 53–4.

19 Ronald Tiersky, 'French Communism in 1976', *Problems of Communism*, January–February 1976, p. 39.

20 On the history of the Communist-Socialist relationship, see François G. Dreyfus, *Histoire des gauches en France 1940–1974* (Paris, 1975); Jean Poperen, *L'Unité de la Gauche 1965–1973* (Paris, 1975); Robert Verdier, *PS–PC: une lutte pour l'entente* (Paris, 1976); Howard Machin and Vincent Wright, 'The French Left under the Fifth Republic: The Search for Identity in Unity', *Comparative Politics*, October 1977, pp. 35–67; Ian Campbell, 'The French Communists and the Union of the

Left 1974–1976', *Parliamentary Affairs*, Summer 1976, pp. 246–67; Frank L. Wilson, 'The French CP's Dilemma', *Problems of Communism*, July–August 1978, pp. 1–14; special issue of *Esprit*, February 1975.

21 The revealing title of a book by Etienne Fajon which appeared in 1975.

22 André Laurens, 'Le choix internationaliste du PC', *Le Monde*, 13–14 January 1980.

23 Speech of Georges Marchais at Bobigny, 10 February 1980.

24 Irène Allier, 'Comment digérer la Pologne', *Nouvel Observateur*, 30 August 1980.

25 See article 'Jamais Ça' in *L'Humanité*, 17 December 1979, and Michèle Cotta, 'Le PCF à fond derrière Moscou', *Le Point*, 24 December 1979.

26 On the latter visit see the somewhat scathing article by Annie Kriegel, 'Le Fils Prodigue', *Le Figaro*, 29 July 1980.

27 *L'Humanité*, 9 May 1980.

28 Anicet Le Pors, *L'Humanité*, 14 March 1979.

29 *L'Humanité*, 22 April 1980.

30 *L'Humanité*, 26 June 1980 (Maxime Gremetz).

31 *L'Humanité*, 8 June 1980 (Charles Fiterman, member of the secretariat of the party).

32 See especially the speech by Gaston Plissonnier, *L'Humanité*, 19 April 1980.

33 *L'Humanité*, 21 August 1980.

34 See also the article by Jean Radvanyi, in *Cahiers du Communisme*, December 1980.

35 Revealing in this respect was the publication by Editions Sociales (the party's publishing house) of *La Nation* by Roger Martelli – a vigorous defender of the nation.

36 See notably the declaration of Marchais to *Le Monde*, 31 May 1979.

37 In Paul Laurent (reputed to be one of the leading liberals of the party), *Le Parti Communiste comme il est* (Paris, 1978).

38 Discussion was allowed in the party press during the period of the 1979 party Congress.

39 See also the apologia of democratic centralism by Paul Laurent in *France Nouvelle*, 7 April 1979.

40 The theme of a perceptive article by Paul Friedrich, 'Légitimité et Représentation', *Esprit*, February 1975, pp. 206–17.

41 Speech of Georges Marchais, 19 June 1980.

42 The catalogue of socialist sins outlined in Georges Marchais, *Parlons franchement* (Paris, 1977).

43 The theme was already contained in the Marchais Report of 29 June 1972 to the central committee after the negotiations on the joint programme of government. The report was made public in June 1975. See also the party's official *L'histoire du réformisme en France* (Paris, 1976), and Burles, op. cit.

44 The autumn by-elections of 1974, local elections and opinion polls.

45 André Lajoinie (member of the *bureau politique*), in *L'Humanité*, 19 April 1980.

46 Cf. the statements of Marchais on Europe I radio station, 23 September 1979, and Lajoinie in *L'Humanité*, 19 April 1980.

47 Tiersky, 'French Communism in 1976', pp. 20–1. Certainly there was a renewed emphasis in party propaganda on the revolutionary role of the party, and *Nous vivons l'époque des Révolutions* was the theme of Marchais's speech to the young communists in February 1980. *Le Monde*, 5 February 1980.

48 Cf. in particular the statement by Jospin in *Le Monde*, 2 January 1980.

49 Resolution of the 23rd Party Congress and that adopted at the meeting of the *Conseil National* which took place on 9–10 February 1980.

50 Although Marchais in his 23rd Congress speech insisted on the need to keep open the door even at the summit.

51 Georges Marchais in a television interview, *Cartes sur Table*, 13 October 1980.

52 There were reported conflicts at Sarcelles, Epernay, Besançon, Dreux, Châlons, Tourcoing, Reims, Nantes, Elbeuf, Villeneuve-d' Ascq, Lille, Montargis, Rennes, Saint-Etienne, Poissy, La Ciotat, Angers, Héronville, Le Mans, Saint-Malo, Saint-Priest.

53 The PS's refusal to vote the PC motion of censure in December 1979 illustrated the division. Cf. Patrick Jarreau, 'Une vieille querelle', *Le Monde*, 21 December 1979.

54 *Le Monde*, 25 June 1981.

55 The text of the agreement is in *Le Monde*, 25 June 1981.

56 *Le Monde*, 1 July 1981.

57 Frédéric Charpier, 'PC: le contre-attaque des prosoviétiques', *Nouvel Observateur*, 11 July 1981.

58 Notably in Marchais's report to the central committee on 25–6 June. Cf. *L'Humanité*, 27 June 1981.

59 22.4 per cent in March 1967, 20.3 per cent in June 1968, 21.3 per cent in March 1973, 20.6 per cent in March 1978, 20.6 per cent in the European elections of June 1979, 15.3 per cent in the April 1981 presidential elections and 16.1 per cent in the June 1981 legislative elections.

60 *L'Humanité*, 8 January 1981.

61 Ronald Tiersky, 'French Communism in 1976', pp. 32–3.

62 Jane Jenson and George Ross, 'The Unchartered Waters of De-Stalinisation: The Uneven Evolution of the Parti Communiste Français', *Politics and Society*, 9 (3), 291.

63 Charles Fiterman in his report to a meeting of the federal secretaries in April 1980 complained that many cells were not functioning at all (*Le Monde*, 23 April 1980), and Marchais made a similar point after the disappointing results of the November 1980 by-elections (*Le Point*, 8 December 1980).

64 Alain Duhamel, *La République Giscardienne* (Paris, 1980), pp. 150-2, and on *L'Humanité*, *Le Monde*, 3 July 1981.

65 George Ross, *Workers and Communists in France* (Berkeley, 1982).

66 On these developments see the articles by Claude-François Jullien in *Le Nouvel Observateur* of 29 October 1979, 14 January 1980, 4 February 1980 and 2 August 1980, and 'L' Embarras du CGT', *Le Point*, 14 June 1980.

67 Michèle Cotta, 'Marchais annonce la riposte', *Le Point*, 15 May 1978.

68 'P.S. Quand l'espoir vient du PC', *Le Point*, 17 December 1979.

69 Denis Jeambar, 'Les verrous de Marchais', *Le Point*, 23 June 1980.

70 *Révolution* was created to replace *La Nouvelle Critique* and *France Nouvelle* which were suppressed because they were judged to be too critical towards the party. The two deputy editors were François Hincker and Serge Goffard. cf. 'PCF: des fuites dans l'appareil', *Nouvel Observateur*, 12 July 1980.

71 These include the mayor of Sèvres (who protested about the party's attitude on Afghanistan), the chairman of the important PC group in the municipal council of Carcassonne and the deputy mayor of Hem (Nord).

72 Paris, 1980. See also his interview in *Le Monde*, 12 June 1980.

73 *Le Monde*, 10–11 December 1979.

74 Notably the petition which emanated from the Jacques Duclos cell of Aix-en-Provence in May 1978, demanding the full implementation of the decisions of the 22nd Congress (see Michel Barak, *Fractures* (Marseilles, 1980)) and which collected 1500 party signatures. Equally important was the petition *Pour l'Union dans les luttes* which advocated left-wing unity and which, by the end of 1980, had collected 140,000 signatures, many of which from well-known party activists (see Irène Allier, 'Tristes bougies pour le PC', *Le Point*, 29 December 1980.

75 Louis Althusser, *Ce qui ne peut plus durer dans le Parti Communiste* (Paris, 1978); Jacques Brière, *Vive la Crise* (Paris, 1979); Hélène Parmelin, *Libérer les communistes* (Paris, 1979); Raymond Jean, *La singularité d'être communiste* (Paris, 1979); Jean Elleinstein, *Une certaine idée du communisme* (Paris, 1979); Gérard Belloin, *Nos rêves camarades* (Paris, 1979); Nina and Jean Kéhayan, *La rue du Prolétaire rouge* (Paris, 1978); Antoine Spire, *Profession: permanent* (Paris, 1980); Jean Rony, *Trente ans de Parti: un communiste s'interroge* (Paris, 1978).

76 These include the writers Hélène Parmelin, Robert Merle and Raymond Jean, the painter Edouard Pignon, the poet Eugène Guillevie, the university professors André Gisselbrecht, Claude Frioux, Claude Mesliand, Maurice Goldring, Alexandre Adler, Jean Rony and Antoine Spire, and Antoine Vitez, Bernard Sobel and Stellio Lorenzi. See Denis Jeambar, 'PC: la fuite des cerveaux', *Le Point*, 5 January 1981.

77 *Le Monde*, 5 November 1980 and 8 January 1981.

78 Interview with Philippe Robrieux, one of the best historians of the party,

in *Le Point*, 24 April 1978.

79 The party also censured a second issue of *La Nouvelle Critique* devoted to the question of pluralism (*Le Nouvel Observateur*, 13 November 1978, which published the three incriminating articles).

80 *Le Monde*, 13 December 1978 (article by Michel Barak, one of the dissidents) and 16 March 1979.

81 For example at Vitry in December 1978 and in Paris in January 1981.

82 Cf. Questions Essentielles, *Esprit*, February 1975, p. 171.

83 The themes of *La crise du PCF* by Daix and *Vive la crise* by Brière.

84 For example, in its attitude to decentralization see Yves Mény, 'Partis politiques et décentralisation', in *L'Administration vue par les politiques* (Paris, 1979), pp. 108-9.

85 Cf. for example, Isaac Aviv, 'Le PCF dans le système français des années 1930 à la fin de la IVe République', *Mouvement Social*, July–September 1978, no. 104, pp. 75-93.

86 Duhamel, op. cit., p. 147.

87 Ronald Tiersky, 'French Communism, Eurocommunism and Soviet Power', in Rudolf L. Tökés, *Eurocommunism and Détente* (London, 1978), p. 143.

88 The theme of much of Tiersky's writing.

89 A point admirably put by Jensen and Ross, op. cit., p. 264. See also Gérard Molina and Yves Vargas, *Dialogue à l'intérieur du Parti* (Paris, 1978).

90 Cf. Notably Jean Elleinstein, 'Que Faire?', *Le Monde*, 23 December 1980.

91 See the well-argued article by Jensen and Ross, op. cit.

92 Georges Marchais on television, 11 June 1980, described it as 'un costume trop étroit'.

7

Historic compromise
or bourgeois majority?
Eurocommunism in Italy 1976–9*

Sidney Tarrow

When Eurocommunism in Italy is compared with its counterparts in other countries, immediately a number of apparent differences appear. First, Eurocommunism, in the shape of the 'historic compromise', appeared in Italy in the early 1970s before the word 'Eurocommunism' existed. Second, the Italian communists were part of a political majority between mid-1976 and early 1979, in contrast to the largely theoretical Eurocommunism of their counterparts elsewhere. Third, the strategy appears to have failed in the country in which it reached its pinnacle of success, as the PCI, losing voters, members and face, went back into opposition after electoral defeats in the June 1979 legislative election and in administrative elections the following year.[1] In Italy Eurocommunism came early; it achieved a semblance of success; and then it met profound defeat – at least judging by Italy's return to a centre-left political formula which separated the communists from their former socialist allies in 1980.

How can we explain the steep parabola of the PCI's historic compromise? I will offer four sets of observations, based both on the Italian case and on the experiences of communist parties in relation to bourgeois majorities elsewhere. First, the historic compromise – and Eurocommunism in general – was far from the radical change in doctrine for the Italian communists that it would have been, say, for the French party.[2] Second, what was involved in Italy between 1976 and 1979 was not the innovative and transformative doctrine put forward by party secretary Berlinguer in 1973, but an Italian version of communist participation in bourgeois majorities familiar from the

* I am extremely grateful to Stephen Hellman for his detailed and perceptive comments on an earlier (1980) version of this article.

past. Third, paradoxically, the strategy itself suffered during the 1976-9 period because of the party's way of linking strategy to tactics; but, fourth, strategic defeat did not constitute the defeat of the strategy, as the PCI - though reeling from its political exclusion - refused to turn to global oppositionism or to the sectarianism that distinguished French communism after September 1977. These points will be taken up in sequence as I turn, first, to the genesis and changes in the historic compromise strategy since 1973; second, to the pattern of the PCI's relationship to the Andreotti governments between 1976 and early 1979; third, to the problems that collaboration brought the party and its strategy; and fourth, to the continuities in its strategic model before and after its electoral débâcle in 1979.

Historic compromise: genesis and dynamics

The event that began the period of Eurocommunism in Italy was the publication in the autumn of 1973 of communist leader Enrico Berlinguer's 'Reflections on the Facts of Chile'.[3] In it Berlinguer painted a stark picture of the prospects for classical revolution in the West, concluded that the only way for a communist party to come to power under such conditions was through coalition with parties of the *status quo*, set out a general programme of reforms to expand the alliances of the working class and deduced the necessity, in Italian conditions, for a great 'historic compromise' between the working class and organized Catholicism. The latter was the most optimistic part of the article: for in the atmosphere of rapid secularization and mass mobilization of the early 1970s, there were currents in the Italian church and among lay Catholics that appeared to augur a new progressivism, or at least a split within Catholicism that could be exploited politically by the left.[4]

The international situation also seemed to be evolving in directions favourable to the PCI. Détente between the superpowers was probably at its height, just as the Italian party was moving towards a line of 'Europe neither in NATO nor in the Warsaw Pact'. In Western Europe there was restlessness with the remnants of American hegemony and the PCI was in the process of accepting the Common Market. The decline of authoritarian regimes in Southern Europe in particular gave the PCI the hope of finding parties of the left in power within a very few years. The party's gradual but determined detachment from Soviet foreign policy positions over the past two decades had prepared it well to meet these new conditions.[5]

Internally, the PCI had weathered its exclusion from power since 1947 quite well. It now had an organization that had adapted itself from a cadre into a mass party, a membership that - after a period of decline - was showing signs of rejuvenation, and a doctrinal flexibility that enabled its programmes, adapted to the problems of 'post-industrial' society, to appeal to young people, women and the new middle class. The party presented a strong contrast to the PCF, which could only with difficulty wrench itself away from its traditional *ouvriériste* mentality and from its reflexive alignment with the Soviet Union.[6]

Berlinguer's pronouncements in 1973 reflected this optimism about the PCI's perspectives. But if one reads his 'Reflections on the Facts of Chile', it becomes clear that this optimistic surface has a more cautious, even defensive, substratum. First, his proposal for a coalition with the Christian Democrats (DC) was put forward tentatively and alongside alliance proposals of a more traditional 'popular front' type.[7] Second, together with the hope of taking advantage of a changing international system, there was the fear of a repetition of the Chilean disaster. Third, as a hand was outstretched to new social actors and prospective political allies, there was a warning to Italy's then-militant trade unions that their aggressive wage claims and 'strategy of reforms' would alienate potential friends and could drive the middle class into the hands of resurgent neo-fascism - in 1973 still a force to be reckoned with. Finally, though the overall tone of the article was conciliatory, Berlinguer was careful to strike a combative note, calling at one point for 'alliances of combat' on the road to a social transformation - a slogan scarcely calculated to seduce the more conservative factions of the DC.[8]

The themes of alliances stretching to the centre-right of the political spectrum and the general climate of unrest in Italy at the time underscored the elements of innovation in the proposal for an historic compromise. But there was an underlying continuity in it too, particularly with the *'politica di Salerno'* that Togliatti had initiated in 1944 and with his 'Testament', published after his death in 1964.[9] Both employed the logic that the type of alliance sought induces the content of reform - rather than vice versa - and both showed a preference for broad, multipolar alliances stretching through the left parties to the DC, rather than an exclusive alliance with any one partner. Although Berlinguer was certainly more explicit in his appeal to the DC than his predecessor, both he and Togliatti recognized that - short of attempting to destroy religion - coming to power in Italy meant coming to terms with at least some sectors of organized Catholicism.

The PCI's electoral windfalls of the mid-1970s - the divorce referendum of 1974, the local and regional elections of 1975, and the legislative election of 1976 - were by some observers accounted to the credit of the new line. But if, as argued above, the line was *not* all that new, then the PCI's electoral gains could not be so clearly traced to decisions in favour of it by the electorate.[10] At least equally important were the country's severe economic crisis, the recent extension of the suffrage to 18-21 year-olds - a group that had been formed politically during the late 1960s student movement - and the series of scandals and strategic mistakes made by the DC in the early 1970s. Although the PCI did make electoral gains in 1976 among key targets of the Berlinguer line - women, Catholics, southerners and young people - there were objective explanations for these changes.[11]

The political implications are obvious. If, as the PCI believed, the new line was really new, then subsequent electoral and political gains could be credited to it and it could safely be pushed to its ideological limits. If, however, the line was a simple extension of the Togliattian synthesis and was not primarily responsible for the party's political gains, then its further extension could lead to difficulties were it to be given too much prominence in the PCI's tactical decision-making. It might particularly lead to problems if its really innovative domestic feature - the proposal for an alliance with organized Catholicism - was interpreted politically as a moderate coalition with the DC, at the cost of the party's more traditional alliance strategy and its relationship with its bastions in the labour movement.

Skilled politicians that they are, the PCI's leaders must have known that their electoral gains in the mid-1970s were largely due to objective factors and to their opponents' mistakes. However, a variety of factors led them to place increasing emphasis on the Berlinguer line after 1973, and to interpret its political proposals as demanding a policy of conciliation with the DC, first at the local and regional, and then at the national levels. These factors may be briefly summarized:

The economic crisis

While it would be wrong to paint too gloomy a picture of the Italian economy in the mid-1970s, it would be a mistake to ignore either its reality or its perception by the PCI. To the worker and student mobilizations of the late 1960s, which had resulted in major increases in both salaries and public spending, there was added a crisis of accumulation after 1973, when the country's economy appeared to be incapable of absorbing both the earlier costs and quadrupled energy prices. As both government spending and industry's costs rose (in the heavily nationalized Italian economy, the two are often the same), a monetary crisis ensued in 1974 and again in 1976, bringing on a degree of capital export and a good deal of international speculation about the possibility of the country's 'bankruptcy.'[12] The crisis not only gave the PCI a weapon with which to attack the DC; it also threatened jobs and appeared to have the potential to reduce Italy to the dependent capitalist nation it had been prior to the 'economic miracle' of the 1950s and 1960s. Especially from the liberal wing of the party could be heard calls for protecting the level of affluence that Italy had achieved over the past twenty-five years.[13] Only in government, it was increasingly argued, could the PCI assume this role.

The political weakness of the DC

Enabled to govern as a 'party of the relative majority' through centrist coalitions in the 1950s and a centre-left coalition in the 1960s, the DC saw the latter evaporate through the socialists' (PSI) defection in the early 1970s. This party, which had been described by Sani as having 'three souls',[14] responded to the worker and student mobilization of the turn of the decade by adopting the most advanced reform proposals of the trade unions and declaring itself unavailable for further coalitions of the centre-left.[15] The leftward turn of the socialists, only definitively reversed in the late 1970s, left the DC temporarily in danger of veering to the right – which it tried unsuccessfully from 1972 to 1974 – and ultimately available for 'more advanced equilibria' which would include the communists. For the PCI, the DC's strategic weakness, far more than the changing electoral balance, was the practical undercurrent to the theoretical wave of Eurocommunism.

The social crisis

Linked in its origins to the political and economic factors sketched above, but – by 1974 at least – distinct in its manifestations, Italy's social crisis appeared to take the form of acute anomie to some and conspiracy to others. The convulsive 'movement' that had carried social unrest into the streets in the late 1960s was, by the mid-1970s, divided into those who had moved into the existing party system, those who were organized into radical voluntary associations and pressure groups, and those who had rejected reform altogether for political terror.[16] The latter appeared to merge with the purely criminal delinquency that flourished during the period. (In fact, political murder was far less frequent than kidnapping for pure gain, but in a social climate that had been turbulent since the late 1960s, ordinary citizens could be forgiven for confusing the two and even equating them.)

For the PCI, the danger was a triple one: first, the immediate danger in which party leaders and trade unionists found themselves as they too became targets of political terror; second, the votes that would be lost if the middle class and part of the working class turned to the parties of 'order'; and, third, the danger that social disintegration, economic crisis and political fragmentation would lead the country into a reactionary revolution of the kind it had experienced in 1922. There was no Mussolini on the scene, but there were figures in both the DC and on the far right that appeared to toy with the idea of a 'strong' government that would be able to repress both criminality and political violence. After these were suppressed, the PCI's turn might be next. The social crisis of the mid-1970s thus led the PCI to emphasize the moderate note in the historic compromise and to translate it into largely political terms that could lead only to the project of an alliance with the DC.

The translation of strategy into tactics

There is an internal feature that the PCI, for all its ideological evolution and tactical flexibility, has not escaped; and that is, though strategy can be interpreted in a variety of ways, once a strategic line has been adopted it becomes a fixed reference point in organizing the behaviour of party leaders, cadres and militants and in legitimating the party's tactics. Though this is true of all communist parties, the strategic models of orthodox parties are generally abstract ('opposition to capital'), historical ('being true to the party's tradition') or distant ('fealty to the Soviet Union'). But the PCI, which long ago left behind the security of Stalinism, substituted for it a strategic model that is politically concrete, contemporary and domestically specific, making it difficult to separate from the party's day-to-day behaviour. The problem is not that, once adopted, a strategy cannot be reversed, but that *as long as* it is the party's strategy it must be referred back to as the main source of party behaviour, and will therefore be judged in terms of the success or failure of the behaviour. In the case of the historic compromise strategy, as we shall see below, the strategy would become identified with some remarkably moderate political behaviour, behaviour which both failed to achieve the party's ambitious claims for it and failed also in the more modest sense of achieving policy goals in competition with the DC and the other parties of the majority.

In summary, with the virtues of hindsight we can see that prior to 1976 the PCI's strategy was the linear descendant of Togliatti's line of the 1940s and the 1960s; it was not the only, or even the *major*, source of the party's spectacular electoral gains from 1974 to 1976; but for the reasons outlined above, it would be invoked increasingly as the source of success and as the strategic model to guide behaviour after the party decided to support a DC government in 1976. Whatever happened after June 1976 was not the result of the strategy's success, but it would be interpreted by the PCI in terms of the strategy's aims. Hence the failures of 1976–9 could not fail to reflect on the strategy itself.

1976–1979: the PCI and the majority

What had its partners to gain by inviting the PCI into the majority? Many reasons have been invoked to justify the taking of this historic step, which, by the way, strained the DC's ties with some of its political allies and with the United States. Some of the PCI's motives outlined above – confronting the economic crisis, the DC's political weakness, and the threat of terrorism – also motivated the governing party. But its major incentive appears to have been industrial: having lost control over its trade union affiliate, the CISL, in the late 1960s, the DC hoped to engage the communists – by far the most influential political element in the labour movement – to argue on behalf of an incomes policy with their representatives in the unions. The idea was not a new one – it was first put forward by republican party leader Ugo La Malfa – but it took on new urgency in the context of the 1976 monetary crisis and gained strength with the accession to power within the DC of party president Aldo Moro and secretary-general Benigno Zaccagnini. Moro and Zaccagnini came to power with the support of the progressive and labour-oriented factions in the party, with the goal of opening a dialogue with the PCI and ending the stalemate in the country's economic policy-making.[17]

Was the DC really ripe for a left-leaning coalition of national solidarity with the PCI? Though reeling from the effects of recent scandals and economic problems, after its 1974 and 1975 defeats the party of relative majority had reasserted its electoral strength in 1976.[18] Its plural internal factions were recomposing themselves into a broad majority, and its ties with domestic and international business were unimpaired. For long years the guardian of both ideological and political anti-communism, and still a formidable political machine with control over most of the levers of state power, the DC was none the less the home of some powerful political notables who could not look kindly upon their party's arch-enemy entering the control room of government.

There were many in the PCI who also doubted whether the conditions for their party's participation in the majority really existed. In addition to distrust of the DC's motives, the PCI had recently acquired – but not assimilated – thousands of new members and hundreds of thousands of voters, many with expectations for rapid change. The cities and regions over which the left gained control in the 1975 administrative elections were in a state of near-paralysis, requiring that many cadres be directed from party and political work into municipal administration and be replaced with often-inexperienced militants. Internationally, the Soviet Union was showing itself restive with the implications of Eurocommunism for its foreign policy and for its control over Eastern Europe, and expressing public doubts about the wisdom of Western parties entering coalitions with bourgeois groups.[19] The trade unions – whose support would be critical for the implementation of any incomes policy – remained cautious and internally divided in their support for the experiment, although the communist militants in the CGIL were mostly in favour.[20]

For the PCI to overcome its hesitation, the DC had first to give some sign that it was prepared to lift the ban on communist legitimation that it had imposed since 1947. This it did by formally consulting the PCI on the choice and programme of the new Prime Minister in July 1976 and by agreeing to PCI leader Pietro Ingrao as president of the Chamber of Deputies. A till-then conservative DC notable, Giulio Andreotti – a *ministrabile* of thirty years' duration – was asked to form a one-party government that would depend on the parliamentary support of the lay parties and on the abstention of the PCI. The choice of Andreotti was a shrewd political move, for he was acceptable to the communists, had worked repeatedly with the centre-left parties, and had close ties to the Vatican and to the USA. Inside the DC, he would balance the Moro–Zaccagnini directorate which was still slightly suspect to the party's right wing.

The PCI remained cautious, abstaining on the investiture of the Andreotti cabinet, calling it only a government of 'democratic and national solidarity' within the 'framework of present-day relations of domestic and international forces'[21] and cautioning its militants that it did *not* represent the historic compromise, but only a response to Italy's desperate social, political and economic crisis. Consultation would take place through meetings among the secretaries of the co-operating parties of the majority, or among designated party 'experts', with the cabinet exercising a kind of implementing role for decisions taken elsewhere. Andreotti was able to mediate skilfully between the committees of party officials and the cabinet, maintaining the support of most of his own party, of the small social democrats (PSDI) and republicans (PRI), of the conservative liberals (PLI) for a time, and of the communists. After programmatic accords were signed in the summer of 1977, the liberals left, but Andreotti carried on as before with a five-party majority accepting PCI support, and not merely abstention, as was the case in 1976.[22]

These were the conditions which would make possible the relative political stability of the next three years. Gianfranco Pasquino writes, 'One single Prime Minister, Giulio Andreotti, was able to survive (and, for that matter, to thrive) through the creation of three different types of governments.'[23] The first was an all-DC cabinet enjoying the abstention of all the other parties with the opposition of only the very extreme right and left. It operated under a 'programmatic accord' hammered out by the secretaries of the six majority parties in 1977 and lasted 536 days, almost twice the length of the average post-war Italian government, resigning in January 1978, when trade union pressure forced the PCI to demand a formal role in the Government. This triggered a long governmental crisis which ended in March with the PCI formally in the majority but still not in the cabinet.

Andreotti's second government lasted for less than a year – the most turbulent in Italy's post-war history – and finally fell because of the communists' renewed demands for cabinet posts. After a long governmental crisis marked by the failure of a compromise which would have admitted 'technicians' acceptable to the PCI into the cabinet, Andreotti formed his third majority – this time with the small parties of the centre in the Government – whose real purpose was to prepare the way for new elections. The stratagem worked: in June,

1979 there would be major gains for the small parties, a stable position for the DC and a large electoral setback for the PCI – which declined from its pinnacle of nearly 35 per cent of the vote in 1976 to just over 30 per cent and a loss of twenty-six seats in the chamber.[24]

Part of Andreotti's success resulted from the fact that he provided a solution to the internal conflict in the DC between its conservative factions, discredited between 1974 and 1976, and a left which had wanted to move much closer to the communists. His success was also due in part to the unique position in which his government placed the socialists: though in the majority, their position between DC and PCI gave the PSI the leverage to criticize both, and the chance for a new leadership group under Bettino Craxi to consolidate its position.[25] Part was also due to Andreotti's ability to calm the Vatican and the American Government, although the latter was increasingly restive as the PCI sought greater leverage within the coalition.

There was no question, however, that without communist support in Parliament, among the public and with the trade unions, the Andreotti government could not have survived. In Parliament, several major pieces of legislation were passed as the result of hard, behind-the-scenes bargaining in the committee of party secretaries that had become the hidden control centre of the majority. In the media, the PCI from mid-1976 on turned its guns away from the DC towards the extreme left and its terrorist fringe. And in the trade unions it was the communist CGIL leader, Luciano Lama, who took responsibility for a bruising fight to support austerity in return for presumed reforms in social policy and a promised increase in public investment, particularly in the south.[26]

Its hold over governmental power reinforced, the DC used the Andreotti governments to recompose its internal majority and to reassure business and the middle class that it was not bent on ceding control to the communists. Though Moro vacillated during late 1977 and early 1978, under American pressure, PCI demands for a direct role in the Government were ultimately resisted. Before long, a 'mini-recovery' could be discerned in the economy as the result of changing international conditions and of a shrewd policy of monetary management. Political conditions had contributed; for the economy, concludes economist Michele Salvati, 'The period from the end of 1976 to the beginning of 1979 saw one of the most stable governmental formations of the whole decade.'[27]

But far from benefiting the communists, whose co-operation had made it possible, the Andreotti governments cost the PCI dear and would ultimately result in their electoral defeat, their return to opposition in 1979, and in the socialists' return to the centre-left formula they had sworn never to repeat. What was experienced between 1976 and 1979 was clearly not the bold and transformative vision of PCI–Catholic compromise that had been put forward in 1973, but a far more traditional model of communist participation in bourgeois coalitions. In retrospect, this conclusion is obvious, true almost by definition. Why, then, did the PCI pay such high costs for its coalitional experience? We will turn to this question after briefly summarizing what these costs were.

The costs of collaboration

The first warning signs were electoral. In administrative elections in both 1977 and 1978, there was a decline in votes for the PCI – in a few cases precipitous – a recovery for the DC, and an increase for both the socialists and the minor lay parties. In several areas, local or regional parties made surprising gains. In 1978 there were referenda on public order and on state financing of the party system, in which all the institutional parties lost face, to the benefit of the radicals, a volatile 'new left' grouping that had gathered together civil libertarians, feminists, environmentalists and dissidents from the main parties. Most disappointing to the PCI were its losses in the south, where in 1976 it had seemed to overcome its traditional weakness in that underdeveloped region.[28]

In industrial relations, though the EUR conference of February 1978 endorsed austerity, there was major dissent among some sectors of the unions and an outbreak of strikes from the so-called 'autonomous unions', mainly in the public sector. Industrial violence recurred sporadically and though the strike rate declined, productivity was still growing more slowly than inflation.[29] The PCI's dilemma was revealed in a CeSPE survey of working-class communists in 1977, only a bare majority of whom felt that the movement's commitment to the factory was sufficient.[30] The unions' attempt to redirect pressure from the shop floor to political goals like increased investment in the south was of little direct interest to the workers, who were more interested in preventing the gains in real wages they had made in previous years being eroded by inflation.

It was through the increasing attacks against law and order that the majority was most sorely tested. A reorganization of the security services revealed widespread disaffection, competition between services and duplication of activities in the fight against terrorism. As party and trade union officials began to be attacked too, communist calls for law and order equalled in stridency those coming from the right. When an extreme left student demonstration in Bologna in March 1977 led police to shoot a demonstrator, the army was called into this model city of central Italian communism and the municipal administration had to suffer an even more imposing demonstration under the windows of city hall.[31]

Both police incompetence and calls for 'vigilance' came to a head in the most dramatic event of the period: the kidnapping in broad daylight and eventual murder of DC president Moro by the Red Brigades between March and May 1978. In the six weeks between the kidnapping and the murder, the DC held firm in the face of its leader's agony, but the most intense pressure against compromising with the terrorists came from the PCI. It was on his way to Parliament to speak in favour of the second Andreotti government that Moro had been seized. As Peter Lange writes,

> The conjunction of the two events was neither accidental nor without its ironies. The entrance of the PCI into the majority was the apogée of success for the policy of accommodation and national unity which the PCI had been pursuing for a number of years ... Aldo Moro had been the chief advocate among Christian Democrats in favour of at least a short-run version of this compromise.[32]

But accommodation to what and national unity with whom? Even the strains outlined above could have been overcome had something akin to the innovative spirit and optimistic tone of the original Berlinguer formulation been felt by party militants between 1976 and 1979. Instead, there was a national economic policy that sought to reassert fiscal conservatism, a social policy that continued to dam up unemployment while making no real effort to provide new sources of jobs, a limited urban policy that made it impossible for left-wing municipalities to finance innovative new projects, and – it goes without saying – a foreign policy that left Italy a stalwart ally of the USA.

The PCI's contributions to policy-making were equally compromising and lacking in imagination. Its role in implementing the regional reform was severely criticized for compromising with the DC's unwillingness to turn over full powers to the regions; it was unable to convince the Government to pump governmental funds through the byzantine bureaucracy to the financially strapped cities it had taken over in 1975; and its economic confusion was summed up in the 'Medium-Term Economic Programme' published in 1977, which was greeted by the other parties and by the press with a loud yawn.[33] Though anti-communists made much of the stranglehold that the communists were supposed to be gaining over policy and appointments, the reality was much less flattering. The party remained tangential to the cabinet; it was exploited for its usefulness in reining in organized labour and for spreading among its supporters a moral revulsion against terrorism that helped the Government to adopt more serious police measures; but it was largely ignored when it made even modest reform proposals.

The result was a number of serious internal problems. The party's organization had grown by leaps and bounds in the wake of the student and worker mobilizations of the late 1960s. By 1976, there were nearly 1,800,000 PCI members, an increase of 20 per cent over 1968. The number of party sections had risen from under 11,000 in 1967 to almost 12,000 in 1975, while the crucial strata of party cadres and parliamentary Deputies were being successfully renewed and rejuvenated.[34] There was no doubt that the PCI, with its flexible and adaptive organizational system, had been able to roll with the punches of the post-1968 period, and – unlike its sister party, the PCF – to grow organizationally as a by-product of the massive mobilizations of that period.

Remarkably, however, two Italian researchers, Marzio Barbagli and Piergiorgio Corbetta, have produced evidence that PCI membership growth in the early 1970s was not particularly strong among the social categories (young people, women and workers) who had been the protagonists of the 'movement' of the late 1960s and early 1970s. Growth was heavily concentrated in central Italy, the party's traditional fortress, where the 'movements' had not been strong. In the urban centres of north-western Italy, where the hot points of the earlier mobilization had been found, PCI growth was less intense, while in sheer percentage terms membership grew most in the south, where the 'movement' had been extremely weak.[35] Although the meaning of these data are open to differing interpretations,[36] what is beyond dispute is that the electoral break-throughs of the mid-1970s were not matched by corresponding organizational growth that could turn the voters of the moment into permanent sympathizers.

The fruits of these ambiguities ripened after 1976, when the PCI's participation in the majority began to produce far less than many of its supporters had expected. Many party members – over 60 per cent in a regional survey in Emilia – doubted that it was possible to have confidence in the DC's willingness to keep its part of the bargain.[37] From 1977 on, there were reports of disorientation and outright dissent in the PCI's ranks. Giorgio Amendola, himself no leftist, saw not so much dissent from the party's line, but an absence of active *con*sent among the militants. The results could be seen in the membership figures for 1977 and 1978, which registered the first reversals since the 1960s.[38]

The PCI's involvement in the majority also gave the socialists an opportunity to reassert their identity by attacking the PCI. This began under the best theoretical credentials, with a debate between socialist and communist intellectuals in 1977 regarding the compatibility between democracy and Marxism-Leninism in the thought of Gramsci.[39] It was followed by a PSI 'Project for a Socialist Alternative' in 1978, which was, unfortunately, buried in the agony of the Moro affair and its aftermath.[40] After the May 1978 local elections, PSI secretary Craxi returned to the attack in an *Espresso* article in which he condemned 'the philosophical thread linking the Jacobin tradition of élitist, centralizing authoritarianism with the Leninist route to power.'[41] It was a classical social democratic attack from the right which was, however, combined with a series of rhetorically radical attacks from the left presenting the PCI as too close to the DC, both in its stances on political–economic policy and on public order.

Though Craxi's broadsides were clearly demagogic, the fact is that both his radical and his moderate attacks contained a portion of truth. The PCI *was* co-operating with the DC in a government that had produced few signs of reform; and it *had* continued to maintain that democratic centralism was the only true form of internal democracy. But there was a logic to this contraposition of moderate external and orthodox internal policies: by maintaining stiff internal control, the PCI was enable to follow its moderate political course without fearing the consolidation of a left-wing faction like the *Manifesto* group that had emerged in the late 1960s. Entry into the majority in 1976 gave this dialectic a new twist; since the PCI *right* was most anxious to demonstrate the party's democratic credentials, there was new pressure for loosening up its internal life, just as the party's moderation in policy matters gave the left more reason to complain.

Some movement could be discerned towards modification of the party statute as the PCI neared its 15th Congress in early 1979.[42] But dissent among the membership and the imminence of new elections made real theoretical departures unlikely. By the time of the Congress, the DC had scorned the PCI alliance by supporting entry into the European Monetary System under conditions that supposed no growth in real wages over the next three years.[43] Given the state of mind of its militants, the PCI could not afford to go along with such a policy, and, indeed, used it as an issue of confidence on which to withdraw its support from Andreotti. The 'liberal' resolutions passed by the 15th Congress were thus no more than cosmetic, with the Congress itself turned into a pre-electoral platform and the theoretical debate reduced to a generic call for a 'third way' for Italy between Soviet communism and Western capitalism.[44]

The June 1979 legislative elections and, even more, the elections to the European Parliament a week later, confirmed the worst predictions of the PCI's internal critics. Not only did the party lose 4 per cent in the Chamber of Deputies and 2.5 per cent in the Senate: its vote for the European Parliament fell to below 30 per cent. It held a much lower percentage of younger voters than either the radicals or the extreme left (PDUP–NSU). Its losses were particularly humiliating in regions in which it had gained local and regional power in 1975 – particularly in Piedmont, Lazio and Campania, where the left controlled, respectively, the cities of Turin, Rome and Naples – and were highest of all in the south, where 1976 had seemed a historic break-through.[45]

There was no doubt that the 1979 elections were a débâcle. In *Rinascita*, Gerardo Chiaromonte wrote,

> We face an important decline in our votes with respect to . . . 1976, and we are well aware of the implications of this decline. It is the first time that such a thing has happened. Like all our cadres and militants, we too feel bitter and disillusioned.

Though Chiaromonte was quick to blame the results on the 'violent offensive that for some time has been unleashed against us' by the DC and its allies, there was no attempt to throw off the party's own responsibility. 'We must reflect on and discuss with great energy', wrote Chiaromonte, 'the paths we have taken, the policy we have followed, our capacity for organization, for action, for propaganda and for ideological struggle.' 'We remain convinced', he went on 'of the validity of our line of democratic solidarity. However,' he concluded, in implied criticism of the recently failed coalition with DC, 'we consider ever more pressing the need to work for collaboration, for a dialogue between programmes, for convergence and for *unity between communists and socialists* in Italy and in Western Europe'[46] (emphasis added).

There was little prospect of a renewed communist–socialist alliance, however, for after a transitional period of posturing and bargaining, punctuated by an outbreak of internal factional fighting, the PSI of Bettino Craxi joined a renewed centre-left coalition with the DC and the republicans, under Francesco Cossiga. This government would survive not only the 1980 administrative elections but also the remarkable Donat–Cattin affair in which Prime Minister Cossiga was himself involved.[47] Not only that, but the PSI made major gains in the 1980 elections – as did the anti-Communist social democrats, reinforcing the impression that the electorate was moving to the right. The communists lost ground in almost all the regions, particularly in the south, with the curious exception of Naples, which they had been expected to lose.[48] To the extent that local and regional elections are a referendum on national politics (and even if they are not, the politicians read them as if they were), the results of June 1980 definitely buried the politics of national unity of the previous three years, and the PCI entered a period of opposition and partial isolation.

When, in 1981, Cossiga's government fell, there was little chance of a return to anything like the Andreotti formula, if only because the muscle-flexing leader of the PSI, Bettino Craxi, would not have gone along. What resulted instead was equally revolutionary in the post-war history of Italy – a five-party government from the socialists on the left to the liberals on the right with a *non*-Christian Democrat, republican Giovanni Spadolini, in the premiership! But the loss of the leading role in government, while it threw the DC into crisis, did not rebound to the benefit of the communists. On the contrary, it seems to have emboldened Craxi's anti-communist polemics and undercut what was until then a hallowed shibboleth to the PCI – that the left cannot gain even a share of power in the absence of the communists. Opposition, it would seem, has not been an unmixed blessing for the PCI, and its nightmare is that a party one-third its size, the PSI, will follow the same incredible trajectory to power as the French PS did in the 1970s.

Assessing the damage

Thus the period 1976-9, and its aftermath, was a failure for the PCI. But why did the party fail so dramatically? How did the defeat relate to its national strategy and to Eurocommunism in general? And, given the present stalled situation and the communists' isolation in the opposition, what are the prospects for the future? These three separate questions can, as yet, only be tentatively answered, though there is somewhat more certainty now than there was in 1979. My general argument will be that, under the surface of tactical adaptations dictated by the twists and turns of current Italian politics, there has been no return to the tough, besieged policies of the Cold War, and that the ambiguities that were traced during the course of the 1976-9 period can still be discerned in the PCI today.

First, the question of the party's failure. In assessing the reasons for the PCI's failures after 1976, it is insufficient, as party leaders did, to bemoan the *implementation* of the party's strategy, which had the double comfort for them of leaving the strategy untouched and of placing the blame further down the ladder of the organization.[49] The major failure was the result of entering the Andreotti majority, and of being outmanouevred within it by a DC whose basic sources of strength - the Catholic electorate, the party's American connection and its links with the state and with business - were unimpaired. Since PCI leaders knew all these things and more, we have to assume that they chose to enter the Andreotti majority because they still thought something was to be gained by doing so, even in the face of the DC's staying power and the PCI's strategic weakness.

The reason they entered, I would maintain, lay in the party's reading of the Italian crisis. Like many on the left, PCI leaders saw the period after 1973 as one of real or potential 'organic crisis', possibly leading to a decline of Italian capitalism, but more likely to lead to a major crisis of the political system. It was through this system - immobile and inefficient as it was - that the PCI had long since chosen to seek an internal and gradual path to power. It could even be said that, for a party that had chosen the democratic path to socialism, defending the democratic system (and Italy *is* a democracy)[50] was not only consistent with theory and strategy but constituted the highest form of enlightened self-interest.

But the interpretation of this need to protect democracy as the party's 'obligation' to join a moderate political majority made sense only if the system was indeed in mortal danger. Of danger signs, both before and after 1976, there were many, and who can say how well the Italian republic would have survived the onslaughts made upon it - for example, the Moro killing - with the PCI in opposition? What seems dubious, however, is that Italy in the mid-1970s was engulfed in the kind of *organic* crisis which grips society, economy and polity in the same stranglehold and threatens the collapse of political democracy itself. The PCI apparently believed this to be the case, and was far from being alone in this conviction. What argues against the organic crisis view is the ease with which an apparently seamless web of crisis was taken apart into separate policy strands after 1976 and the degree to which both the political dominance of the DC and the economic dominance of management were re-established.[51] This is not to argue against the sincerity of the PCI's belief in the gravity of the Italian crisis in 1976, but only to question its accuracy and the party leaders' inference that it obliged them to join a political majority whose reform prospects were bound to be slim. Indeed, the more loudly they broadcast their fears about the gravity of Italy's crisis, the less likely were they to extract reform concessions from their allies, who could always respond that, as the PCI well knew, the crisis was far too serious to permit 'experimenting' with expensive or structually upsetting social reforms.

Second, the question of the defeat, national strategy and communism. Why could the PCI's failures during these years be laid so securely at the doorstep of the historic compromise? Earlier in this paper I hinted at one reason that was political in the most elementary sense: between 1973 and 1976, both friends and enemies had pointed to the Berlinguer line as the reason for the PCI's electoral successes. How natural, then, that the strategy itself should bear the brunt of the blame for the failures of 1976 to 1979? Berlinguer himself admitted as much as he began to trim his sails in preparation for the 15th Congress and as he took a harder line with the DC in local and regional administrations in late 1978.

But there is a more fundamental reason for the strategic defeats of these years, and it involves the combination of rigidity and flexibility with which the PCI relates political behaviour to party strategy. A communist party (perhaps any organized mass party) needs a strategic model to mediate between its internal life and its political behaviour. Especially when engaged in dispersive and potentially compromising governmental participation, a party must turn to its strategic model as source of signals for its leaders' behaviour and as a symbol of assurance for its primary constituencies – labour, party sympathizers and militants – that what it is doing in government bears a legitimate relationship to its strategic goals. Thus, however aware it may be of the gap between long-term strategic perspectives and the objective conditions surrounding its accession into the majority, the party *must* invoke its strategy – or some other strategy –

to organize its actions in power and mediate between its external behaviour and its internal life.

It may be remarked that communist parties have always possessed strategic models, but this has not prevented them from making strategic reversals of almost galactic proportions. Leaving aside the fact that such reversals have often been extremely costly to the parties involved, what distinguished the historic compromise from more orthodox party strategies was that right from the beginning it was couched in concrete *political* terms which specified not only the political and social alliances to be sought, but also the political and social policy goals to be expected from them. Therefore, for as long as the strategy lasted, the party's political behaviour had to live up to some extremely specific criteria in order to match the strategy's goals. Compared to the hopes raised by the historic compromise, the paucity of what could be realized through the PCI's participation in the Andreotti majority was bound to increase the party's problems.

During much of the first year of the arrangement, little was tested because little was attempted, with the parties manoeuvring around one another as the Government responded to periodic crises and prepared the programmatic accord that would be signed in July 1977. It was only when the terms of this accord were published that the truly moderate character of the experiment was made plain. Yet the expectations raised by its strategy were such that the PCI had to emerge triumphant from the months of bargaining that had led to the accord. *Rinascita* gave it weeks of positive coverage, concluding that 'Even if we have not yet arrived at a turning point, it can nonetheless be affirmed that the orientations which have emerged constitute *the basis for a new political phase*, one of broad democratic unity'[52] (emphasis added).

Amid the general euphoria, some PCI leaders gave a more measured assessment, for the accords had said nothing concrete about a general reform of the public sector, nor was there a firm commitment to implement economic planning or to give organized labour the role in investment that it was demanding. The reforms of the tax system were designed to render it more efficient, not to penalize profit or unearned income; the educational reform attempted was equally innocuous. The only real change was the one regarding the defence of the public order.[53] Referring specifically to the economic planks of the accord, Luciano Barca noted the PCI's approval, but also observed that 'we are conscious of all the limits of the programme, particularly given what we were able to verify from the outside about its construction and given that the same sentences could disguise different meanings'. The crux of the programme he found in the problem of '*how to shift resources from consumption to investment without stimulating a further process of inflation*',[54] not a markedly different goal from what the Bank of Italy had been urging for years (emphasis added).

Given this sober assessment, it is hard to see what basis the party had for regarding the programmatic accord as a turning point towards a new type of society. Yet it was so described only two weeks later, in a special issue of *Rinascita* entitled 'Thirty Years that Signal an Epoch', Recalling how the left had been ejected from the post-war government of national solidarity in 1947, Berlinguer's powerful lieutenant, Gerardo Chiaromonte, asked: 'How have we arrived at an event [the signing of the programmatic accord] which seems to close, or to begin the closing, of that historic period that began thirty years ago with the breakdown of the governments of democratic unity?'[55]

In his editorial in the same issue of *Rinascita*, editor Minucci appeared to attempt an answer to Chiaromonte's question. He wrote: 'the sense of a historical cycle ended, between the two poles of 1947 and 1977,' is due not 'to the fact that the communists themselves have changed, and in changing have resigned themselves to renounce who knows what obsolete "authoritarian" character.' The party had indeed changed, but for Minucci these changes 'have taken place in an increasingly tight and organic matrix of a process of growth of the working class, of its influence and hegemony in Italian society, of its contractual and political strength'. Such changes should be seen in their international, economic and class contexts: internationally, 'from the rise of American hegemony to its first signs of decline'; economically, in the 'exhaustion of the peculiar mechanism of development' chosen by the Italian Government in the early post-war years; and, in class terms, in the failure of the dominant groups to translate their economic power into 'an adequate capacity of social and political control'. The result, he concluded, is that:

the choice of the economic directions on which a new phase of ex-pansion will depend cannot be separated from the identity of the forces that will guide this new phase or from *a qualitative change in the class equilibrium in the very composition of the ruling elite* (emphasis added). This is the theme of today, the element that gives meaning and historical significance to the accords agreed upon over the past few weeks by the democratic parties.[56]

The most extraordinary transmutation had occurred! A set of programmatic accords, which at best could be described as an attempt to modernize and assist Italian capitalism to revive, were being described as the harbinger of 'a qualitative change in the class equilibrium in the very composition of the ruling elite'. Between Barca's and others' realistic assessment of the economic core of the programme and *Rinascita's* triumphant interpretation of its import for the social coalition underlying the ruling élite, there was a profound difference. The accord was the programme of a bourgeois government with left-wing external support; what Minucci described was akin to the optimistic tone of Berlinguer's 'Reflections on the Facts of Chile'. There was little objective basis to link the one to the other. However, the PCI is a traditional enough communist party to have no policy without a strategy to justify it, and modern enough to have made its strategy so concretely political that the contradictions between its strategy and the reality of what it was doing were palpably clear.

This brings us to the final question raised at the beginning of this paper: 'What had happened to the historic compromise strategy?' Or, to put the question in more general terms: 'Is Eurocommunism dead in Italy?' I have already made clear my opinion that the Berlinguer line adopted in 1973 was basically a continuation of Togliatti's strategy of the 1940s and 1960s. If I am correct, then the power of tradition alone would prevent any very different strategy emerging from the defeats that the PCI suffered towards the end of the 1970s. Georges Marchais could turn away from Eurocommunism so easily (though not without cost) in 1977 because the theoretical departures on which it was based had never taken root in his party; but the fundamental precepts of the historic compromise – though in new and innovative forms developed by Berlinguer – were so deeply rooted in the PCI's basic strategic model that they could not be easily changed, even if the party's leaders wanted to do so. As Joseph LaPalombara has written in a recent issue of *Foreign Affairs*, 'Just as Togliatti was not Thorez, Berlinguer is a far cry from Georges Marchais.'[57]

Some serious observers of the PCI have seen in the policy directives of its leadership after 1979 the signs of a *svolta*, or turning point.[58] For example, in a press release in November 1980, the leadership defined as 'inadequate to the gravity of the present situation' 'the search for solutions that are limited to the sphere of the parties that have governed Italy during the last few decades'.[59] Barbagli and Corbetta, who have done some of the finest empirical work on the PCI, have defined this decision as 'a true turning point', concluding that 'the prospects for the historic compromise are closed for the immediate future'.[60] Even Berlinguer, the apostle of the historic compromise, called soon after for a 'democratic alternative' to the DC, a line that he had summarily rejected when it became the rallying cry of the socialist left in 1976.[61]

But if the prospects for anything resembling the historic compromise are closed off for the immediate future, is this because of a change of strategy on the part of the PCI's leadership or because of the political situation in which the party found itself after 1979? The militants, as Barbagli and Corbetta clearly show, had never been enthusiastic for the Berlinguer line; the party's electoral stagnation was continuing; on the industrial relations front, a crushing defeat was inflicted at the FIAT works of Turin as the automobile industry – still the linchpin of the Italian economy – began to fire workers. My own view is that the exclusion of the PCI from the Government and the success of the socialists produced what I would regard as a tactical *svolta* that left the essentials of Berlinguer's strategy still in place. As LaPalombara concludes:

> The PCI is relatively free of Stalinist residues; it remains relatively friendly toward Catholicism and ready to pursue a strategy of broad alliances at home and in Europe; it is in favor of the institutions of the European Community, has accepted NATO, and has avoided declarations that strike fear into the hearts of others.[62]

By the beginning of 1982, there was still no sign of the 'strategic' *svolta* that observers had seen coming since the fall of the Andreotti government in 1979. Most of the combative language of PCI leaders is, in fact, directed at Craxi's socialists and not at the DC, while a minority, reformist faction in the party prefers a softer line, even towards Craxi.[63] But what has demonstrated far better than internal political sparring that the *svolta* had severe limits was the party's reaction to the Polish crisis, which went far beyond criticism of Poland's military leadership or the support that the coup enjoyed from the USSR. In a formal statement in December 1981, reinforced by press releases in January 1982, the PCI, in LaPalombara's words, 'issued a bombshell statement': 'not just excoriating the military coup and repression in Poland but, more important, announcing that *the historical phase ushered in by the October Revolution had ended* and that a new phase of socialist development must begin'[64] (emphasis added). Though nothing in politics is ever final, the depth of the PCI's current alienation from the USSR – and the disrepute into which this has thrown pro-Soviet leaders within the party – indicate that no real alternative to the historic compromise has yet been adopted by the Italian party. In December 1982, in response to the formation of a new centre–left government by DC leader Amintore Fanfani, Berlinguer – while refusing to admit it – renewed all the themes of his earlier strategy.

Moreover, even the terms in which the party secretary had announced the PCI's return to opposition in 1979 simply gave a more combative tone to what had become a fundamental strategic direction. In an important *Rinascita* editorial, Berlinguer recalled an article of Togliatti's from 1946 in which his predecessor had described as a 'precise compromise' the post-war governments of national unity that had ushered in the Italian republic.[65] He used the parallel to warn the Italian bourgeoisie of the dangers of excluding the working class from government, as De Gaspari had done in 1946.

> Do the conservative forces of Italy in the 1980s demonstrate the same blindness and political incapacity that they showed three decades earlier in ending the 'precise compromise'? Do they, too, fail to understand the law of intelligent conservatism? ('Lose something methodically every day so as to avoid losing everything.').

He feared that the same might be true today, warning that DC attacks on the PCI threatened not only the communists but 'all the parties which attempt to organize the masses and to lead the society in new ways in search of particular ideals' – in other words the DC itself.[66]

But despite the political defeat of 1976–9 and his new and more combative tone, Berlinguer was *not* calling for a return to oppositionism, for he reminded his comrades that, though going into opposition, it was incumbent upon them '*to return to and to make explicit and deeper the terms of the compromise that is necessary today*'[67] (emphasis added). Though deeply compromised by the defeats of 1976–9, the Berlinguer strategy has remained the theoretical basis of the PCI's future action. Of course, under a new leadership – both in Rome and in Moscow – all this could change, but the strategic prospects for PCI power in Italy are unlikely to improve sufficiently to produce an outright rejection of the policies we have analysed during the period of Eurocommunism.

Conclusions

Eurocommunism existed in fact, though not in name, in Italy well before 1973, when Berlinguer's 'historic compromise' line was unveiled. The line was an extension and refinement of the party's entire post-war strategy, and made explicit its links with the early post-war period. But communist participation in the majority between 1976 and 1979 did not really implement the historic compromise, since the underlying conditions of that period were not those that would have permitted major social and economic reforms to be achieved. They were conditions that encouraged the communists to support a bourgeois majority whose task was to resolve a series of interrelated crises – social, economic and political – where the greatest need was to involve organized labour in a recovery programme. As in other cases of communist support for bourgeois majorities, the conditions encouraging the party to participate disappeared as soon as remedial and stabilizing goals had been reached.

In assessing the whole pattern of PCI strategy during the 1970s, one question which is crucial for the future remains unanswered: how can we explain the optimism of the PCI about moving towards socialism through coalition with a Christian Democratic party that has shown itself to be not only moderate but a truly formidable opponent? Three possible reasons can be adduced for the party's stubborn persistence in a line that, at least between 1976 and 1979, did not seem to apply to the conditions of Italian life.

First, there is the PCI's continuing underestimation of the DC, a party which is poorly understood in general, but which the left in particular has tended to classify as a party of clienteles, a party of the state, even as a *non*-party of factions.[68] But the DC, apart from its extraordinary record of heading every government from 1946 to 1981 has proved strategically able as well, using rather than being consumed by its factional heterogeneity to adapt to different political situations. Thus, the Andreotti government was a government of technocrats led by a centre-right-wing leader supported within the DC by a centre-left majority! No wonder that Gianfranco Pasquino can characterize the DC as 'the case of a continuous and successful adaptation of a complex organizational structure to environmental changes and political challenges'.[69]

Second, a hallmark of the PCI's departure from classical communist practice in bourgeois democracy has been the relative precedence it gives to the political superstructure in its strategic thinking. The argument appears succinctly in Minucci's 1977 *Rinascita* article, and is worth reproducing in detail for what it tells us about the party's optimism about the possibilities of gaining political power through a coalition with the Christian Democrats. He begins with the bourgeoisie, which he sees, after World War Two, as 'clearly demonstrating its preference for a pure and simple restoration of its own domination, without posing the problem of a new type of relationship with society'. The result has been to increase profits and disequilibrium, but also 'to transfer to the political system the burden of aggregating that which monopolistic expansion tended to disaggregate'. As well as accelerating the process of integration between economics and politics, this also had the effect of 'giving politics as such . . . a *degree of autonomy that it doesn't have in other capitalist countries*'[70] (emphasis added). This recognition of the autonomy of the political has taken the PCI a long way away from economic orthodoxy, but it perhaps underestimates the structural constraints on politics in a society like Italy's.

Third, all political parties need to connect their primary constituency - in this case the working class - with a secondary constituency reached through social and political alliances - mainly from the middle class. The PCI attempts to link the two constituencies ideologically, calling for a government of reforms (to appeal to the middle class) leading to socialism through working-class hegemony. The ideological syncretism that results is evident; the PCI cannot expect to construct a secular alliance for modernization and social justice with a party that contains a strong traditional religious and cultural base and maintains links with some of the most conservative elements in Italian society. Working-class hegemony, as the PCI correctly argues, need not take the narrow and sectarian ideological and organizational forms that it has usually had in the history of Marxism, but it seems unlikely to be compatible with a 'consociational democracy' in partnership with a Christian Democratic partner whose power is based upon hegemony of a very different sort.[71]

Notes

1 For a thorough analysis of the 1979 elections, see the American Enterprise Institute's *Italy at the Polls, 1979*, ed. H. Penniman (Washington, DC, 1981).

2 Michel-André Gadbois, 'Alliance Strategies and the French Communist Party's Concept of "Rapport de Forces"', ICES Research Report No. 1, Interuniversity Centre for European Studies, Montreal, Canada, March 1980.

3 'Riflessioni sull 'Italia dopo i fatti del Cile', *Rinascita*, 28 September, 5 October and 9 October; republished in Berlinguer's *La 'questione'*

comunista: 1969-1975, vol. 2, ed. Antonio Tatò (Rome, 1975), pp. 609-39.

4 For example, the once-conservative Association of Italian Catholic Workers (ACLI) split during this period, with its former leader, Labor, leading a group of progressive Catholics out of the Vatican-linked organization and aligning himself with the left.

5 The now-classical source is Donald L.M. Blackmer's *Unity in Diversity: Italian Communism and the Communist World* (Cambridge, Mass., 1968). No book-length study really attempts the same job for the 1970s, but see Joan Barth Urban's 'Moscow and the PCI: Kto Kovo?', paper presented to the Annual Meeting of the American Political Science Association, Washington, DC, 1977.

6 For a synthetic treatment of the differences between these two parties, see my 'Communism in Italy and France: Adaptation and Change', in Donald L.M. Blackmer and Sidney Tarrow (eds), *Communism in Italy and France* (Princeton, 1975), pp. 575-640. For a recent treatment of the changes in the French Communist Party, see George Ross and Jane Jenson, 'Eurocommunism and Democratic Centralism: The *Parti Communiste Français*', paper prepared for the Annual Meetings of the Canadian Political Science Association, UQAM, Montreal, Canada, June 1980.

7 Berlinguer, 'Riflessioni', op. cit., pp. 628-31.

8 Ibid., p. 622. For a brief analysis, see my 'Italy in 1978: "Where Everybody Governs, Does Anybody Govern"?', in B. Denitch (ed.), *Legitimation and Delegitimation of Regimes* (London 1979), pp. 230-5.

9 On the *politica di Salerno*, see Harald Hamrin, *Between Bolshevism and Revisionism: The Italian Communist Party, 1944-1947* (Stockholm, 1975), pp. 120-9. On the Togliatti line in the 1960s, see Grant Amyot, *The Italian Communist Party* (New York, 1981) and, for a different view, my *Peasant Communism in Southern Italy* (New Haven, 1977), ch. 5.

10 Giacomo Sani, in his analysis of the Italian electoral changes in the mid-1970s, writes: 'Electoral results are often interpreted as the response of the electorate to the alternatives proposed by the parties in a given political situation. The hypothesis advanced here is that the results of a particular election, beyond the situation of the moment, also reflect the characteristics of the political culture at the time when different cohorts of votes were socialized politically.' 'Ricambio elettorale, mutamenti sociali e preferenze politche', in Luigi Graziano and Sidney Tarrow (eds), *La crisi italiana*, vol. 1, *Formazione del regime repubblicano e società civile* (Turin, 1979), p. 303.

11 Arturo Parisi and Gianfranco Pasquino have advanced a cogent hypothesis which enables them to both understand the growth of the electorate of the left in the mid-1970s, and its qualitatively new relationship to the parties, especially to the communist party. See their 'Changes in Italian Electoral Behavior: The Relationship between Parties and

Voters', in Peter Lange and Sidney Tarrow (eds), *Italy in Transition* (London, 1980), pp. 6–28.

12 For two excellent summaries of Italy's economic problems during this period, see Raymond Lubitz, 'The Italian Economic Crisis of the 1970s', International Finance Discussion Paper No. 120, United States Federal Reserve Board, June 1978; and Michele Salvati, 'Muddling Through: Economics and Politics in Italy – 1969–1979', in Lange and Tarrow, op. cit., pp. 31–48.

13 The historical leader of the liberal wing, Giorgio Amendola, put this – as usual – in most extreme form. But it was central to the PCI's growing support for a policy of austerity, though the latter was couched, in official party language, in the need 'to initiate a grand policy of social transformation'. As Peter Lange writes, the Italian economic crisis was 'exposing in dramatic form the structural weaknesses of the economic order': and 'threatening to create severe divisions within the bloc of social alliances which lay at the heart of the party's strategy'. See his 'Crisis and Consent, Change and Compromise: Dilemmas of Italian Communism in the 1970s', in Lange and Tarrow, op. cit., esp. pp. 122–3.

14 For a summary of the twists and turns of the PSI strategy during this period, see David Hine, 'The Italian Socialist Party under Craxi: Surviving but Not Reviving', in Lange and Tarrow, op. cit., pp. 133–47. Excellent summaries of particular periods are found in Gianfranco Pasquino's contributions to Howard Penniman (ed.), *Italy at the Polls, 1976*, and *Italy at the Polls, 1979* (Washington, 1977 and 1981).

15 On this period of the PSI's evolution, and on its effects on the political balance, see Salvati's 'Muddling Through' in Lange and Tarrow, op. cit., pp. 35–36.

16 Francesco Alberoni's 'Movimenti e istituzioni nell'Italia tra il 1960 e il 1970', in Graziano and Tarrow, op. cit., vol. 1, pp. 233–47 describes the genesis and differentiation of many of these groupings. For a more detailed development of the same theme, see his *Movimento e istituzione* (Bologna, 1977).

17 Pasquino's 'Italian Christian Democracy: A Party for All Seasons?', in Lange and Tarrow, op. cit., pp. 97–102, deals with this period of *'rifondazione'* of the DC's internal factional alignment.

18 The DC's electoral recovery in 1976 is dealt with in Giuseppe Di Palma's contribution to Howard Penniman's *Italy at the Polls, 1976* (Washington, DC, 1977). The reasons for this recovery are not easily understood. For a first, able attempt, see Pasquino, 'Italian Christian Democracy', in Lange and Tarrow, op. cit., pp. 102ff.

19 See Urban, op. cit., for a detailed press analysis. For more general observations, see Leonard Schapiro's 'The Soviet Response to Eurocommunism', *West European Politics*, 2, May 1980, pp. 3ff.

20 This distinction, which has been evident in the reactions of different strands of the labour movement to government attempts to achieve an

incomes policy, has not yet been adequately analysed by students of Italian trade unions. For example, Marino Regini, in his fine article 'Changing Relationships between Labour Unions and the State in Italy: Towards a Neo-corporatist System?', in G. Lehmbruch and P. Schmitter (eds), *Variations in the Pattern of Corporatist Policy-Formation*, vol. 2 (London, in preparation) explicitly limits himself to the CGIL.

21 Gerardo Chiaromonte published the party's official reaction in 'Il governo e il PCI', *Rinascita*, 6 August 1976, p. 1.

22 This period is covered in very general terms in my 'Three Years of Italian Democracy', the introduction to Penniman, *Italy at the Polls, 1979*.

23 Gianfranco Pasquino, 'In Search of a Stable Governmental Coalition: The Italian Parliamentary Elections of 1979', unpublished paper, 1980, p. 1.

24 Ibid., p. 3; for the 1979 results see Giacomo Sani, 'Italian Voters, 1976–79', in Penniman, *Italy at the Polls, 1979*.

25 Hine, 'Surviving or Reviving?', in Lange and Tarrow, op. cit., p. 140; also see Pasquino's contribution on the socialists to Penniman's *Italy at the Polls, 1979*.

26 Marino Regini, 'Labour Unions, Industrial Action and Politics', in Lange and Tarrow, op. cit., pp. 49–66.

27 Salvati, 'Muddling through', in Lange and Tarrow op. cit., p. 44.

28 For analyses of the local elections and referenda of these years see Arturo Parisi and Maurizio Rossi, 'Le relazioni elettori-partiti: quale lezione?', *Il Mulino*, July–August 1978, pp. 503–47, and Gianfranco Pasquino, 'Referendum: l'analisi del voto', *Mondoperaio*, July–August 1978, pp. 18–24.

29 OECD, *Main Economic Indicators*, August 1979, pp. 110–13; Salvati, 'Muddling Through', in Lange and Tarrow, op. cit., pp. 44–45.

30 R. Mannheimer, M. Rodrigues and C. Sebastiani, *Gli operai comunisti* (Rome, 1979), p. 110.

31 The shrillness of the response of the PCI's municipal élite can be heard in an interview with Mayor Renato Zangheri entitled 'Perché Bologna?', *Rinascita*, 18 March 1977.

32 Peter Lange, 'Crisis and Consent, Change and Compromise', in Lange and Tarrow, op. cit., p. 110.

33 PCI, *Proposta di progetto a medio termine* (Roma 1977); for a critical analysis, see Alberto Martinelli, 'The Economic Policy of the Italian Communist Party', *Challenge*, September–October 1976.

34 Marzio Barbagli and Piergiorgio Corbetta, 'Partito e movimento: aspetti del rinnovamento del PCI', *Inchiesta*, January–February 1978, tables 2, 7, 9 and 10. Part of this important article is republished in Alberto Martinelli and Gianfranco Pasquino (eds), *La politica dell' Italia che cambia* (Milan, 1978), pp. 144–70.

35 Ibid., tables 12 and 13.

36 The Barbagli and Corbetta model appears much less applicable at the local level, or so it can be concluded from Stephen Hellman's fascinating

'Il PCI e l'ambigua eredità dell'autunno caldo a Torino', *Il Mulino*, March-April 1980, pp. 246-95.

37 Barbagli and Corbetta, 'Una tattica e due strategie: inchiesta sulla base del PCI', *Il Mulino*, November-December 1978, pp. 911-67.

38 A number of articles and letters to the editor in *Rinascita* during 1978 revealed a state of anxiety in the party about the state and morale of membership. For an example, see the round table discussion on 'Il partito oggi: Il rapporto con le istituzioni e le masse', *Rinascita*, 6 January 1978, pp. 9-13.

39 Most of the articles appeared in *Rinascita* and in *Mondoperaio* during this period. The most important have been collected in Federico Coen (ed.), *Il marxismo e lo stato*, Quaderni di Mondoperaio (new series), no. 4, 1976.

40 The Project appears in *l'Avanti*, 29 January 1978. For an analysis, see Hine, 'Surviving or Reviving?', in Lange and Tarrow, op. cit.

41 *L'Espresso*, 27 August 1978.

42 See the draft theses for the Congress which appeared in *l'Unità*, 20 March 1979.

43 Salvati, 'Muddling through', in Lange and Tarrow, op. cit., p. 42.

44 The 'Terza Via' line was first aired by Berlinguer in a speech at the *Festival dell'Unità* in Genoa in September 1978. See *Corriere della Sera*, 18 September 1978, p. 1.

45 Sani, 'Italian Voters, 1976-1979', in Penniman, *Italy at the Polls, 1979*.

46 *Rinascita*, 8 June 1979, pp. 1-2.

47 The crisis, which raised the tone of the 1980 administrative elections to a much higher pitch than they otherwise would have had, involved a former cabinet minister and DC notable, Carlo Donat-Cattin, whose son – wanted for questioning by the police in connection with a political terrorism investigation – managed to escape the country about the time his father met with Prime Minister Cossiga. The latter was accused by the PCI of complicity, was subjected to a parliamentary inquiry and was eventually cleared.

48 For the PCI's position during the electoral campaign, see Massimo Ghiara, 'Tutti i dubbi sul caso Cossiga', *Rinascita*, 6 June 1980, pp. 3-4.

49 *Corriere della Sera*, op. cit., p. 2. A more critical version was given by Armando Cossutta in commenting on Berlinguer's speech. *Corriere della Sera*, 20 September 1978, p. 1.

50 Though it may seem self-evident to some that Italy is a democracy, such an observation is noticeable by its absence in works on the country in the 1970s, which appeared with titles such as 'Surviving without Governing', and 'Republic without Government'. My view is that the last decade of Italian political life – warts and all – can best be understood as a period of democratization. Indeed, by some standards, Italy, however unstable, is one of the more representative democracies in Europe. For an essay that is flawed only in not having yet been published, see Gianfranco Pasquino's

excellent 'Italian Democracy in a Period of Change', prepared for presentation to the First Conference of Europeanists, Washington, DC., 1979. For a similar perspective in somewhat different form, see my 'Italy: Crisis, Crises or Transition?', in Lange and Tarrow, op. cit., pp. 166–86.

51 See my 'Three Years of Italian Democracy', ibid. for this argument spelled out in more detail.

52 'I punti fermi dell'intesa', *Rinascita*, 1 July 1977, p. 3.

53 Ibid., pp. 3–6, for articles on the economic, regional and local, educational and anti-terrorist aspects of the accord.

54 Luciano Barca, 'Le scelte economiche nell'accordo di programma', *Rinascita*, 8 July 1977, p. 3.

55 Gerardo Chiaromonte, 'L'avanzata dell'egemonia operaia e le sue contradizzioni', *Il Contemporaneo*, *Rinascita*, 15 July 1977, p. 13.

56 Adalberto Minucci, 'Il caso italiano', ibid., pp. 11–12.

57 Joseph LaPalombara, 'Socialist Alternatives: The Italian Variant', *Foreign Affairs*, Spring 1982, p. 927.

58 See, for example, Marzio Barbagli and Piorgiorgio Corbetta, 'La svolta del PCI', *Il Mulino*, January 1981, pp. 95–130.

59 'Un'altra Italia deve governare', in *L'Unità*, 28 November 1980.

60 Op. cit., p. 95.

61 Ibid.

62 Op. cit., p. 927.

63 Ibid., p. 926.

64 Ibid., p. 937. For the evolution of the PCI's statements on the Polish crisis, see *L'Unità*, 10–31 December 1981. *Pravda's* response was reported in *L'Unità* on 25 January 1982, and the PCI's firm rejoinder on 26 January.

65 Togliatti's article, 'La Politica di Corbino', appeared in *Rinascita*, August 1946, pp. 177–81.

66 Enrico Berlinguer, 'Il compromesso nella fase attule', *Rinascita*, 24 August 1979, p. 1; Togliatti, op. cit., p. 178.

67 Berlinguer, op. cit., p. 3.

68 Mario Caciagli, 'Il partito conservatore di massa', in M. Isnenghi and S. Janaro (eds), *La DC dal fascismo al 18 aprile* (Venice, 1978), pp. 267–73.

69 Pasquino, 'Italian Christian Democracy', in Lange and Tarrow, op. cit., p. 88.

70 Minucci, 'Il caso italiano', op. cit., p. 12.

71 For a clear, scholarly, but somewhat partial, exposition of this view, see Luigi Graziano's 'Compromesso storico e democrazia consociativa: verso una "nuova democrazia"?', in Graziano and Tarrow, op. cit., vol. 2, pp. 719–63. For a lively criticism of 'consociationism' as applied to Italy, see Barbagli and Corbetta, 'La svolta del PCI', pp. 96–8.

8

The PCE in the struggle
for democracy in Spain*

Paul Preston

When the phenomenon of Eurocommunism first began to attract attention in the mid-1970s, hostile journalists, politicians and scholars tended to denounce it as a Trojan Horse designed to breach the gates of democratic Europe. After all, it was not just the suspicious right-wing opponents of Eurocommunism who saw it as a cynical tactic to win votes by waving the flag of socialism with a human face and then to erect a regime of totalitarian communism. For years in the Italian Communist Party, for example, old Stalinist hard liners reconciled themselves to moderation, democratic competition and the non-Soviet road to socialism by considering it as a clever duplicity to cheat the bourgeoisie. Even Santiago Carrillo, at a rhetorical level the most outspoken of all Eurocommunists, admitted that his own party contained those who thought that once in power the sheepskin could be cast aside, although he admonished them for this *doppiezza* and clearly regarded them as an insignificant minority.[1]

Of the four Southern European communist parties, Carrillo's PCE is, by a sizeable margin, the furthest away from power. Since, in addition, the PCE has outdone the others in verbal commitments to democracy and condemnations of the USSR, it is hardly surprising that there have been abundant accusations that its Eurocommunism is merely electoralist.[2] There is therefore a strong case for assessing the position of Spanish communism not in terms of verbal attacks on the Soviet Union and pious commitments to a future pluralistic socialism, but rather in terms of its practice. An examination of the PCE's role in Spanish politics in the last decade and of its own internal evolution in that period is not only likely to be more useful than an

* I would like to acknowledge the assistance of the Sir Ernest Cassell Educational Trust and the Twenty Seven Foundation in the preparation of this paper.

exegesis of Carrillo's public declarations for the obvious reason that actions speak louder than words. There is another more powerful reason.

One of the central features which unites the Italian, French and Spanish parties is the conviction that they are capable of finding a third road between Soviet communism and Western capitalism. Accordingly, spokesmen for all three parties have stressed that their evolution towards the positions known loosely as Eurocommunism has been a response to developments in both the capitalist and communist blocs. It is clear that the European communists have been dramatically affected by fissures in the world communist movement provoked by Yugoslav or Chinese rejection of Soviet tutelage and by revulsion at Soviet suppression of Hungarian or Czechoslovak manifestations of independence. However, what gave an intense relevance to the emergence of Eurocommunism was the growing economic and political crisis of the Western world in the 1970s. The ending of the post-war boom, the energy crisis and the onset of the second slump were matched politically by the weakening of US hegemony in the Far East, the Middle East and in Southern Europe.[3]

The position of Eurocommunism as a potentially dynamic response to crisis in both superpower blocs led to a shift in thinking among its opponents. Emphasis on the sincerity or cynicism of Eurocommunists gave way to concern about their inadvertent capacity to disrupt the world order.[4] Shortly before the death of General Franco, Santiago Carrillo made a declaration that was intended to increase his respectability among Spanish conservatives and in the eyes of the Western powers. He claimed that the triumph of moderate, pluralistic socialism in France, Italy and Spain, demonstrating that socialism and liberty were not incompatible, could lead to Czechs, Poles and Hungarians calling their Russian masters to account.[5] Contrary to Carrillo's intentions, the State Department was as thoroughly alarmed by the prospect as was the Kremlin. Heavy-handed Russian attacks on Carrillo were only the sequel to equally crude hints from Henry Kissinger and Helmut Sonnenfeldt that the USA would not tolerate communists in the governments of Italy or France. In other words, Eurocommunism, especially in the optimistic outbursts of Carrillo, was beginning to imply a serious challenge to the post-war settlement, threatening as it did both Western capitalism and Eastern communism at a time when recognition of their respective inviolability was central to détente between the superpowers. Neither America nor Russia wanted the areas of their hegemony treated to the sight of capitalism being successfully undermined by a truly democratic socialism.

Nevertheless, it remains arguable that excessive attention has been paid to the conflict between the Soviet Union and the PCE which arose out of Russian sensitivity to Spanish criticism of the nature of Eastern bloc socialism. It is understandable that the acrimonious exchanges between Carrillo and the Kremlin should attract media attention and that the Spaniards should make efforts to publicize the rift, given the extent to which it provided evidence of the PCE's independence.[6] Yet the fact remains that there are more revealing perspectives from which to view the PCE. After all, much as Eastern European communists may be envious of the ideological flexibility and national autonomy of Carrillo and other Eurocommunist leaders, Moscow's control of the Soviet bloc remains firm in both economic and military terms. In the last resort, Carrillo's potential impact inside the Eastern bloc was small by comparison with the importance of his role within Spain itself and, by extension, given the special circumstances of Spain, within the Western bloc.

At a moment of crisis in the USA's hegemonic capacity, both economic and ideological, Spain in the 1970s assumed a special importance both strategically and as a potential launching pad into the EEC for Spanish-based American companies. American investment in Spain, either direct or through subsidiaries in Switzerland, Liechtenstein or other countries, rose dramatically throughout the decade except for the period of political uncertainty between 1975 and early 1977.[7] Having underpinned the Franco dictatorship both militarily and economically since the early 1950s, the USA clearly had a vested interest in controlling Spain's inevitable transition to a different form of regime. This was manifested not only in terms of continued investment but also in terms of positive political intervention. During the transition to democracy, the Spanish representatives of important American-owned multinational corporations emerged from the shadows to play important roles in the foreground of Spanish politics at ministerial level. Similarly, there is reason to suppose that key decisions of the transition period taken shortly after visits by King Juan Carlos and premier Adolfo Suárez to the USA were influenced by American advice.[8]

In the light of the PCE's performances in the elections of 1977 and 1979, with 9.2 per cent and 10.9 per cent of the vote respectively, it is perhaps difficult to see that, at the beginning of the decade, the communists constituted the greatest political obstacle to the sort of political transition likely to be satisfactory to the USA. The modesty of communist electoral success is, in part, a tribute to the success of American and West German sponsorship of the two mass parties of right and left which have dominated the politics of democratic Spain – the *Unión del Centro Democrático* and the *Partido Socialista Obrero Español*. Carrillo's critics on the Spanish left would argue that the poor communist vote was to be attributed to working-class disillusionment at a degree of PCE moderation which was being sold too cheaply.[9] Of course, there are many reasons for the results of Spain's first two elections: the enormous disproportion between propaganda budgets; a loaded electoral law favouring the conservative countryside; the fears consciously engendered for forty years by the virulently anti-communist Franco regime; Carrillo's aged leadership team and its inadvertent tendency to awaken memories of the Civil War, to name but a few. However, taking up the leftist critique of communist moderation, it might be argued that from mid-1976 until mid-1979, the PCE, not entirely disinterestedly, perhaps even making a virtue of a necessity, took the longer term view and sacrificed its vanguard position in order to strengthen the new democratic regime. The anti-democratic stance of powerful elements of the Spanish army, culminating in the attempted coup of 23 February 1981, has provided a retrospective justification for Carrillo's caution.

That caution, and the relative eclipse of the PCE after 1977, should not obscure the fact that prior to mid-1976 the main burden of pressure for democratic change in Spain fell upon the PCE. This is not to deny the contribution made to the anti-Franco struggle by a wide spectrum of political groups, but rather to acknowledge the extent to which many of them had fallen by the wayside since 1939. Of course, communist prominence was not unchallenged on the left at the time of Franco's death, especially in the Basque country. Nevertheless, when spontaneous mass pressure for amnesty and political change became a crucial factor in 1976, the PCE was in a particularly good position from which to direct it. As a result of its unbroken tradition of opposition to the dictatorship, of growing communist influence in the organized working class through the *Comisiones Obreras* and of the existence of its nation-wide clandestine network, the PCE was able to play an important role in orchestrating mass action. In 1976 many unaligned activists, except in Euzkadi, tended to turn for guidance to the communists. Thus, despite its own difficulties and the problems of securing widespread opposition unity, the PCE became the crucial mediating influence on the plans laid by Spanish and American capitalists to direct a process of transition which would not damage their interests.

Until the end of 1976, the initiative in this tacit struggle to mould the post-Franco regime in Spain lay with the communists. After the elections of June 1977 and the transfer of the political arena from the streets to the Cortes, the importance of the communists diminished considerably. Nevertheless, the fact remains that the communists' combination of mass strength and reasonableness was a central factor in making possible Spanish democracy in its present form. Even if it is believed that, in the last resort, Suárez out-manoeuvred Carrillo in regaining the initiative within the transition process,[10] there can be no doubt that the UCD leader would not have gone as far as he did down the democratic road without the pressure orchestrated by the PCE. In that sense, an examination of the PCE's contribution to the coming of democracy in Spain provides a more meaningful example of Eurocommunism in practice than would an analysis of its verbal discrepancies with the Soviet Union or of its rhetorical commitment to a future pluralistic socialist utopia.

The process whereby the Spanish Communist Party developed in such a way as to permit its prominent role in the transition was long and complicated. It dated back to 1954 and, despite a number of interruptions and wrong turns, had become virtually irrevocable by the beginning of the 1970s. Nevertheless, it was a long and painful process. With its leadership dependent for funds and hospitality on the Soviet Union and with its rank-and-file involved in a clandestine struggle with a fiercely reactionary dictatorship, it is hardly surprising that the PCE was firmly Stalinist in both its thinking and its organizational methods in the fifteen years following the Spanish Civil War. After the death of Stalin, a slow and grudging effort was made to de-Stalinize. The lead in this was taken at the PCE's 5th Congress, held in Prague in September 1954, by the party's organization secretary, Santiago Carrillo. Worried by the rigidity of the aged party leadership in exile, Carrillo called for a renovation of the apparatus within Spain. By introducing younger militants from the interior into the central committee, Carrillo was not only enhancing his own position for a future power struggle, but also preparing the party for a search for a politically wider alliance against the dictatorship.[11]

Carrillo's ideas were supported by other, then young, PCE leaders like Fernando Claudín and Ignacio Gallego. They received a boost with Khrushchev's revelations to the 20th Congress of the CPSU. It is perhaps ironic that the de-Stalinizers were to find their own aspirations paralleled by those of the Russian leadership. A more flexible policy was applied as Carrillo grew in strength and confidence. Efforts were made to meet the demands of the militants within Spain for links with other opposition forces by means of the formulation of a new policy known as National Reconciliation.[12] In fact, 1956 was to be the high point of Carrillo's efforts to de-Stalinize the PCE until the events of 1968 provoked a further surge of liberalization. Indeed, when the new line of national reconciliation did not immediately secure the overthrow of Franco by a wide coalition of democratic forces, Carrillo was to react with an almost Stalinist rigidity and with excessive subjectivism. His determination to see a confirmation of the correctness of the new line in every event inside Spain eventually would lead him into conflict with his erstwhile ally, Fernando Claudín, who began to call for greater sensitivity to the changing situation in the interior. In the meanwhile, however, the PCE elaborated the notion that the first fruit of national reconciliation should be a national pacific strike to bring down the dictatorship.

Efforts to bring about such strikes failed in 1958 and 1959. The failures were attributed to organizational deficiencies. Accordingly, the 6th Congress of the PCE, held once more in Prague in December 1959, recognized the limitations of the clandestine cell structure. It was acknowledged that reconciliation and the national pacific strike necessitated the widening of party recruitment to the middle and professional classes. Party statutes were altered to permit looser conditions of membership.[13] The transition from a party of cadres to a mass party, along with national reconciliation and the pacific strike, was a substantially correct, albeit somewhat premature, concept which was only to come finally to fruition between 1975 and 1977. Not only did these concepts put the PCE firmly in the vanguard of the anti-Franco struggle, but they also signified irreversible progress towards the liberalization of the party. In the short term, however, the limits of de-Stalinization were about to be starkly exposed.

A series of strikes in the spring of 1962 were interpreted by Carrillo as evidence of a wide alliance of social forces coming together to overthrow the backward Francoist clique, of national reconciliation leading to a national pacific strike. In fact, the strikes were a response to the birth pangs of a major industrialization process. Claudín, in alliance with Jorge Semprún, the director of the PCE's interior organization, argued that the fundamental changes being undergone by Spanish capitalism required a major re-think of party strategy. If they were right, and events were to show that they were, then national reconciliation would only materialize at the point of future economic development when the industrial bourgeoisie began to find the Franco regime an impediment to its continuing prosperity. Unable to countenance the possibility of having to tell the party rank-and-file that, after twenty-five years of struggle against Franco, the dictatorship could well last another twenty-five years, Carrillo used his control of the PCE apparatus to silence Claudín and Semprún and then, in 1965, to expel them.[14] Carrillo's handling of the Claudín–Semprún crisis was distasteful and not without its Stalinist overtones. Nevertheless, a case could be made to the effect that he was simply ensuring that the necessary new party line be imposed gradually without the risk of splitting the party.

This became clear at the PCE's 7th Congress held near Paris in August 1965. The Congress was held in near secrecy, even within the usual norms of clandestinity, largely because its primary objective was to wrap up the loose ends of the Claudín expulsion. Although Carrillo was soon to adopt the positions for which Claudín and Semprún had been vilified, his report to the Congress, which took him a day and half to deliver, reaffirmed his view that a wide front of forces could rapidly overthrow the isolated Francoist clique of landowners and financiers.[15] Over the next two years, however, Carrillo's stance was to evolve considerably. A number of influences came to bear upon him. In the first place, he cannot have been totally unmoved by the strength of the arguments mobilized by Claudín who was, after all, the party's leading theoretician and Carrillo's closest collaborator before 1964. The extent to which the specific points made by Claudín and Semprún were taken up on a European scale by Togliatti in his Yalta memorandum seems also to have affected Carrillo. Nevertheless, the key factor in impelling Carrillo towards a realistic and flexible line based on the Spanish situation was probably the fall of Khrushchev.

The revelations of the 20th Congress of the CPSU had convinced Carrillo that the USSR was on the road to democratization. One of his greatest differences with Claudín and Semprún was what he saw as their dangerous and gratuitous efforts to examine the nature of Soviet socialism. Indeed, during the campaign against them, Carrillo declared in the course of a barely veiled attack upon them that the PCE would never adopt anti-Soviet positions merely to facilitate an alliance with bourgeois elements.[16] Having based his own form of disciplined and limited change on the model of Khrushchev, Carrillo was confused by the manner of his mentor's demise.[17] Henceforth, until the dramatic change of 1968, Carrillo's attitude to the Soviet Union was ambiguous. Increasing evidence of independent thinking derived partly from his unease with the new dour Russian leadership, but also from recognition that national reconciliation required that the PCE convince potential allies within Spain that it was untainted by the dictatorial tendencies of the Russians.[18]

The realization that the Russians were less than reliable guides coincided with growing evidence of the sort of capitalist growth within Spain that had formed the basis of the Claudín–Semprún positions. With the PCE still in clandestinity and in need of international communist solidarity, Carrillo's first steps towards the Claudinist position were hesitant. In 1966, he cautiously criticized the Siniavski and Daniel trial. In 1967, he began to talk of the lack of democracy in Eastern Europe. At the same time, references to the narrow Francoist clique started to disappear from his writings. Instead there emerged a more realistic assessment of the fact that the bourgeoisie was benefiting from economic growth under Franco but might well come to resent the regime's archaic political machinery.[19] The combination of a critical approach to the Soviet bloc with a more flexible line regarding relations with other groups inside Spain was clinched by the developments in Czechoslovakia after the fall of Novotny. After the great enthusiasm expressed by the PCE for the Prague spring, Carrillo was placed in an extremely awkward position by the Soviet invasion in August.[20]

After the tentative progress towards an independent position since 1964, Carrillo seems to have realized that he had reached a major turning point. The invasion was condemned and the not inconsiderable rank and file sympathy for the Russian action was effectively silenced. When the Russians sponsored pro-Soviet factions, first under Eduardo García and Agustín Gómez and later under Enrique Líster, Carrillo's resolve was hardened. He was fortunate in that the PCE president, Dolores Ibárruri, was reluctant to see the party split and, despite her own pro-Russian sympathies, could see that the PCE's long-term survival within Spain depended on the adoption of the more open positions now held by Carrillo. The brutality of the Soviet response pushed the PCE nearer to the Italian and Romanian parties, something which was to have a liberalizing effect on the Spaniards. Moreover, as Russian attacks on Carrillo continued, he reacted by using his control of the party machinery to eliminate pro-Soviet elements from the PCE. Hard-line veterans of the Civil War resident in the East were replaced at all levels of the party apparatus by working-class militants from within Spain. This renovation of cadres accelerated the process of modernization and intensified the PCE's sensitivity to developments within Spain.[21] Carrillo's unilateral co-option of these new cadres smacked of Stalinism. As organization secretary, Carrillo had used the accumulated bureaucratic wisdom of the Stalinist apparatchik to prepare the ground for the renovation of 1954-6. Now, during 1969 and 1970, impelled on the one hand by Russian hostility and on the other by the need to respond to the changing situation inside Spain, Carrillo resorted to the same trusted and efficacious methods to give the PCE the sort of image which he believed to be essential to its survival. Whatever the methods, the changes which he imposed had the effect of opening up the PCE, of making it more attractive to intellectuals and students and ultimately of reducing the average age of militants.

It was pointed out by Claudín at the time that the pro-Soviet elements could have been defeated in open debate and that the PCE would have been healthier for the experience. Yet even leaving aside a possibility that the number of veteran Stalinists still in the PCE in the late 1960s obliged Carrillo to act as he did, the fact remains that the party came out of the crisis of 1968-70 considerably changed. The effect of the Claudín–Semprún crisis had been, at enormous cost, to make the party more aware of the need to respond to Spanish realities. Now, at greater numerical cost, albeit at lower intellectual and moral cost, the Czechoslovak crisis left the PCE less rigid. Throughout the 1960s, in response to the reforms introduced at the 6th Congress, the PCE extended its membership in the universities and the factories of a rapidly modernizing Spain. When the strategy of national reconciliation was renamed the Pact for Liberty in 1969, the PCE had become altogether more modern, moderate and responsive than it had been ten years earlier.

The emergence of a highly politicized student movement and of powerful semi-clandestine unions was largely a reflection of the vertiginous economic growth of Spain in the 1960s. No other anti-Franco group was able to react to the changed situation with anything like the efficacy of the PCE. As the communists became increasingly involved in the mass struggle against the regime, Carrillo began to talk of conquering 'zones of liberty' and 'bases for democratic struggle'. By the end of the 1960s, such areas were to be constituted by the growing scale and frequency of strikes, demonstrations and meetings held in defiance of police repression. At the September 1970 meeting of the PCE central committee, Carrillo reported on the party's return to the surface and the beginning of the 'capture of democracy'. In 1970, the PCE launched a massive recruitment drive called the 'Lenin Promotion' which saw the party expand not only in the big industrial areas but also, to a lesser extent, in the countryside.[22] At the same time, party members became more involved in legal associations – housewives' groups, consumer pressure groups, parent–teacher associations, neighbourhood groups – while party lawyers took a prominent role in the defence of trade unionists on trial for their syndical activities. All this constituted, within the limits of the dictatorship, an attempt to emulate the successes of the Italian communists in municipal government, that is to say to demonstrate to ordinary Spaniards that communists were efficient, reliable and helpful.

The PCE thus entered the 1970s in sound shape, ideologically flexible and in a phase of organizational expansion. There is little doubt that communists enjoyed considerable prestige within Spain among non-partisan opponents of the Franco regime. Moreover, the strength of the Workers' Commissions ensured that key figures in the economic élite had little choice but to take the communists into account when they elaborated their own strategy for survival after Franco. Already in the late 1960s, negotiations had taken place between top industrialists and leaders of the Workers' Commissions to by-pass the regime's antiquated vertical syndicates.[23] This tendency increased rapidly in the 1970s. The Pact for Liberty seemed to be gaining wider relevance than ever before when the *Assemblea de Catalunya* was founded in November 1971. The Assembly movement included a wide range of left-wing parties, of which the most important was the Catalan Communist Party, the *Partit Socialista Unificat de Catalunya* (PSUC); a number of working-class organizations, of which the dominant one was the Workers' Commissions; and a broad span of legal associations. The Assembly was represented all over Catalonia and, apart from its enormously wide spectrum of popular support, included bankers among its leaders. It soon revealed a capacity for mass mobilization in the form of amnesty demonstrations which were to reach their apogee in 1976.[24]

The Assembly was just the sort of vehicle for the conquest of 'zones of liberty' and the PCE began to make efforts to emulate the PSUC's success in other parts of Spain. And as the PCE grew nearer to representatives of the Spanish bourgeoisie, so it grew further away from the USSR. At a central committee meeting in September 1973, the executive committee received formal permission to establish contacts with 'representatives of neo-capitalist groups'. In the same session, Azcárate delivered the report on the PCE's international policy which was to provoke a broadside from the Soviet party.[25] Perhaps inspired by this evidence of the PCE's independence of Moscow, important figures of the capitalist élite, representing both Spanish and multinational corporations, took part in discussions with the communist leadership.[26] At the same time, democratic round tables and juntas, rather like the Catalan Assembly, were springing up all over Spain. This was far from being an all-communist movement, but the fact that the PCE, alone among opposition groups, had a nation-wide organizational network ensured for it a dominant co-ordinating role.

The onset of the energy crisis in 1973, presaging as it did future labour discontent as prosperity diminished, was a considerable stimulus to capitalists in Spain. They realized that the antiquated and semi-fascist structures of the dictatorship would be incapable of resolving the forthcoming economic crisis without damaging confrontations. Accordingly, their readiness to accept some kind of political reform began to coincide with popular pressure for change. This convergence of interest gave the Pact for Liberty a new relevance and thus enabled the PCE to play a crucial role in the events of 1975-7. Nevertheless, the Franco regime was hardly helpless. The armed forces and the police were intact and Franco's plans for the succession of Juan Carlos under the tutelage of Admiral Carrero Blanco were well laid. In an outright conflict between the forces of reaction and those advocating change, the odds lay with the dictatorship.

That situation changed dramatically in December 1973 with the assassination of Carrero Blanco. With an eye on their own futures, various Francoist elements began to jockey for power. As the regime's forces began to fragment, the Pact for Liberty began to assume greater importance. Several events elsewhere in Europe in early 1974 – the Italian divorce referendum and the defeat of Fanfani, the Portuguese revolution, Mitterrand's good performance in the French presidential elections and the fall of the Greek colonels – increased the impression that the initiative was slipping away from the right. In particular, the events in Portugal were an immense boost to PCE morale. The victorious alliance of workers, the army and the 'most dynamic and liberal sectors of capitalism' was seen by Carrillo as an indication that the Pact for Liberty could and would dominate the transition from dictatorship to democracy in Spain.[27]

It was not simply events abroad which boosted Carrillo's confidence. Contacts with businessmen, other left-wing and also Christian Democrat opposition forces and even with representatives of Juan Carlos's father, Don Juan de Borbón, were proceeding throughout the spring. At the same time, Carrero Blanco's successor, Carlos Arias Navarro, was making a series of errors which cast considerable doubt on his capacity to head the regime's campaign for survival without serious risk of bloody conflict. Arias's position was, in fact, virtually impossible. His function was to adjust the political forms of the Franco regime to a changed social and economic situation – a job for which he had neither the will nor the power. The ability of the Francoist old guard, the so-called 'bunker', to mobilize the dictatorship against any sign of reform was to be Arias's undoing. In trying to placate the 'bunker', he destroyed his own credibility and convinced broad sectors of the population that the communist strategy for change was the most realistic one.

When Franco fell seriously ill in the early summer of 1974, the Arias government had already seen its position weakened. In February, an attempt to silence Bishop Añoveros of Bilbao had led to a humiliating climb-down and to an acceleration of the withdrawal of ecclesiastical support for the regime. The execution of the anarchist Salvador Puig Antich on 2 March in the face of international protests revealed the limits of Arias's reforming zeal. The remainder of the year saw a number of triumphs for the 'bunker', culminating in October with the resignation of Arias's most liberal minister, Pio Cabanillas, whose relaxation of censorship led to him being accused of opening the door to the reds. This merely underlined the internal crisis of the regime. Resignations abounded and the stock market was falling. Communist predictions were assuming an aura of inevitability. In fact, in an effort to force the pace, the PCE had responded to news of Franco's illness by launching, on 30 July, the *Junta Democrática*, along with the Workers' Commissions, the small *Partido Socialista Popular*, the Carlists and numerous individuals of whom the most notable was the monarchist Rafael Calvo Serer. [28] Despite the non-participation of the *Partido Socialista Obrero Español* (PSOE) and the various Christian Democrat groups, the *Junta* was a very considerable publicity coup for the communists. The Pact for Liberty now had a focus. Opposition circles in Madrid and Barcelona buzzed with excitement. Non-aligned individuals looked to the *Junta* as a potential alternative at the moment when the regime's legitimacy was crumbling. Skilful diplomacy gained the *Junta* widespread recognition as the main opposition force and placed the PCE at the centre of the transition process.[29] Events were to show, however, that communist optimism that a *Junta*-inspired national strike could establish a provisional democratic government was misplaced.

Indeed, with Franco still alive, there was something of a stalemate. Ultimately confident in its powers of repression, if somewhat confused about its future evolution, the Government adopted an increasingly hard line throughout 1975. A three-month state of exception in the Basque country decreed on 25 April unleashed an operation of mass police terror against the population at large. On 26 August, the Government passed a sweeping anti-terrorist law which exposed the entire left to indiscriminate and draconian police action. Along with intensification of censorship and the seizure of many publications, the regime seemed to be returning to the habits of the 1940s, something made brutally clear by the execution of five leftists on 27 September. A wave of fear and distaste thus accompanied the death agony of Franco and strengthened the prestige of the *Junta*. Nevertheless, despite the relative success in Madrid of the three days of democratic action convoked by the *Junta*, it was not possible to attain anything near the great national strike which might begin the job of toppling the regime.[30]

In the meanwhile, however, the PSOE and the various Christian Democrats had formed the *Plataforma de Convergencia Democrática*. In the hope of breaking the stalemate with the regime, frantic efforts were made to unite the *Junta* and the *Plataforma*. Impelled by the intransigence of the regime, a liaison committee was set up and a joint communiqué was issued on 30 September calling for a 'democratic rupture' with the dictatorship.[31] The opposition's confidence grew after Franco died on 20 November. Despite a notable increase in right-wing terrorist activity, the PCE stepped up its calls for 'national democratic action' as it now denominated what had once been the national pacific strike. The first half of 1976 was dominated by a series of such actions, partly a response to the PCE's calls but, in the main, the reflection of a massive popular urge for political change. In January 1976, Madrid was paralyzed by a strike wave mounted by the Workers' Commissions. In February, the *Assemblea de Catalunya* mobilized 100,000-strong amnesty demonstrations on successive Sundays.[32] In March, there was a general strike in the Basque country, organized by a wide spectrum of local forces including ETA, ELA, LAB and LAIA, in protest at the killing by the police of five people in Vitoria. The PCE leadership had to come to terms with the fact that possibilities for 'national democratic action' were effectively limited to Madrid and Barcelona, the situation in the Basque country being beyond their control. Closer unity with the *Plataforma* was thus an urgent task.

To achieve it involved the PCE in an acute problem. Already, in the quest for opposition unity, the communists had moderated their declarations to such an extent that they were exposed to virulent criticism by groups to their left that they were simply playing the game of the oligarchy.[33] Too much moderation could interrupt the momentum of the mass mobilization campaign as well as blurring the PCE's identity. Equally, there were fears that the relative success of the campaign might provoke the government into trying to buy off the PSOE or the Christian Democrats. Juan Carlos's first government was presided over by Arias but it contained nominally 'liberal' Francoists like Manuel Fraga and José María Areilza. If it had hoped to be able to resolve the crisis by means of a timid and cosmetic reform, the evidence of popular militancy was forcing it to accept that the survival of the monarchy required a more positive commitment to democratic change. This could well involve some sort of compromise with those forces that were incorporated in the *Plataforma* and the exclusion of the PCE from the subsequent arrangements.[34]

Carrillo was living clandestinely in Madrid and was following the situation closely. Aware of the possibility of being edged out of the game, he decided to modify the PCE's position on a number of issues in order to pre-empt a government effort to capture the moderate left. Dropping the party's hitherto insistent calls for an outright break, the departure of Juan Carlos and the creation of a provisional government, he was rewarded on 4 April by the fusion of the *Junta* and the *Plataforma* into *Coordinación Democrática*. This really meant the end of mass mobilization and the hopes of overthrowing the regime.[35] Henceforth, the emphasis would be on negotiation with the government and the widening of the opposition front to include centre and right-of-centre groups until the government was isolated By this sacrifice, Carrillo ensured that the PCE would not simply be ignored. Moreover, having proved the party's capacity for popular mobilization, Carrillo was ensuring that negotiations would carry more weight. In other words, the PCE's moderation facilitated the coincidence of popular pressure for change with the economic élite's dissatisfaction with Francoist structures which had been predicted twelve years previously by Claudin. The combination of the communist tactic of mass mobilization with the emergence of a wide and respectable coalition of forces was to ensure that there would be change and that it would take place without bloodshed.

Incontrovertible evidence of a unified opposition with the capacity to call strikes and mass demonstrations obliged Juan Carlos to speed up his programme of political liberalization. At the beginning of July, apparently on American advice, the King called for Arias's resignation and replaced him with Adolfo Suárez. In view of Suárez's Falangist past, the opposition was horrified. Massive demonstrations for political liberties and amnesty were thus called in the second week of July with considerable success. Suárez was left in no doubt that swift and thorough-going reform was necessary if the crisis was to be resolved without massive violence.[36] If fact, having expected that Juan Carlos would replace Arias with Areilza, the PCE expected little from Suárez. Carrillo declared that the most Suárez could do would be to make a small contribution to the negotiations for the *ruptura pactada*, the central objective of *Coordinación Democrática*, which had replaced the *Junta*'s more decisive aim of overturning the regime by strike action, the *ruptura democrática*. At this stage, it is clear that Carrillo conceived of this in terms of negotiations between government and opposition leading to agreement on a provisional government to preside over free elections to a constituent Cortes.[37] Carrillo's lack of optimism regarding Suárez derived in part from a minor incident towards the end of July. He applied for a passport at the Spanish embassy in Paris, was received by the ambassador, Miguel Maria de Lojendio, and revealed to him that he had been clandestinely inside Spain already. Immediately on receiving Lojendio's report Suárez relieved him of his post. It was hardly surprising when the PCE greeted Suárez's programme of government with incredulity, denouncing his intentions of seeking dialogue with the opposition as mere words.[38]

Carrillo kept up the pressure by holding a plenum of the PCE central committee in Rome from 28 to 31 July. As well as being a significant publicity coup, it formed part of the PCE's long-term policy of 'coming to the surface', capturing democracy by challenging the Government either to tolerate the party's existence or else reveal its true colours by taking repressive action. As it was, none of the delegates from Spain was arrested on return to Spain, perhaps because of the presence at the plenum of numerous Italian and Spanish political personalities. Carrillo used the occasion to cast doubt on the reforming capacity of Suárez and to call for amnesty, for a provisional government of national reconciliation and for the election of a constituent assembly. He also made it clear that the process of the 'return to the surface' would continue by announcing that the PCE would begin the open distribution of party carnets in the autumn.[39] This threat, which was in fact carried out, was shortly after backed up by another. Carrillo informed Suárez via intermediaries that, if he did not receive a passport, he would hold a press conference in Madrid in the presence of Oriana Fallacci, Marcel Niedergang and other influential correspondents.[40]

A struggle was thus developing between Suárez on the one hand and Carrillo and the rest of the opposition for control of the transition process. Suárez could only take the initiative by a combination of substantial concessions and efforts to split the united front of the opposition. Carrillo would thereby be forced back from setting the pace of opposition demands for change to a more defensive position of trying to ensure that the PCE would not be isolated. Throughout August, Suárez interviewed a wide range of opposition personalities and made a favourable impression on them.[41] He was also in contact with Carrillo through José Mario Armero and urged the PCE leader not to make the transition impossible by provocative actions.[42]

Nevertheless, the pressure was on Suárez. On 4 September, a wide range of liberal, social democrat and Christian Democrat groups gathered in Madrid's Eurobuilding to discuss unity with *Coordinación Democrática* and with a number of regional opposition fronts.[43] All that came out of the meeting was the creation of a liaison committee but Suárez was obliged to hasten his preparations for the presentation of his project of political reforms. His plans were revealed to the high command of the army on 8 September. Enjoying the backing of Juan Carlos, Suárez's plans were reluctantly accepted but the military insisted that the PCE be excluded from any future reform.[44] Suárez seized on the issue of legalization of the PCE with great skill and was to use it to drive wedges into the opposition and to impose a certain caution on Carrillo.

On 10 September, having gained the acceptance of the army, Suárez presented his project for reform to the country. Since it was his government that proposed to hold elections before mid-1977, and since there was to be no question of Suárez resigning and being replaced by a provisional government of government and opposition forces, the PCE denounced the project as an 'anti-democratic fraud'.[45] The PCE demanded the prior legalization of all political parties, but Suárez simply continued with his project. Many within the opposition were pleasantly surprised by the extent to which daily life was being liberalized. The press was functioning normally, political groups to the right of the PCE were unhindered, the PSOE was preparing to hold its 28th Congress and even the PCE was allowed unofficially to go about its business inside Spain. The initiative was swinging Suárez's way. He was able to insinuate to socialists and Christian Democrats that he could make greater concessions to them if only they would not rock the boat and provoke the army by insisting on legalization of the PCE.[46] Faced with evidence of the impossibility of imposing change against the will of the army and of the fact that things were moving along steadily under Suárez's guidance, the opposition could do little but acquiesce.

In the meanwhile, on 23 October, *Coordinación Democrática* united with five regional fronts, the *Taula de Forces Politiques i Sindicals del País Valenciá*, the *Assembleas de Mallorca, Menorca e Ibiza*, the *Assemblea de Catalunya*, the *Coordinadora de Fuerzas Democráticas de las Islas Canarias* and the *Taboa Democrática de Galiza*. Knowing that Suárez intended to hold a referendum on his reform project, the new united opposition front, called the *Plataforma de Organismos Democráticos* issued a statement on 5 November that it would boycott the referendum unless the Government conceded the legalization of political parties and trade unions, amnesty for political prisoners and exiles, recognition of the freedoms of expression, reunion and manifestation and repeal of the anti-terrorist law.[47] Suárez, however, simply proceeded with steering his project through the Francoist Cortes. When the referendum was held on 15 December, despite the *Plataforma de Organismos Democráticos* and particularly the communists calling for abstention, the project was approved by 94 per cent of the vote.[48] The fact that such a project was being put to a referendum was in general terms a great triumph for the opposition. Nevertheless, the tactical error of the abstention call highlighted the extent to which Suárez was now setting the pace.

Henceforth, the central objective of PCE policy would be legalization. Precisely for this purpose, Carrillo, who was still living semi-clandestinely in Madrid, called a press conference on 10 December. It was a deliberate effort by the PCE executive committee to bring pressure to bear on the Government. The press conference was in itself a provocation, but Carrillo's words were conciliatory. He insinuated that, provided the PCE were allowed to take part in the elections, it would collaborate in the elaboration of a social contract to deal with the economic crisis.[49] The Government was furious and ordered Carrillo's arrest, although it took the police until 22 December to find him. The PCE executive used the time to prepare a massive campaign in favour of Carrillo's release.[50] Under arrest for eight days, Carrillo posed a dilemma for the Government and no matter what they did he stood to gain. If he was not released or was tried, it would have damaged Suárez's liberal credibility. If he was released, it would constitute a major step towards legalization.

Throughout January 1977, Carrillo and Suárez negotiated through José Mario Armero and Jaime Ballésteros of the PCE's Madrid apparatus. The PCE pushed for authorization for its meetings; the Government pressed for the PCE to use its influence in the Workers' Commissions to restrain industrial militancy. Then, on 24 January, right-wing terrorists murdered five people, including four PCE labour lawyers, in the Atocha district of Madrid. The PCE called for serenity and organized a gigantic display of silent solidarity at the funeral of the victims. Not only was Suárez personally impressed by the demonstration of PCE strength and discipline, but much popular hostility to legalization of the party was dissolved by the restraint of its response to the tragedy.[51] By 27 February, Suárez was prepared to meet Carrillo. An eight-hour meeting at the home of Armero resulted in a basic agreement for legalization. In return, Carrillo undertook to recognize the monarchy, adopt the monarchist red-yellow-red national flag instead of the republican tricolour and offer his co-operation for a future social contract.[52] To remind the Government of the PCE's capacity to cause an international scandal if it were excluded from the elections, on 2 March it played host at the Hotel Meliá-Castilla in Madrid to a Eurocommunist summit meeting of Carrillo, Berlinguer and Marchais. On 9 April, with most of the Madrid political élite out of town for the Easter week-end, Suárez announced the legalization of the PCE.

The communists were understandably delighted with the completion of their 'return to the surface'. Nevertheless, Carrillo's announcement to the first legal plenum of the central committee that the PCE would drop the republican flag caused some discontent. He went on to counsel moderation. Given the delicate nature of democracy in Spain, he said de-stabilization and military intervention were a risk to be avoided at all costs. Far from seeking partisan benefit, he wanted the PCE to form part of a wide 'constitutional pact', until a new democratic constitution was established.[53] Carrillo's readiness to sacrifice immediate profit in order to consolidate the democratic process was

visible during the election campaign. Communist fire was concentrated not on Suárez's UCD nor on the PCE's immediate rivals, the
PSOE, but on the neo-Francoist *Alianza Popular*. This was one of the
reasons why, on 15 June 1977, the PCE received only 1,634,991 votes,
9.29 per cent of the total. Given the pre-eminent role that the party
had played in thirty-eight years of struggle against the dictatorship, it
was a disappointing result. There is a case for arguing that the PCE,
in the interests of establishing democracy, let themselves be the
victims of their own moderate and accommodating policies. The
PSOE, as well as putting to great use the semi-paralysis of the PCE
while awaiting legalization, used its ample financing to present a
more positive left-wing image and, with 34 per cent of the vote,
seemed to harvest the fruits of the PCE's long struggle for democracy.

Despite the disappointments accruing from party moderation,
Carrillo continued with the same line until the autumn of 1979 when
evidence of dwindling membership and belief that the democratic
process was sufficiently advanced not to need further coddling led
him to opt for a more dynamic policy. In his first speeches in the new
democratic Cortes, he called for a government of national concentration on the grounds that the country was economically too weak and
the health of the new-born democracy too fragile to stand right–left
polarization.[54] Then, in late October 1977, he took part in Spain's
social contract, the *Pacto de la Moncloa*, risking the accusation that
the communists were collaborating in an operation to make the
working class suffer the costs of the economic crisis. All of these
policies sat ill on a party which was ostensibly revolutionary.
Combined with the falling off of excitement after the establishment of
the parliamentary regime, they led to a dramatic fall of PCE membership. Members of the communist youth complained that the only
political activity left for them was to stick posters on walls or sweep out
party headquarters. Veterans of the anti-Franco struggle joked
nostalgically that 'Contra Franco, vivíamos mejor'. Party strength
dropped off from the 1977 high point of 201,757 to 171,332 in 1978.[55]
This 15 per cent drop became all the more dramatic when weighed
against the steady increase of membership throughout the 1970s.

The loss of 30,000 members by the end of 1978 reflected the
continuing caution of Carrillo's policy. At a time of increasing
unemployment and rampant inflation, his moderation seemed like a
betrayal to working-class party members. Moreover, after years of
struggle against the dictatorship and the apparent triumphs of 1976

and 1977, inordinate hopes had been pinned on the establishment of a democratic regime. It was difficult for the average rank and file militant to accept that the party had to maintain a low profile and even to give its parliamentary support on occasions to the UCD. Yet events in 1978, 1979 and 1981 suggested that Carrillo's moderation was not misplaced. Terrorist activities, first by the ostensibly ultra-leftist, but almost certainly police-manipulated, GRAPO, and then by the Basque revolutionary separatist organization ETA, ensured that as the new constitution was being elaborated great strain was put on the fragile loyalties of the forces of order. The various attempts at a military coup which finally culminated in the *Tejerazo* of 23 February 1981 all gave credence to Carrillo's assertion that Spanish democracy was in need of all cosseting it could get.[56] Oddly enough, while this caution necessitated curtailing rank and file militancy, it was rewarded in the elections of 1 March 1979 by a small increase in the PCE vote from 9.2 per cent to 10.9 per cent which was to be set against a 2 per cent drop in the PSOE vote. However, in the wake of the *Tejerazo*, the PCE vote was as likely to be hit by fear among the electorate that communist success could provoke the military as by disquiet at the internal disarray of the PCE.

Such disarray has been the consequence of the fact that the PCE's moderation in the period of Spain's democratization left it as junior partner to the PSOE. The element of sacrifice in the PCE's self-imposed moderation, together with Carrillo's heavy bureaucratic style, led to considerable internecine dispute which surfaced at both the 9th and 10th Congresses of the PCE, held in Madrid in April 1978 and July 1981. At the 9th Congress, discontent centred on the dropping of Leninism. Along with the incorporation of substantial numbers of working-class militants into the central committee, this constituted an attempt by the PCE to adjust both its theoretical positions and its organizational composition to its day-to-day political practice. This was not possible without loud rumblings of rebellion, especially in Asturias and Catalonia.[57] Thereafter, the Carrillo leadership was challenged on two fronts. On the one hand, a Soviet-sponsored opposition, which attained considerable success within the PSUC, pushed for a return to a harder line. On the other, an 'ultra-Eurocommunist' group, known as the *renovadores*, with the support of Roberto Lertxundi of the Basque Communist Party, demanded that Carrillo go further towards the Eurocommunist ideal of internal democracy. Since this implied the removal of the aged leadership team that Carrillo had brought from Paris in 1976, it led to a bitter fight in both the *proceso precongresual* and in the Congress itself.[58] In both cases, Carrillo dealt with the problem by so-called 'administrative sanctions', in other words, by reverting to the Stalinist instincts of his youth and simply expelling his opponents.

Aside from the fact that both the *pro-soviéticos* and the *renovadores* made significant errors of timing and tactics, Carrillo was able to justify his repressive stance against them by reference to a political situation dominated by the threat of a coup. That context was used to back up Carrillo's claim that the time was not ripe for adventurous experiment and that he thus had no choice but to clamp down on both sets of opponents. If that argument was plausible when applied against the Leninist positions of the *pro-soviéticos*, it was less so where the *renovadores* were concerned. There can be little doubt that, had the *renovadores* triumphed, the PCE would have been a remarkably open and moderate party, not to say unrecognizable as a communist party. Thus, in crushing the *renovadores*, Carrillo was drawing the limits of the Eurocommunist modernization of the PCE which he had begun in 1954. Arguably, he was doing so in order to leave the PCE on undisputably communist ground. However, the fact that, in order to do so, he had to expel the most creative and enthusiastic party cadres suggested that his perception of communism was out of touch with the changing face of Spanish political life.

There were three periods, 1954–6, 1967–70 and 1974–9, during which Carrillo contributed both to the modernization of the PCE and to the consolidation of its position within the democratic struggle. However, by the time of the 10th Congress, it seemed that Carrillo had little left to offer. With an ever narrower group of apparatchiks, he was more concerned to hold on to his own position at any cost rather than permit the opening of the party to changing currents. Discredited by the constant blood-letting of expulsions and the drifting away of party intellectuals, the PCE suffered badly in the elections of 28 October 1982. The drop from 23 to 5 parliamentary deputies could not be explained simply by voters' fears of the army. Unable to avoid some responsibility for the débâcle, Carrillo was obliged to resign as secretary-general. He chose his own replacement, the Asturian leader, Gerardo Iglesias, hoping to be able to manipulate him. The exclusion of more able and popular candidates, such as Nicolás Sartorius, opened the way to internecine struggles. In fact, at every point in his moulding of the PCE since 1954, Carrillo had similarly used his control and knowledge of the party apparatus to achieve his ends. His enemies have claimed that this invalidated the process; his friends that, without such methods, there would probably have been no communist party at all, and certainly not a Eurocommunist one. The truth certainly lies between those two extreme views. In the last resort, the PCE's behaviour during the transition to democracy, rather than the occasionally Stalinist reflexes of its erstwhile leader, must be taken as the yardstick by which to judge its Eurocommunist sincerity.

Notes

1 Apart from the celebrated remarks of Sir Harold Wilson and David Owen on the subject, see also Rudolf Tökés (ed.), *Eurocommunism and Détente* (Oxford, 1979), p. 3. Santiago Carrillo, *'Eurocomunismo' y Estado* (Barcelona, 1977), pp. 16–17.

2 See especially the respectively ultra-rightist and pro-Soviet accounts: Angel Ruiz Ayucar, *El partido comunista: treinta y siete años de clandestinidad* (Madrid, 1976) and Julio Luelmo and Henry Winston, *'Eurocomunismo y Estado' o la desintegración del PCE y la ruptura con el movimiento comunista internacional* (Madrid, 1978).

3 Manuel Azcárate, 'The Prague-Moscow-Madrid Triangle', in G.R. Urban (ed.), *Communist Reformation: Nationalism, Internationalism and Change in the World Communist Movement* (London, 1979); Azcárate, 'What Is Eurocommunism?' and Jean Elleinstein, 'The Skein of History Unrolled Backwards', in G.R. Urban (ed.), *Eurocommunism* (London, 1978); Enrico Berlinguer, 'Report to Central Committee of PCI on Preparations for XIV Congress', in *El PC español, italiano y francés cara al poder* (Madrid, 1977).

4 Tökés, 'Éastern Europe in the 1970s: Détente, Dissent and Eurocommunism', in *Eurocommunism and Détente* (Oxford, 1979); Archie Brown and George Schöpflin, 'The Challenge to the Soviet Leadership: Effects in Eastern Europe', in Paolo Filo della Torre, Edward Mortimer and Jonathan Story (eds), *Eurocommunism: Myth or Reality?* (Harmondsworth, 1979); Godfrey Hodgson, 'The US response', ibid. In November 1977, the Italian dissident communist group, *Il Manifesto*, organized a congress to discuss the links between the European left and the working-class opposition in the Soviet bloc. Cf. *Power and Opposition in Post-Revolutionary Societies* (London, 1979).

5 *Il Manifesto*, 1 November 1975.

6 In February 1974, the CPSU organ, *Partiinaya Zhizn*, made a virulent attack on Manuel Azcárate as a result of a report that he made to the PCE central committee in September 1973 in which he deplored the lack of true socialist democracy in the USSR. The executive committee of the PCE quickly published and distributed a substantial and well-produced

pamphlet containing Azcárate's report, the Russian reply and the PCE's counter-reply, thereby both publicizing the rift and also managing to give the impression that the PCE conducted all its affairs in public. See Comité Ejecutivo del PCE, *Documentos: Informe de Manuel Azcárate; Artículo publicado en la revista soviética 'Vida del Partido'; Acotaciones al artículo* (n.p., n.d.). Similarly, when Carrillo was attacked in *Novoye Vremya* after the publication of his *'Eurocomunismo' y Estado* in the spring of 1977, the PCE hastened to publish a similar dossier. See Comisión de Información y Propaganda del Comité Provincial de Madrid del PCE, *Dossier sobre la polémica en torno al artículo de la revista soviética 'Tiempos Nuevos'* (Madrid, 1977).

7 Manuel Vázquez Montalbán, *La penetración americana en España* (Madrid, 1974) pp. 203-4, 253-350; Juan Múñoz, Santiago Roldán and Angel Serrano, *La internacionalización del capital en España 1959-1977* (Madrid, 1978) *passim* and especially pp. 127-30, 146-56, 190-4; Carlos Berzosa and Francisco Arbell, 'Inversiones extranjeras en el postfranquismo', *Revista Mensual*, 2 (516), December 1978-January 1979.

8 Genaro Campos, 'Los dos primerós gobiernos de la monarquía y sus relaciones con el poder económico', *Cuadernos de Ruedo Ibérico*, nos. 51-3, May–October 1976. The crucial turning-point in the transition process was the King's dismissal of his first prime minister, the Francoist Carlos Arias Navarro, in the summer of 1976 shortly after a visit to Washington. It is an interesting comment on the evolution in US attitudes to Spain that whereas in 1976 American influence was used to urge Juan Carlos to speed up the reform process, in 1961 a semi-official source could worry that Franco was going soft on communism. Cf. Arthur P. Whitaker, *Spain and the Defence of the West* (New York, 1961), pp. 184-90.

9 Juan Martínez Alier, 'El Pacto de la Moncloa, la lucha sindical y el nuevo corporativismo', *Cuadernos de Ruedo Ibérico*, nos. 58-60, July–December 1977; G.I. Marti, 'El gran *show* politico o las trampas de la comunicación: las elecciones del 15 de junio de 1977', *Cuadernos de Ruedo Ibérico*, nos. 61-2, January–April 1979; Rafael Bosch, *La revolución democrática: ¿Quo vadis? Tamames* (Madrid, 1978), p. 145-81.

10 This is the view propounded by Jonathan Story, 'El pacto para la libertad: The Spanish Communist Party', in Filo della Torre, Mortimer and Story, op. cit., pp. 177-8, and by Eusebio Mujal León, 'Spain: The PCE and the Post-Franco Era', in David E. Albright, (ed.), *Communism and Political Systems in Western Europe* (Boulder, Colorado, 1979) pp. 153 ff.

11 Santiago Carrillo, *Informe sobre problemas de organización y los estatutos del Partido* in *Actas del V Congreso del Partido Comunista de España*, 4 vols, typescript, vol. III, pp. 775-826. Cf. Fernando Claudin, *Documentos de una divergencia comunista* (Barcelona, 1978), p. ii.

12 Partido Comunista de España, *Declaración por la reconciliación*

nacional, por una solución democrática y pacífica del problema español (n.p., n.d., but Paris, 1956), pp. 3, 29-31, 37-40; Dolores Ibárruri, *Por la reconciliación de los españoles hacia la democratización de España* (Paris, 1956), *passim*.

13 Federico Sánchez, 'Informe al VIo Congreso del PCE', *Nuestra Bandera*, no. 25, March 1960, pp. 63-74; Eduardo García, 'La organización de las masas', *Nuestra Bandera*, no. 27, July 1960; *Estatutos del PCE aprobados en su VI Congreso* (n.p., n.d., but Prague, 1960), pp. 13-14; VI Congreso del PCE, *Programa del PCE* (n.p., n.d., but Prague, 1960), p. 17.

14 For accounts of the Claudín-Semprún schism, see Claudín, *Documentos*; Jorge Semprún, *Autobiografía de Federico Sánchez* (Barcelona, 1977); *Nuestra Bandera*, no. 40, January 1965; Paul Preston, 'The Dilemma of Credibility: The Spanish Communist Party, the Franco Régime and After', *Government and Opposition*, 11 (1) (1976).

15 There were no references to the 7th Congress in PCE periodical publications and none of the reports were published as such. This was in large measure a consequence of the fact that, after the relatively well-publicized 6th Congress, many delegates were arrested on their return to Spain. It also reflected a desire for a discreet resolution to the expulsions. Carrillo's report, *¿Qué queremos los comunistas para España? Hacia una democracia política y social* in *VII Congreso del Partido Comunista de España* (3 vols, unpublished typescript) was published with minor alterations as *Después de Franco, ¿Qué?* (Paris, 1965). Cf. especially pp. 11, 23, 32-6.

16 Santiago Carrillo, *Discurso ante una asamblea de militantes del Partido* (n.p., but Prague, 1964), p. 39.

17 *Mundo Obrero*, 15 October 1964; Azcárate, 'The Prague-Moscow-Madrid Triangle', p. 174.

18 Santiago Carrillo, *Nuevos enfoques a problemas de hoy* (Paris, 1967), pp. 140-59.

19 Interview with Carrillo in *Nuestra Bandera*, nos. 47-8, February-March 1966, pp. 15-17; Carrillo, *Nuevos enfoques*, pp. 26, 58-9, 101-6.

20 Santiago Alvarez, 'La renovación en Checoslovaquia', *Mundo Obrero*, 1ª quincena de mayo 1968; Santiago Carrillo, 'La lucha por el socialismo hoy', *Nuestra Bandera*, supplement to no. 58, June 1968, pp. 32, 38-40.

21 Probably the most complete account of the Czechoslovak crisis of the PCE is Fernando Claudín, 'La crisis del Partido comunista de Espana', *Cuadernos de Ruedo Ibérico*, nos. 26-7, August-November 1970; see also Enrique Lister, *¡Basta!* (n.p., n.d.); *Nuestra Bandera*, no. 65 3er trimestre de 1970, pp. 3-24.

22 Ignacio Gallego, *El partido de masas que necesitamos* (Paris, 1971), pp. 7-9; Santiago Carrillo, *Libertad y socialismo* (Paris, 1971), pp. 56-66; *Nuestra Bandera*, no. 62, October-November 1969, pp. 22-5.

23 Apparently contacts between Marcelino Camacho and various business-

178   *National Communism in Western Europe*

men were arranged by Antonio García Trevijano. Information supplied to the author by Rafael Calvo Serer.

24 *Mundo Obrero*, 24 December 1971; Santiago Carrillo, *Hacia el post-franquismo* (Paris, 1974), pp. 57-62; Josep María Castellet and Lluís María Bonet, *¿Cuáles son los partidos políticos de Catalunya?* (Barcelona, 1976), pp. 40-4.

25 *Mundo Obrero*, 5 September 1973; *Nuestra Bandera*, no. 72, 4° trimestre 1973, pp. 15-30; Carrillo, *Hacia el post-franquismo*, pp. 29-30.

26 'El espíritu del Ritz', *Cambio 16*, no. 134, 10 June 1974; Ramón Tamames, *Un proyecto de democracia para el futuro de España* (Madrid, 1975), pp. 7-10.

27 *Mundo Obrero*, 8, 22 May, 4 July 1974; *Le Monde*, 23-5 June 1974; Carrillo, *Hacia el post-franquismo*, pp. 5-6.

28 *Mundo Obrero*, 31 July 1974; Rafael Calvo Serer, *Mis enfrentamientos con el poder* (Barcelona, 1978), pp. 119-21, 248-65.

29 *Mundo Obrero*, 19 March 1975.

30 *Mundo Obrero*, 1ᵃ y 2ᵃ semanas de junio de 1975.

31 *Mundo Obrero*, 4ᵃ semana de septiembre de 1975.

32 V. Díaz Cardiel *et al. Madrid en huelga, enero de 1976* (Madrid, 1976); *Cuadernos de Ruedo Ibérico*, nos. 51-3, May–October 1976.

33 Francisco Lasa, 'La oferta de la Junta Democrática: Lenin ha muerto' and Colectivo 70, 'Interpretaciones políticas en la declaración de la Junta Democrática', *Cuadernos de Ruedo Ibérico* nos. 43-5, January–July 1975; *Frente Libertario*, no. 45, September 1974; *Vanguardia Obrera*, no. 90, 2ᵃ quincena de agosto, no. 91, September 1974; *Servir al Pueblo*, no. 30, August 1974.

34 The fear of being betrayed by other opposition groups was very noticeable in conversations with senior officials of the PCE held by the author throughout 1976.

35 *Mundo Obrero*, 9, 17 April 1976.

36 *Mundo Obrero*, 14 July 1976.

37 *Mundo Obrero*, 7 July 1976.

38 *Cambio 16*, no. 246, 23-9 August 1976; *Mundo Obrero*, 26 July-2 August 1976; Joaquín Bardavío, *Sabado santo rojo* (Madrid, 1980), pp. 42-4; Gregorio Morán, *Adolfo Suárez: historia de una ambición* (Barcelona, 1979), p. 337.

39 *Mundo Obrero*, 1 September 1976; Santiago Carrillo, *De la clandestinidad a la legalidad* (n.p., n.d.); Gian Piero Dell'Acqua, *Spagna: cronache della transizione* (Florence, 1978), pp. 136-58.

40 Bardavío, *Sabado santo*, p. 52.

41 *Cambio 16*, No. 245, 16-22 August 1976; Morán, *Suárez*, pp. 331-2.

42 Bardavío, op. cit., pp. 51-8.

43 *Cambio 16*, no. 249, 13-19 September 1976; *Mundo Obrero*, 8 September 1976.

44 Bardavío, op. cit., pp. 59-60; *Cambio 16*, no. 250, 20-6 September 1976.

45 *Mundo Obrero,* 15-23 September 1976.
46 Morán, op. cit., p. 334.
47 *Mundo Obrero,* 1-7 November 1976.
48 *Mundo Obrero,* 15-21, 22-8 November 1976.
49 *Mundo Obrero,* 20-6 December 1976; Bardavío, op. cit., pp. 88-90.
50 Bardavío, op. cit., pp. 91-111.
51 *Mundo Obrero,* 31 January-6 February 1977; Bardavío, op. cit., pp. 142-7.
52 Morán, op. cit., p. 338; Bardavío, op. cit., pp. 158-68.
53 Santiago Carrillo, 'Intervención en el Pleno ampliado del C.C.' *Escritos sobre Eurocomunismo,* 2 vols (Madrid, 1977), vol. II, pp. 29-51.
54 Cf. Carrillo's speeches in the Cortes on 27 July, 14 September and 24 September 1977, reprinted in *Escritos* II.
55 For complete membership figures broken down by regions, see Carlos Elordi, 'El PCE por dentro', *La Calle,* no. 95, 15-21 January 1980.
56 On the destabilization of Spanish politics throughout 1978 and 1979, see José María Mohedano and Marco Peña, *Constitución: cuenta atrás* (Madrid, 1978) and Paul Preston, 'Walking the Terrorist Tightrope', *Contemporary Review,* 234 (1358) (March 1979). The extreme moderation displayed by Carrillo is evident in his articles and parliamentary speeches in 1978; see Santiago Carrillo, *El año de la Constitución* (Barcelona, 1978).
57 On the 9th Congress, see PCE *9° Congreso del Partido Comunista de España: Resoluciones* (Madrid, 1978); *Nuestra Bandera,* no. 93, 1978; *El País,* 20-3 April 1978; *Mundo Obrero,* 20, 23 and 27 April 1978. Cf. Fernando Claudín, 'Las tesis del IX Congreso', *Triunfo,* no. 795, 22 April 1978 and Fernando López Agudín, 'Un paso adelante dos pasos atrás', *Triunfo,* no. 796, 27 April 1978.
58 On the 10th Congress, see *Mundo Obrero,* 24-30 July, 28 July 1981 and *Suplementos* 1,2,3, and 4. See also *La Calle,* no. 176, 4-10 August 1981.

9

The Portuguese Communist Party:
the weight of fifty years of history

Manuel Villaverde Cabral

For most of its existence, the Portuguese Communist Party (PCP) was a clandestine illegal organization. Until the recent changes in Portuguese politics, very little research on the PCP had been carried out. During the dictatorship access to communist publications and documents was very difficult and even dangerous. Furthermore, since 1974 the party itself has been reluctant to open its own archives. Hence, the author has been obliged to rely on 'current knowledge' in Portugal about the history of the PCP for the long period when it was outlawed. Such 'current knowledge', irrespective of the good faith of the author, cannot be either completely accurate about historical details or politically unbiased. In short, only a few years after the fall of the longest dictatorship of recent times it is not yet possible to provide an objective academic analysis of the developments of the PCP. The interpretation of this author is presented with great hesitancy and no claims to scientific rigour. It is, however, important to examine the long and troubled development of the party if one wishes to understand its actions since 1974.

Before 25 April 1974 when Caetano fell, the communist party had seldom been obliged to face public criticism or to strive for mass public support. Hence, like many other communist parties in clandestinity, the Portuguese party developed largely as a result of its own internal dynamics. This does not mean, however, that the party evolved independently and in isolation from the changes taking place in Portuguese society as a whole. Indeed, one aim of this chapter is to relate the history of the party to the major social changes of the last five decades and to demonstrate the deep roots of the PCP in the Portuguese working class. A further aim of this paper is to show how the fifty years of authoritarian and reactionary dictatorship helped to prolong social and economic backwardness and to embitter opponents of the regime with the result that the PCP became notable for monolithism, dogmatism and conspicuous loyalty to the Soviet Union. It is a curious paradox that the dictatorship partly resulted from the apparent *weakness* of industrialists and large farmers when faced with strong pressures for change from the working class: instead of agreeing to some form of liberal reformism, scared employers turned repeatedly to the more conservative rural groups to form alliances to stop any change from taking place.

After the fall of the dictatorship in 1974, it was once again the apparent superior strength of the organized working classes which engendered yet another alliance between scared employers and rural conservatives to attempt to block reform.

The beginnings of the Portuguese Communist Party

One significant difference between the Portuguese party and most other communist parties in Western Europe is that the PCP was not born as a result of a split in the socialist party. The Portuguese Socialist Party had been created in the mid-1870s, but by the end of the First World War it had lost the small influence it had previously built up, to the ruling Republican–Democratic Party (on whose favour the socialists had depended) and to the syndicalist movement. In 1919, when the first communist groups were organized in support of the Russian Revolution, perhaps coincidentally a socialist was appointed to the Labour Ministry. This new attempt to introduce some sort of political reformism, however, failed as pitifully as earlier similar attempts had. For by that time, a national trade union movement, the General Confederation of Labour (CGT) had been founded after a period of rapid working-class organization in labour unions. The CGT claimed a membership of over 100,000 (if accurate, this figure represented almost a quarter of the southern urban and rural proletariat) and was controlled by anarchists and revolutionary syndicalists.

In these circumstances, it was not surprising that the first communist grouping, the Maximalist Federation, began life in 1919 as an offspring of the syndicalist movement under the auspices of intellectuals and trade union leaders like Manuel Ribeiro and Carlos Rates. It is interesting to note that the Maximalists intended to operate as a kind of pressure group within the CGT. They did not challenge the CGT leadership of the working-class movement. The ideology of the Maximalists, as seen in their newspaper, the *Red Flag*, had its origins in the pre-war debate between *pure* syndicalists and *pure* anarchists. It was close to the *ouvriérisme* expressed by such men as Pierre Monatte in the French CGT and Andrés Nin and Joaquín Maurín in the Spanish CNT. Hence, it would be inaccurate to describe the future founders of the PCP as a consciously Leninist group of professional revolutionaries aiming at a seizure of power. Only when the anarchist leaders of the CGT clearly dropped their support of the Russian Revolution, particularly after the Kronstadt episode, did the communists decide to face a split and create the new party, in March 1921.

In spite of these strong ideological differences over the evaluation of Bolshevik rule in Russia the PCP still did not want, or dare, to challenge the CGT as the dominant organization of the Portuguese working class. Until the 1920s the activities of the PCP appeared rather ineffective. A good deal of time seemed to be wasted by the main communist leaders debating and falling out amongst themselves. In fact this was a common feature of communist parties in Latin countries throughout that decade, after their initial take-off and the subsequent setbacks of all working-class movements.

During that period, however, two groups emerged as more directly involved in the current social warfare, and more relevant for the future of the PCP. The first of these groups was the so-called 'Sympathizers of the Trade Unions' Red International' (ISV). These were workers who were active in the CGT but hostile to the anarchist leadership. When the syndicalist movement began to face a series of serious set-backs and to lose members, the leaders of the CGT reacted to the challenge of the ISV Sympathizers and tried to expel them.

The latter proved, nevertheless, strong enough to gain control of some important trade union federations, and notably the Seamen's Federation which was a significant segment of the Lisbon proletariat, as it included all the different groups of dock workers, as well as the navy shipyard workers. From this federation a young turner called Bento Gonçalves was to emerge a few years later to lead the 'Bolshevik reorganization' of 1929. Thus, by the mid-1920s, despite its divisions and small membership, the PCP was already able to challenge the anarchist leadership of the CGT and to attract the support of some important segments of the urban workforce.

The second group of the two groups referred to above was the Syndicalist Youth movement. Like the ISV Sympathizers, some young workers were radically critical of the old leadership of the CGT. Unlike the ISV people, however, the Syndicalist Youth did not maintain the *ouvriériste* outlook common to Portuguese workers' movements, but turned towards violent action. Their recruitment from among the huge numbers of young unemployed of that period (rather than among young trade union members) perhaps accounts for their ideology which resembled a mild version of the terrorism of the *Federacion Anarquista Ibérica* (FAI) in Spain.

In Portugal though, the anarchist CGT leaders very strongly resisted the use of violence. Hence these armed bands of young unemployed were driven into contact with the small PCP. Moreover, after 1923, the party appeared to offer more institutionalized channels for these forms of radicalism. This development in turn created several difficulties, and in the years immediately prior to the military take-over in May 1926, the delegate of the Comintern, Humbert-Droz, had a hard fight to prevent the Youth leaders from winning leadership of the PCP from the man he had helped to install, Carlos Rates.

Apogee and decline of the PCP

The period of the Rates leadership, under the direct sponsorship of the Comintern through its delegate, Humbert-Droz, was a very interesting period and represented the peak of the PCP's influence before the dictatorship. The PCP developed then a programme of alliances virtually alien to the tradition of the Portuguese working-class movement; it tried to deal both with the small peasantry, traditionally left out of working-class politics by the syndicalists, and with the democratic left of the ruling republican party. It also made repeated offers to the CGT and the remnants of the socialist party to unite in a common anti-fascist front.

In retrospect, one feels that the real strength of the PCP did not match the sophistication of these policies, which required a mass membership which the party was then far from having. There had been a brief period of euphoria early in 1925, when the PCP helped to gather popular support for the left-wing cabinet of Domingues dos Santos. After that its weaknesses were overwhelmingly exposed in the disastrous results of the November election, and later on, much more cruelly, when it failed to add any significant strength to the opposition to the military coup of 28 May 1926.

The advent of authoritarianism, even before Salazar came to power (in April 1928 as Minister of Finance), proved fatal for Rates and his Comintern policy of alliances, and it plunged the PCP into complete disarray. Indeed, the military coup actually interrupted the progress of the party's 2nd Congress (the 1st had taken place in 1923) and only in 1943 was it able to call, in clandestinity, its 3rd Congress. It should be noted that the PCP's disarray was also shared by the CGT, as well as by the entire political class.

In the later years of that decade the history of the PCP is extremely obscure. Somehow it survived, although it failed to establish any stable alliance with the other forces trying to operate among the working classes. Nonetheless, the party was still in a position to send to the Soviet Union a small group of young activists who were briefly trained there. These men were later able, under the leadership of Bento Gonçalves, to implement the '1929 reorganization', the Portuguese version of the 'Stalinization' of communist parties outside the Soviet Union.

Equally little is known about the party in the 1930s. Most of the energy of the PCP seems to have been spent in maintaining itself from repression. Nevertheless, this was undoubtedly a crucial period for the future of the Portuguese working-class movement, and indeed for Portuguese society as a whole. In the first place, the CGT went into rapid decline from which it was never to recover; hence the communist-type of organization seemed superior for coping with repression and clandestinity. Secondly, the almost complete·halt to industrialization and urbanization, imposed by the combined effects of the world depression and the deliberate social and economic policies of the regime, led to a 'crystallization' of the political composition of the working classes. In other words there were no new jobs but little overt unemployment, no new industries but a heavy dependence on old skills and seniority at the shop floor level, no social mobility but an increasing gap between factory workers and other workers.

Finally, the 1930s were also the period of disenchantment for large sections of the middle classes, which had initially put a good deal of hope in the authoritarian regime. By the middle of the decade a new anti-fascist alliance, sponsored by the Comintern after 1934, provided the basis for membership expansion and even for some recruitment of leaders.

In January 1934, as the country was painfully recovering from the economic crisis, the communists and the remnants of the CGT joined in an uneasy front against the fascist takeover of the trade unions and launched a 'general strike'. This failed completely, in the face of harsh repression, but it led to the episode of the twenty-four-hour rising of Marinha Grande, a glass-manufacturing town seventy miles north of Lisbon on 18 January. For the CGT the collapse of the strike meant an end to its existence; most of its leaders and activists were arrested or deported, and the syndicalist movement never recovered from the blow. The PCP was also greatly hit by the repression. Bento Goncalves, its Soviet-trained general secretary (the only Portuguese communist leader to have attended the Comintern congresses) was deported with many other PCP leaders to the Camp of Tarrafal (Cape Verde Islands) where he died in 1942.

From Gonçalves' writings in exile emerges a PCP view of the events of 1934. The 18 January uprising was described as a typical anarchist error, *uma anarqueirada*. The lesson for the party was to avoid any kind of 'all out' action of this kind, and to concentrate on the organization of the party itself. This attitude (which the defeat of the Spanish Republic only confirmed) encapsulates the way in which the PCP dealt for the next few decades with repression, managing to survive all blows, and it became a dominant feature of PCP strategy until the present day.

The reorganization of the early 1940s

From the limited information available, it appears that the party was again in serious trouble, if not in total disarray. Often *ad hoc* leaders had taken over from the better-trained ones in prison or exile. It seems that by and large the PCP had lost any organized contact with the working class in the factories. As a result various groups of middle-class intellectuals found themselves, with virtually no training or preparation, having to assume the task of leading the party. According to some views, this may have accounted for the complete ideological confusion prevailing in the late 1930s and early 1940s, when the PCP was eventually expelled from the Comintern and its leadership accused of indulging in all kinds of 'opportunistic' moves.

It is interesting to note the role of middle-class intellectuals during this period. Several literary sources of the time, particularly novels by Carlos de Oliveira and Soeiro Pereira Gomes – the latter a full-time party organizer in the 1940s – describe a situation of serious economic difficulties for small businesses in competition with the few big concerns protected by the policies of the regime. The fears the middle classes had nurtured towards the syndicalist threats of the 1920s were now a thing of the past; indeed, a minor feature as compared to the threats of Nazism and war.

This context favoured the rapid growth of *Neorealism*, a left-wing literary and artistic movement that became the intellectual trend in the country until the late 1950s. This movement was important not only in exposing the social injustice and authoritarian activities of Salazar's regime, but also in expanding the influence of left-wing ideas, including communist ones, amongst the middle classes.

One feature of this intellectual movement was the replacement of 'the working class' as a category by 'the people' or 'the poor'. Naturally 'the people' is full of noble qualities, but it does not have any clear political identity of its own. This is not to dispute the sincerity of the middle-class intellectuals who joined the PCP in the 1940s, but only to underline the vanishing of 'the working class' as a political concept in the descriptions of Portuguese society at the time. More importantly, this populist approach also pervaded the PCP on more than one occasion, and one can still detect a good deal of it in post-1974 populist activities especially among the politically uneducated army officers of the 25 April movement.

However pervasive and persuasive, populism (which as usual went along with *putschism*) did not finally prevail. By the early 1940s, the PCP was involved in a terrible internal struggle which is still virtually unknown to the general public. International issues about the involvement of Portugal in the war seem to have played a role in the split that divided the party. It has also been argued that British pressures were determinant in forcing Salazar to free some of the Tarrafal political prisoners. Many former communist leaders were freed, and, once back in the country, these activists were instrumental in ousting the so-called 'opportunistic' leaders then in charge of the PCP's organization.

The 3rd Congress, in 1943, witnessed the complete defeat of the 'putschist faction' led by Dr Velez Grilo. The better trained and more working-class oriented faction took over under the leadership of Militão Ribeiro (a worker) and his ideological intellectual comrade, Alvaro Cunhal. Unqualified anti-fascism, openness to middle-class recruitment and to democratic ideas, and broad sympathies for both the Soviet Union and the Allies, were soon to create new problems inside the PCP. Immediately after the war the party leaders had to overcome a strong wish (inside the central committee itself) towards the disbanding of the party and its dilution in a large anti-fascist front.

During the war, between 1941 and 1944, a wave of strikes took place, the first since the fall of liberalism. Although the PCP did not inspire the first strike movements, the party soon proved its ability to capitalize on the social unrest in order to re-establish its working-class links. At once it began to recruit, to organize and to reinforce the factory struggle. These episodes of the early 1940s seem to contain many of the formative elements of the post-war character of the PCP. The repression against the strikers and the communist activists was extremely harsh, and once again this repression was a crucial determinant of the attitudes of Portuguese communists.

In any event, after its 4th Congress in 1946 (where Cunhal appeared unofficially as the successor of Bento Gonçalves) the organizational structures as well as the ideological outlook of the PCP were already those demonstrated after the end of the dictatorship. In the first place, the party had developed a tight network of full-time clandestine officials, *funcionários*. This network was one of the largest in a country outside communist rule. The role of these *funcionários* was not primarily to organize strikes, demonstrations, or influence in society, but rather, first and foremost, *to organize the organization*, to recruit and train members, to raise financial support, to print and to distribute the clandestine press (published continuously from the 1940s inside the country by a network of mobile printing shops). This is, I believe, what the PCP was about, and the failure by commentators to contemplate seriously the identity of the party *as an organization* – cadres led by a co-opted hard core of professional political organizers – has led, in my opinion, to many misunderstandings.

Furthermore, the Portuguese party remained such an organization of co-opted cadres even when it attained mass membership. Today the PCP claims more than 100,000 members, but the party is organized in such a way that rank-and-file members have no means of interfering with the decision-making process and with the recruitment of cadres. Mass membership thus does not make any difference to the way the organization is run by the professional hardcore of co-opted cadres.

From 'frontism' to isolation

Thanks to this structure and this organizational capacity to survive, the party was able to appear to many Portuguese people, from the 1940s until the late 1960s, as the 'party of resistance to fascism', as well as the 'party of the exploited and the oppressed'. Dogmatism, rigidity and blind loyalty to the Soviet Union – in one word, Stalinism –

seemed natural in a country where fascism had divided one and all into black and white, right and wrong.

The PCP in fact expressed the hopes of large numbers of anti-fascists. It is necessary to comprehend this peculiar feeling in order to understand what Cunhal once meant when he talked of the 'moral superiority' of Portuguese communists. Just as the French Communist Party capitalized for years on its achievements in the resistance to Nazism, the PCP never hesitated to advertise the fact that the twenty-odd members of its first legal central committee, set up in 1974, had together spent some 300 years in jail!

At the end of the war, however, the dictatorship was facing serious difficulties in international relations, which had repercussions in national politics. There were many who believed that the regime would not be allowed by the Allies to survive the fall of fascism and Nazism. In retrospect, it is not impossible to detect a sentiment of 'liberation' similar to that felt in France and Italy immediately after the war. This sentiment was most evident amongst members of the broad gathering of anti-fascist forces united, under the auspices of the PCP, in the *Movimento de Unidade Nacional Anti-Fascista* (MUNAF 1943) and in the *Movimento de Unidade Democratica* (MUD 1945). For the first time in twenty years the regime seemed under a real threat. Hence, in order to present a more respectable façade to the Allies, the government decided to hold elections.

The 1949 presidential election was not only a complete fraud by any democratic standards, but it symbolized the transition from the 'euphoria of liberation' to the suspicions of Cold War in two different ways. Firstly, it soon became obvious that the regime was not going to fade away and that the election was only held 'for the English to see'. Secondly, when the election was eventually held, although the PCP had not supported a candidate of its own, most of the non-communist leaders of the opposition (especially the candidate himself, the old general Norton de Matos) made clear their differences with the PCP and accepted only its 'passive support'. In short, a split was created among the opposition to the dictatorship which would never be completely overcome, despite the strong feelings of unity among most people in the anti-fascist movement.

In 1951, when Marshal Carmona, who had been re-elected two years earlier, died, the regime decided to hold a new election, but this time Salazar was already in a stronger position and refused to allow even the few liberties conceded in 1949. In addition, the split between communists and non-communists had become deeper than ever, each group presenting its own candidate. Predictably, the candidate of the regime was elected. The 1950s began and were to continue for the PCP as years of great isolation. The only unitarian movement which managed to struggle through the period was the youth branch of the MUD (MUD-Juvenil), which at its peak claimed a membership of 20,000. By the end of the decade, however, very little was left of it.

From an organizational standpoint the PCP underwent serious difficulties. Cunhal was arrested in 1949, along with several other cadres, and Militão Ribeiro died in prison, on hunger strike, in 1950. The isolation of the party reflected both the isolation of the Soviet Union internationally and the isolation of the working class in Portuguese society. For, in Portugal, the pressure of over-population and unemployment, which reached their peaks in the mid-1950s, conflicted strongly with some slight improvements in wages and conditions among factory workers due to the beginning, however modest, of a new industrializing trend, initiated by the 1953 Six Year Plan. Job security – an essential feature of the corporative social policy – seems to have played a crucial role, keeping apart the more or less communist-organized workers in factories and transport from the vast numbers of the unemployed, both in towns and in the countryside, who engaged only in casual labour. At this time, if my recollections are accurate, a factory worker was looked upon with envy by a casual labourer who might move overnight from an unskilled job on a building site to a plain dependence on charity.

This seems to have been a period for the PCP of significant recruitment among the middle classes. These included students and intellectuals as usual, but also small businessmen and clerical workers, and even some professionals, lawyers and doctors in particular, both in Lisbon and in the provinces. According to the recent memoirs of a former full-time party organizer, J. Silva Marques, most of the few party members in small provincial towns were rather well-off local *notables* even in the late 1960s. It is hard to say whether this trend can be correlated to the so-called 'right-wing deviation' of which the leadership of that time was later accused.

During the 1958 presidential campaign the PCP failed totally, despite significant working-class militancy, to impose its own candidate and had to back General Delgado in the end, after initally opposing him on the grounds of his political past. Moreover, the PCP failed to impose any specific working-class demands or to raise any social issues within the movement supporting Delgado's candidacy. In that sense, the 1958 campaign can be said to mark both the peak and the end of anti-fascim as a cross-class and unqualified movement of opposition to the dictatorship. As such, the Delgado campaign meant a relative decline of the PCP's symbolic domination within the opposition, despite its acknowledged capacity for mass mobilization.

The new peak of the PCP

The communist party was again quick to recover from this decline because of its organizational powers. While the non-communist leaders of the opposition, including Delgado, proved ineffectual after the election was over, the PCP was able to capitalize on the wave of militancy and recruit massively, ultimately regaining control of the activities against the regime. The spectacular escape from prison of Cunhal and nine other members of the central committee in early 1960 also affected the growth and radicalization of the party rank-and-file. Realizing the radical trend already under way, Cunhal persuaded the central committee to issue a very strong attack on the 'right-wing deviation' of the 1950s and to set down a series of proposals for organizing the overthrow of the dictatorship by means of a 'national uprising'. Altogether, it was a subtle return to the hard line, but it excluded neither an appeal to anti-fascist unity nor an allusion to the need of defeating the regime by force.

This period was one of intense social and political warfare. In 1961 Portugal was thrown out of Goa, in India, and war broke out in Angola. These events seriously affected the regime, especially as they provided the roots for the first significant split in the army. Military leaders (including General Costa Gomes, an Under-Secretary of State) seem to have envisaged waging a coup against Salazar on the grounds of his colonial policy. But such erratic ideas were quickly defeated by the dictator, who was able to remove these generals and to replace them by more loyal ones. At the time, these events had little public impact. It was only several years later that the colonial wars became a major plank in the movement of opposition to the dictatorship. In retrospect it also appears that the troubles of the regime in 1961 may have contributed in an indirect way to the relative success of the communist mobilization in the campaign for the National Assembly elections. More directly, this mobilization linked up with the student agitation and the first important strikes since the war.

The PCP, already prominent in the organization of the election campaign, was also able during those years to regain influence, and sometimes full control, among the students and workers. During the

1962 strike for an eight-hour working day by the rural labourers of Alentejo (in the south of the country), the PCP showed a political and ideological influence not dissimilar to the one it held in the same area after 1974. The 1962 May Day demonstrations, particularly in Lisbon and its 'industrial belt' where several people were killed in clashes with the police, showed the party at its maximum strength. It had achieved an organizational success which proved impossible to sustain in the following years.

By the end of May 1962, it had become clear that such an agitational effort was too big for a clandestine organization, and the police launched a wave of arrests which continued in 1963. By the end of 1963, activists, especially among students drafted for the war in Angola, started escaping abroad in large numbers. As a result, political agitation in the universities declined until 1968, when the impact of the May events in France led to spontaneous outbursts and made it more difficult for the PCP to keep control.

Moreover, dissent and disillusionment with the PCP's policies could also be detected among segments of the working classes. This was most apparent after the party refused to support the attempt led by General Delgado to seize the barracks of Beja in Southern Alentejo. It was only too easy for the PCP to show *a posteriori* that the Beja attack was doomed to failure, but there were many amongst the working classes who began to feel that the PCP was unwilling or unable to implement its own programme of 'national uprising'.

According to the memoirs quoted above, even before the turning point of the late 1960s, many working-class members of the PCP either gave up political involvement or emigrated, and by 1965 the PCP was, in organizational terms, back to the situation prior to 1958. Even in Alentejo, after the eight-hour strike of 1962, massive arrests and migration had led to a decline of organized control of the area. The 6th Congress of the party in 1965 reflected these difficulties and went by unnoticed in an already declining movement.

As a result of the events of 1958 to 1962, the political debate, particularly among the first wave of exiles abroad, heated up as it had never done before. Also due to the conflict between China and the Soviet Union, part of this discontent was channelled towards the mounting of a strong left-wing criticism of the alleged 'pacifism' and 'reformism' of the PCP, which led to the first significant organized split the party had known for years. At the same time, non-communist intellectuals opposing the colonial wars also entered into competition with the PCP and created a small left-wing movement along lines similar to the French *Parti Socialiste Unifié*.

However, the PCP was not ignorant of these challenges, nor of the changes affecting Portuguese society. Its awareness was expressed in a lengthy and sophisticated document issued in 1964 and written by Cunhal himself (*Rumo a Vitória*). This document remains crucial for an understanding of PCP thinking about both national politics and party organization. In this widely publicized analysis of party tasks, Cunhal skilfully conciliates a general concept of anti-fascism, which could appeal to large strata of the middle classes, with a more specific view of anti-fascism as a step forward towards socialism.

Although the book failed to overcome the criticisms both of left-wingers, who considered it too 'reformist', and of social democrats, who considered it too 'progressive', Cunhal's analysis of Portuguese society was not greatly inaccurate; his 1964 programme for a 'national democratic revolution' was virtually achieved ten years later by the 'April revolution'. He seems to have been right in believing that in the specific conditions of Portuguese society, the anti-fascist movement did contain a social and economic dynamic which went well beyond the mere overthrow of the dictatorship.

The PCP and the modernization of Portugal

Throughout the 1960s and early 1970s there were deep changes in society, due to the combination of massive emigration, industrialization, urbanization and mass education, and the continuation of the wars in the colonies. These put severe strains on the regime as well as on the forces of the opposition.

The PCP was constantly under attack from several groups of the extreme left. It eventually responded by undertaking a few token military actions. Hence, this period of quite marked economic recovery led not to a downgrading of political conflict, as might have been expected, but, on the contrary, to increasingly radicalized politics.

On the whole the PCP still proved a more effective organization than any of the other anti-fascist groups. Those to the right of the PCP found it very hard both to sustain underground activities and to engage in mass action. Those to its left proved eventually unable to achieve anything outside the ghetto of clandestinity. In general the PCP remained more worried with the challenge from the far left than from the right. This seems clear, in retrospect, from Cunhal's 1971 pamphlet against 'radicalism', which was widely publicized among party members. Cunhal's pamphlet was a ruthless but clever attack on 'petty-bourgeois intellectuals', but between the lines the worry of the PCP over the effects of 'radicalism' among its own members is quite apparent.

The late 1960s and early 1970s had seen the PCP in a relatively defensive position, facing strong competition both on its left and its right. Marcelo Caetano had replaced Salazar as the head of government, but had failed in his attempt to 'liberalize' the regime. The continuation of the war in the colonies – where Caetano would rather have contemplated a 'glorious' defeat than an open negotiated peace – coincided with new difficulties in the social and economic area, where the international crisis prevented many important concerns from considering the abandonment of traditional policies of colonialism and high tariffs. The result was that the new dictator surrendered virtually without struggle to the 'hawks' of the regime. In consequence, elements of the middle classes started organizing to challenge the dictatorship and to create a reasonable alternative to it. Several middle-class groups, especially those connected with big business, only materialized as political parties after the coup of 25 April – parties like the PPD (*Partido Popular Democratico* now *Partido Social Democrata*) and the CDS (*Centre Democratico e Social*). Others in the tradition of the liberal middle classes had already succeeded in creating a socialist party in 1973 under the auspices of the Socialist International. The links of the socialist party with a military alternative to the regime, led by General Spinola, were apparent several months before the coup. This was indicated in a series of *Libres Opinions* published in the French newspaper *Le Monde* by its leader, Mário Soares.

The PCP in the revolution

The events of the Portuguese revolution are both too complex and too well known for a cursory description. In the present context, however, it should be noted that the 'April revolution' was the culmination of the protracted process of modernization and liberalization which the country had undergone in the previous decade. As to the radical turn taken by political events, it can be accounted for by the long period of authoritarianism imposed on Portuguese society (the revolution was all the more radical because it had been delayed for so long) and by the need of the military left and its civilian allies for radicalization to accomplish the basic task of the coup – the decolonization. Once the colonial question was settled in November 1975, with the independence of Angola, the radical social movement quickly faded away and left few traces. The civilian left opted for the consolidation of democracy under a kind of 'military protectorate' with the President of the Republic drawn from the officer corps.

The PCP has been conspicuously reluctant to adhere to the tenets and strategies of 'Eurocommunism'. The history of the party and the backwardness of Portugal by European standards seem sufficient to account for its Stalinist outlook, but in reality, before 1974 the PCP had developed an extremely cautious set of policies and had been careful to put forward realistic demands. Indeed, at that time many people on the left judged the PCP too moderate. On the whole the party's approach did not differ substantially from those of the communist parties which did adopt the 'Eurocommunist' positions. This explains the relative ease with which Mário Soares persuaded General Spinola to legalize the PCP, and the agreement of Soares and Spinola to PCP participation in the first provisional government.

In the aftermath of the military coup of 25 April there was little evidence of unrealistic demands by the PCP. Many observers noted that the party spent the first weeks of the revolution trying to curb the huge wage demands made in most factories at the shop floor. PCP leaders feared that these demands, as well as the 'wild purges' carried out by the workers and employers in the administration and management of many firms, would 'de-stabilize' the institutionalization of democracy. There is therefore considerable evidence to suggest that the PCP only departed drastically from the cautious and moderate policies for which it had been known in the past when forced. The spontaneous radicalization of the social movements and the goals of the 'military left' together offered the PCP a real share in state power after the dismissal of Spinola in September 1974. Political events took a further swing to the left on 11 March 1975. The banking system and most big businesses were nationalized and the party was given a legal monopoly over trade unions by the military 'Revolutionary Council'. At that moment, however, the communist party overtly showed its anti-democratic position and tried to oppose the call for elections. It failed. When eventually these elections were held, on 25 April 1975, the PCP and its allies won no more than 18 per cent of the popular vote. It was successful, in contrast, in confining the elected Assembly to the task of drafting the new constitution. In alliance with the MFA (Movement of the Armed Forces), the communist party continued to influence the composition of successive cabinets until July 1976.

Although the PCP did not play a direct role in decolonization policy, the decolonization problem and the social unrest put the PCP under pressure. The party was pushed by the social agitation into radicalizing tactics. It was also pulled by the military left (in the MFA and the 'Revolutionary Council') into the centre of the political arena. This combination led the communist party to depart from its previous cautiousness and adopt an anti-democratic strategy clearly oriented towards the Soviet model. This strategy, however, pushed the socialist party to the right of the political spectrum. In the face of the leftist 'peril', the liberal forces in society gathered behind Mário Soares and the socialist party. Even the more conservative settled for democracy as the best alternative to authoritarian rule. These developments proved later to be decisive in the strengthening of Portuguese democracy, for the representative institutions were the conquest of liberals and conservatives (rather than of leftists as in many democratization processes after dictatorships).

The confrontation between 'democratic' and 'revolutionary' forces reached its peak in the summer of 1975. The installation of General Vasco Gonçalves, at the head of the fifth provisional government on 8 August 1975, was the last victory of the military left and the PCP. The conservative backlash, particularly in the north of the country, proved too strong to be dealt with except by sheer repression. The MFA discovered that it had neither the strength nor the legitimacy to carry out overt repression. The fall of Gonçalves a month later came as the natural result of the political rebalancing brought about by the conservative mass mobilization in the north. Subsequently, the PCP and its radical allies tried to prevent the functioning of the sixth government led by Admiral Azevedo, and the work of the Constitutional Assembly. They tried to oppose the elimination of the radicals from the Revolutionary Council in the 'coup' of 25 November but met a strong reaction from the army 'moderates' led by Ramalho Eanes (the future President). In short, the revolutionary process was stopped by the army. The protection of General Costa Gomes (the President) and of some members of the Revolutionary Council (including Major Melo Antunes) prevented the new 'moderate' military leaders from making an all-out attack on the PCP. Since then, the PCP has been slowly evolving towards a much more moderate political stance, but without giving up much of its rhetoric of revolutionary days, needed for consumption by its own rank and file. The PCP suffered a significant defeat by Otelo de Carvalho, the charismatic leader of the populist left, in the presidential election of

June 1976. Half of the electorate of the PCP voted for de Carvalho, despite the strong attacks of the party against the populist leader. He won 16 per cent of the poll, almost twice as much as Octavio Pato, the communist candidate.

The PCP in the new democracy

The communist party has clearly found it very difficult to adjust to the new democratic institutions. Its moderate approaches before 1974 had been completely subverted by its role in the revolutionary events. Whether this role illustrated the party's 'true nature' or was a temporary departure from its 'normal nature' is unclear. For years to come, however, both party members and Portuguese society at large will remember the events of the revolutionary period. José Pacheco Pereira, one of the few Portuguese experts on the party, has noted that the PCP is still today internally divided into two clearly distinct 'cultures': the cautious and bureaucratic one (represented by the hard core of ageing professional cadres led by Cunhal) and the populist and utopian rhetoric of the PCP's unofficial daily newspaper *O Diario*. He forecasts that in the long run the populist rhetoric will fade away. He also believes that, at the moment, the *apparatchiki* rely heavily on this rhetoric to legitimize the party's tactics in the eyes of the rank-and-file. Finally, Pereira sees that the emergence of a modernized alternative leadership is extremely improbable.

It is then surprising only to observers unaware of Portugal's political culture of bitter conflict that the PCP emerged after the 1974 coup as a major force, particularly amongst the urban and rural workers of the south. Moreover, some apparently mistaken moves made by the PCP during the revolutionary period, as well as the conservative backlash of the so-called 'Hot Summer' of 1975 in the north of the country, can be understood in the context of an old and deep cleavage of Portugal in two bitterly divided halves. Extremely polarized political attitudes are reflected in a pattern of electoral behaviour, with no parallel elsewhere in Europe, of great localization of party strengths. Communist rank and file and the left-wing activists in some areas may well have been mistaken about the reality of their national strength – low – by their actual strength – great – at the local level. For, where communists and the far left are strong, they tend to be *very* strong but in areas of weakness they are virtually non-existent. The combined vote of the PCP and the far left varies between virtually zero in some areas of the Catholic north and nearly

70 per cent in strongholds of the industrial belt of Lisbon and Setubal and the small towns and villages of Alentejo.

In all the eight elections since April 1975, the total national PCP vote (either alone or in alliance) has fluctuated between 15 and 20 per cent of the poll. Recently, the party seems to have increased its electoral appeal, particularly in a series of local by-elections, such as the 1981 elections in Loures, the third largest constituency in the country. As the memories of the revolution fade away, the PCP has been collecting the votes which used to go to minor groups of the far left. At the same time the failures of the socialist party, both in government and in opposition, have pushed segments of the original socialist electorate to the communist party. However, despite these marginal gains, the PCP remains very much a sectional political force both in regional and social terms. We know little of the PCP's social composition (except what the party wants the public to know) but it seems clear that the PCP is mainly based in the southern parts of the country and recruits primarily among the working class and the lower clerical workers, often in nationalized firms. The party seems to have made few inroads either north of Lisbon or among the peasants and the more affluent middle classes.

The increasing stabilization of democratic institutions seems to have led the communist party to adopt new electoral tactics. The PCP appears to foresee the 'Italianization' of Portuguese electoral politics which are increasingly dominated by a large centre-right coalition and a strong communist party, both built at the expense of the socialists and the groups of the centre-left which have lost a quarter of their votes since 1975. These tactics are accompanied by repeated offers of a 'popular front alliance' to the socialist party, although the first sign of 'Italianization' was the reaction to the formation by Dr Mário Soares of the first constitutional government in July 1976. After a few months the PCP combined its votes in Parliament with those of the centre and the right, to bring down the socialist minority cabinet. In fact, the communists are still reluctant to play the democratic game and to accept the popular verdict. The communist party gave support, albeit disguised, for the increasing interference of President Eanes (elected in June 1976) in parliamentarty politics, as the President's cabinets weakened the socialist party and because 'presidentialism' appeared – and still appears – as a means of by-passing the parliamentary framework. The PCP's overt support for Eanes's second mandate in December 1980 was also part of its strategy of clinging to the present constitution, which offers a possible way out of its present isolation in a kind of populist political movement under Eanes and the remnants of the Revolutionary Council.

The PCP thus opposes any changes to the 1976 constitution both in political institutions and in economic arrangements. The party now appears as the only significant political force opposed to the demilitarization of the regime by, say, the curtailment of the President's powers or the suppression of the Revolutionary Council. The party also opposes the privatization of any enterprise national-ized in March 1975, and is predictably hostile to Portugal's candidacy for membership of the EEC. This strategy, however, seems doomed to failure given the present agreement of the ruling coalition and the socialists to end the 'military protectorate' over the democratic insti-tutions, and to limit the dangers of 'presidentialism'. It is true, however, that this 'constitutional' alliance between the socialist party and the centre-right coalition may prove to the electoral advantage of the communist party and to the high cost of the socialists. The worsening economic situation will also aid the electoral position of the PCP.

Cunhal continues to dismiss Eurocommunism as 'a fashion' which will fade and his party retains Stalinist structures, Leninist dogmas and a touching loyalty to the USSR, notably over the invasion of Afghanistan and over Poland. In practice, of course, piecemeal compromises are profitable in domestic matters and the PCP has been increasingly willing, in recent months, to make deals – in both industrial relations and in politics. Indeed, the PCP seems today to have resumed its pre-1974 cautious and moderate outlook. It concentrates on expanding its electorate but also on the consolidating of its regional and class bases. In other words, as 'a society within society' with a long tradition, the PCP is already building up, precisely because of its opposition to 'bourgeois democracy', the structure of a *parti de pouvoir* rather than a *parti de gouvernement*. Its growth increases its strength but also its isolation – and makes a 'popular front' less likely in the near future.

Note

The initial version of this paper was presented in a seminar on 'Communism in Southern Europe' at St Antony's College, Oxford, in 1978, at the encourag-ing invitation of the Warden of St Antony's and Dr Juan Pablo Fusi. It was later discussed with Professor Thomas Bruneau and his students of the McGill University, Montreal, Canada. And finally, a closer version to the present one was discussed at the Department of Government of the London

School of Economics and Political Science, at the friendly invitation of Dr Howard Machin. I am indebted to the chairmen and participants of these meetings for their useful comments, but I must take full responsibility, however reluctantly, for the 'final product'. I am also thankful to my colleague, Dr Jaime Reis, for his attempts to help me with my English style.

Bibliography

Cunhal, A. (1964) *Rumo à vitória* (available in a 1974 edition), Lisbon.
—— (1971) O radicalismo pequeno-burguês de fachada socialista (available in a 1975 edition), Lisbon.
—— (1974-81) *Discursos Políticos*, vols I-XIV, Lisbon.
—— (1976) *A revolução portuguesa - o passado e o futuro*, Lisbon.
Marques, J.A. Silva (1976) *Relatos da clandestinidade - o PCP visto por dentro* (*testemunho e análise crítica da acçao do PCP nos anos da ilegalidade*), Lisbon.
Partido Comunista Português (1974) *Programa e estatutos do PCP*, Lisbon.
—— (1975) *O PCP e a luta sindical* (1935-1973), Lisbon.
—— (1975) *Documentos do Comité Central do P.C.P.*, Lisbon.
Pereira, José Pacheco (1980) 'Problemas da história do PCP', *O fascismo em Portugal* (Actas do Colóquio da Faculdade de Letras de Lisboa), Lisbon.
—— (1981) 'Os três discursos do PCP', *Diário de Notícias*, 27 October, Lisbon.
Quintela, João G. (1976) *Para a história do movimento comunista em Portugal: a construção do Partido* (*1919-1929*), Oporto.

10

The Polish experience:
reflections and reactions

George Schöpflin

The relationship between the West European parties and the East European communist-ruled states has been an uneasy one in recent years. Once the West European parties concluded that their own political roots were more relevant to them than the existing political systems of Eastern Europe, they automatically gave themselves a range of options in their strategies. By, in effect, rejecting the totality of the Soviet experience, they claimed the right to choose – and they felt that this right applied as much to the East European variant of neo-Leninism as it did to their own heritage.[1] As far as the former was concerned, however, the West European parties, which were by no means as homogeneous as this term implies, had also to decide which parts of the East European experience were authentically part of socialism and which were extraneous or more properly internal to the national traditions of the countries concerned.[2]

As far as Poland during the *Odnowa* (renewal) was concerned, the sifting out had to be directed at the different components of the events that took place. In other words, each Western party had to decide whether a particular action or set of actions, or trend, was 'Polish' rather than 'socialist'. Naturally, analyses of this kind would be difficult, more difficult than analyses of the Czechoslovak reform movement of 1968, which had emerged under the leadership of a ruling party. In Poland, the renewal took place in the teeth of party opposition and was aimed at the dismantling and transformation of the inherited Leninist structures.

In the *Odnowa* the Poles in general largely ignored the distinction between 'Polish' and 'socialist', not least because the very word 'socialist' had acquired undesirable connotations. Nevertheless, Solidarity, and more specifically Solidarity's advisers, regarded the independent movement as 'socialist' (whatever that may have meant in real terms as distinct from a façade use of language for purposes of legitimation) and they accepted too the existing structures of the state, including the nationalization of industry, the leading role of the party and the link with the Soviet Union.

In the overall context of the *Odnowa*, numerous trends and currents of action emerged that can be seen as common to the experience of societies suddenly experiencing liberation through the disintegration of the state. In other words, the events in Poland 1980–1 could be interpreted as an instance of revolution, and the actions of the participants and the political values of the time as part of the revolutionary experience of Europe.[3] Whether this experience was to be included in the compass of socialism was very largely a matter for each observer. Although the categories used here to interpret the *Odnowa* are artificial, overlapping and not wholly satisfactory, they are useful as a device for clarifying the events and the extraordinary variety of political values that sprang up. The three categories employed are religion, political values and political institutions.

Religion

It is important not to misunderstand the nature and function of religion in Poland. There was a certain tendency on the part of some Western observers to label the Polish events 'clerical' and thus dismiss their significance. This showed complete misunderstanding of the significance of religion in the Polish context which has two main aspects. The first is the church as an institution, the aspect of religion that tends to receive emphasis and is exemplified by the displays of symbols and the presence of clerics at Solidarity gatherings. The second is religion as a system of values competing with those of the state. The latter function is arguably far more important in understanding the ramifications of Polish political values.

First, the nature of the communist revolution must be considered. This revolution was perceived by the bulk of Polish society as alien (imported from the Soviet Union), as implemented in an alien way (enforcing a concentration of power on the Russian model) and as ignoring or destroying Polish values. Because this revolution lacked legitimacy, Polish society resisted it and the resistance cohered around the most effective and most deep-rooted alternative value system, Roman Catholicism. This explains one of the more striking ironies of the situation, namely that the communist revolution acted as a force for de-secularization. Had Poland followed the Western model of development, industrialization would gradually have brought about a decline in faith. For the reasons given, this has not happened and around 70 per cent of the people regard themselves as religious and a further 20 per cent are non-believers but accept the authority of the church. A word of warning against a literal interpretation of 'religious' is in order here. It is quite evident that the point of attraction to the church has been the role of Roman Catholicism in maintaining the national political identity during the Soviet revolution carried out in Poland.

Armed with this understanding of religion in Poland we can now examine its role in four areas during the renewal. First, in no sense was Solidarity a Christian Democratic movement, and the proposition that the renewal was an attempt to shift Poland from a socialist to a Roman Catholic utopia was false. The role of the church was largely ceremonial. The ritualistic aspects of religion were used because they were the simplest and most familiar means of self-expression. An obvious instance of this was the holding of mass in the Lenin shipyard in August 1980. Second, there was the role of the hierarchy during the renewal. By and large, the church was a force for moderation and compromise and tended to press Solidarity to refrain from overt political action and from issuing challenges to the state. Third, the area of ideology was where the role of religion was limited, not least because the bulk of Catholic thought in Poland concentrated on philosophy, rather than social or economic questions. The explanation for this lay in the popular, even populistic, character of the church in post-war Poland, which had been stripped of its material power and found itself entrusted with spiritual ascendancy and moral authority over the Polish people. This made considerations of social issues less urgent, albeit during the 1970s the hierarchy repeatedly criticized the Government's failure in this field. Finally, there is the crucial role of religion in the realm of values and the self-confidence to insist on those values. One of the more surprising developments in 1980 was the sight of Polish workers holding out for what, until 30 August, was unthinkable - a free trade union. The reserves of endurance available to the workers must at least in part have derived from the sense of an absolute standard of right and wrong encapsulated in Roman Catholicism. Precisely because the Soviet revolution in Poland was alien and the everyday experience of the individual in the temporal realm was one of deception by the state, the spiritual and, indeed, even practical experience of religion was all the more powerful, indeed in many senses it was a more authentic experience than his experience of the state, which was felt to be permeated with falsity. In this respect, religion was a vital component of the *Odnowa*.[4]

Political values and behaviour

The clearest value to emerge from the Polish renewal was the determination of society to regain its autonomy from the control of the state and through this autonomy to make the state accountable for its stewardship of power. The evidence for this derives both from what Solidarity did and from its aspirations, as expressed in the Solidarity programme adopted at the 1981 Congress. In this it was explicitly stated that Solidarity's activities were determined by four sets of values: Christian ethics, the Polish national working-class tradition and the democratic traditions of the labour movement in the world, as well as control by society over the state. It was remarked when the Solidarity programme was published that nowhere does it mention the word 'socialism', yet as even a superficial examination shows, its value system is firmly within the socialist tradition.[5]

The central dilemma – possibly even contradiction – in the programme is the tension between individualism and egalitarianism. Both values are strongly stressed. The solution mooted by the programme is that of social control through self-management, which presumably would overcome potential conflicts. Underlying this proposal appears to be belief in a very high degree of collective consensus in Polish society and in the ability of Polish society to subordinate individual and sectional or group interests to a higher societal rationality. This, of course, suggests a highly idealistic concept of socio-economic planning and can be regarded as close to the Marxian tradition of collectivism.

The principle enunciated by Solidarity sought to vest real sovereignty in society and to insist upon the subordination of the state to the people. Experience of thirty-five years of Soviet-style concentration of power also helped to infuse the programme with a strong commitment to anti-monopolistic pluralism as the guarantee that the efforts of the workers would not be wasted. But pluralism was not to be restricted to the economic and labour sphere. It was to encompass politics as well, albeit not to the extent of reintroducing a multi-party system. The key texts here are points 19, 20 and 22 of the Solidarity programme.

Point 19 deals with pluralism and insists upon changes in state structures and the development of 'independent, self-governing institutions in every field of social life'. Point 20 dealt with the current excessively close relationship between political and economic power and argued that 'the system which ties political to economic power, based on continual party interference in the functioning of enterprises' was the main reason for Poland's economic crisis. Furthermore, the *nomenklatura* system, by which the party controlled appointments (preferring political loyalty over expertise), was strongly attacked as undermining rationality and reducing millions to the status of second-class citizens. Solidarity's answer, in line with the commitment to social control, was the creation of self-management committees, in order to vest real power in the hands of enterprise personnel. Although the text of the programme did not say so explicitly, there was more than a hint in point 20 that the Solidarity programme was demanding a separation of political and economic decision-making. The justification of bad economic decisions by political criteria buttressed by the misuse of ideology had led to a situation where the holders of political power had been able virtually to appropriate the state for their own benefit and self-aggrandise-ment. Examples of the power élite disregarding the advice of the country's technocrats were numerous and the absence of either political or economic constraints on the élite had contributed largely to Poland's economic crisis. Again, the point contains an implicit assumption that pluralism can only be guaranteed if political and economic decision-making were kept strictly separate. Solidarity saw self-management as the answer to the excessive concentration of economic power and had nothing to say on the possible alternative of private enterprise.

Point 22 can be regarded as a central demand in the realm of political power. It in effect called for the restoration of parliamentary sovereignty to the Sejm (Parliament), although this is not entirely clear from the formulation which uses the term 'supreme power in the state'. Thus it is far from certain how the Solidarity programme envisaged the party's leading role. However, it can be deduced that the monopoly position of the party in politics would not be tolerated and that a representative Sejm, based on genuine representation, would be the ultimate repository of power in a reformed Poland. This assumption is strengthened by another of the proposals in point 22, namely that trade unions, as defined in the programme (i.e. as something much wider than unions in the West), should have the right of legislative initiative. This must be regarded as a very radical demand, for the right of political initiative had been jealously guarded by the party as a crucial part of its monopoly. Indeed, had the Solidarity programme been implemented, it would have been hard to see what role would have been left to the Polish Communist Party at all – at best, it would have been reduced to a guardian of ideology and a force for persuasion. The implication of the programme is that the party would have lost control over the instruments of coercion to the state administration, now made responsible to the Sejm and probably also to an independent judiciary. It would also have lost control of economic strategy and the implementation of economic planning, and the *nomenklatura* system would have been wound up or at any rate enormously reduced. These reforms would have left the party so weakened that its main political function, presumably, would have been to act as an ideological fig-leaf in Poland's relations with the Soviet Union.

Points 23, 24 and 25 deal with the problem of legality and carry far-reaching implications for the exercise of political power. The demands of the programme involved the re-establishment of the rule of law, administered by an independent judiciary; respect for the constitutional provisions on equality of all before the law sustained by an independent, newly-created constitutional court; the abolition of secrecy; the abolition of the right of the state to intervene arbitrarily in the economy; and the democratization of the administration of justice by the employment of the principle of self-management. Judges would not be permitted any role other than their judicial one (i.e. they must remain outside politics), and they would be subject to recall. The programme demanded a new law on the militia (police), which would ensure its depoliticization and 'there must be a new law on the secret services, precisely defining their area of competence and providing for social control over their activity'. Point 25 demanded amendments to the Penal Code in order to prevent the party from having the right to prosecute citizens for their (dissident) political views.

The programme makes analogous demands in the areas of the media and education and culture, generally calling for greater openness, accessibility and democratization. Thus censorship in the mass media was regarded as a necessary evil to be tolerated 'only for the time being and out of necessity'; it was to be scrapped entirely in science and the arts. A characteristically Polish demand was point 31, section 2: 'The very language of propaganda, which damages the way in which we want to express thoughts and feeling, is a dangerous instrument of falsehood. The union will seek to give back to society the Polish language, which permits people genuinely to understand each other.' Concern over the use, imposed by the communist party, of an alien political language whereby political alternatives were prevented from emerging had long been expressed at all levels of Polish society.[6] This was fully in the historical tradition inherited by the Poles, for whom language was not just a means of communication but also a badge of identity and an object of semi-mystical reverence.

Overall, the thrust of the Solidarity programme was in the direction of deconcentration of power. Power would be diffused throughout society and Solidarity, the representative of society, would act as the guarantor of deconcentration. The underlying frame of values in the programme, therefore, can be described as a reaction against a generation of living under the Soviet-type system of concentrating power. There was also an assumption of a high degree of social homogeneity and that conflicts of interest would be relatively easily resolved by the proposed system of self-government. The programme also assumed both an existing equality within society coupled with manifest inequality *vis-à-vis* the state, together with a sustainable identity of purpose for the future. The programme made no mention of denationalization, indeed on the contrary it avoided any discussion of private enterprise, so that it can, again, be assumed that the post-war communist revolution, involving the abolition of private capital and land reform, was the starting point. On the other hand, the Soviet features of that revolution were to be utterly expunged.

The Solidarity programme was significantly more radical in its aims than either the Czechoslovak reform programme of 1968–9 or the somewhat inchoate aims of the Hungarian Revolution of 1956. It clearly sought to build upon those features of the post-war legacy that were regarded as desirable, albeit the bulk of the programme was derived from the circumstances of the early 1980s and the experiences of the 1970s. For those who regarded socialism as identical with the concentration of state power, the Solidarity programme could not be reconciled with their perceptions of socialism – this obviously included the Soviet Union, for whom the Polish experience was counter-revolutionary.

Political behaviour in Poland during the renewal can be broadly divided into spontaneous action and organized initiatives. Spontaneous action was extensive and testified to the years of accumulated resentment against the state and the local representatives of the state – the enterprise managers, the local party secretaries, the police and other members of the privileged bureaucracy. The aims of local action were, therefore, twofold. Some were directed at the removal of unpopular figures who had behaved arbitrarily and against the then prevailing climate. An instance of this was the determined action against the *voivod* (i.e. prefects) of Częstochowa, Miroslaw Wierzbicki, in November–December 1980. Wierzbicki had sought to ban the strike action called on 10 November 1980 and intended to bring pressure on the authorities to sanction the legal registration of Solidarity. Wierzbicki became the first prominent target of local action. The events in Częstochowa pointed towards another significant feature of the mood of Polish society – the radicalism of the grass roots. Time and time again, the local tail tried to wag the central dog, which it found comparatively easy to do, given the looseness of Solidarity's organization and its consensual roots. That in turn gave rise to a personalized style of politics, whereby the charismatic Lech Wałęsa would again and again have to use his personal prestige to resolve local flare-ups. The second broad set of aims by local activists was intended to promote the implementation of policies rather than the interdiction of persons. The demonstrations in the summer of 1981 at the persistent food shortages could be cited as an example of this. And, although not strictly within the framework of Solidarity, the pressure by rural activists for the sanctioning of a peasants' union could be said to fall into the same category.

Organized initiatives were likewise a feature of the Polish renewal and were so from the outset – the wave of rolling strikes from one enterprise to another which culminated in the founding of Solidarity itself were examples. Thus the establishment of factory strike committees, later of inter-factory strike committees, became the foundations for Solidarity itself and helped to explain its heterogeneous nature in later months. The strike committee is, of course, a standard and logical feature of industrially-based political action. In the Polish case, its roots may be sought in the committees which sprang up in 1970-1, the workers' councils of 1956-7, the enterprise councils of the post-war era and the pre-war labour movement. Subsequently, membership of Solidarity was made contingent upon having taken part in a strike and having created a strike committee. In that sense, the strike became a symbol of the renewal and a badge of entry to the renewal process.

The territorial rather than the sectoral principle of organization was adopted by Solidarity in order to differentiate it from the official, communist party-controlled unions. This was a reaction against the over-centralizing philosophy of the Leninist tradition and it sought to anchor the principle of grass roots control and of accountability in Solidarity. Elections at every level were made a pre-condition of office and these elections, unlike the façade elections run by the party, were predicated on the possibility of recall by the electors.

If anything, the system of organization adopted by Solidarity tipped the scales too far against the union leadership and in favour of the localities, so that the leadership was more than once held responsible by the party (via party manipulation by public opinion as well) for activities over which it had only the minimum of control. The sixteen months of Solidarity's existence gave the impression of a gradual transformation from Solidarity as a trade union to Solidarity as a socio-political movement. This was at one and the same time accurate and inaccurate – the Gdańsk–Szczecin–Jastrzębie agreements all included overtly political stipulations, but the leadership of Solidarity initially sought to steer clear of politics as such and even tended to treat it in a somewhat offhand and contemptuous fashion as the responsibility of the party, 'them', the politicians who were involved in a dirty game. This rather populistic approach gave way to a deeper understanding of the nature of the communist system over the months as it became evident that Solidarity could not avoid being drawn into the political arena; the party, in effect, failed to exercise its governing functions. The response was initially *ad hoc*, but over time and under the pressure of events, Solidarity came to formulate the coherent set of proposals embodied in the programme.

Light was also shed on the political values of the Polish reforms by the demands of the party reform movement. This set of pressures for the reform of the communist party itself had its origins in the large-scale recruitment into the party of working-class, particularly of skilled working-class, members, who were, of course, expected to subordinate themselves dutifully to the organizational traditions of Leninism. With the defeat of the party in the summer of 1980, the shop-floor members responded either by leaving the party or by insisting on reforms aimed at ensuring that the defeat – something which had left party members exposed to personal responsibility for actions over which they had had no control – would never be repeated. To this end, the party reform movement, which took off spontaneously in the aftermath of the strikes and the founding of Solidarity and was encouraged by the party leadership's initial strategy of penetrating Solidarity by party members, pressed for a complete transformation of Leninist structures.

The aim was to make the leadership accountable to the members and to sustain a genuine unity of purpose and action thereby. This lay behind the emergence of the horizontal movement from the autumn of 1980 onwards. The horizontalists broke with one of the strictest rules of Leninism, that power flows vertically, by forging links laterally with other party organizations in the same locality and including non-members in the horizontal structure. Horizontalism gave the membership a much broader perspective and access to more extensive information, whereby the party functionaries could be supervised.

As in Solidarity, free elections became a fundamental demand of the reformers. Nominations to all offices were to be completely free of pressures from above and the system of candidates arriving in someone's briefcase (to use the Polish expression) would cease. Party leaders, even at the very highest, would be subject to recall and there would be limits on the length of office holding, in order to prevent any re-emergence of the neo-feudal concentrations of power. Information would flow freely in both directions and the leadership would be unable to discount the wishes of the grass roots. These demands brought into question the concept of a 'party career', again one of the fundamentals of Leninism. The reformers felt that the communist party should be an organization of genuinely convinced activists, where there was no place for career bureaucrats, not least because they tended to become more concerned for their bureaucratic futures and to ignore the grass roots. In particular, career officials paid more attention to the wishes of their superiors than to the membership or their ostensible duties. Furthermore, the existence of a career bureaucracy made it possible for bureaucrats to defend their personal, non-political decisions in the name of party ideology and the infallibility of the party.

The concept of the leading role of the party put forward by the reformers would again have made serious inroads into Leninism. The party was to wield power not directly but through the authority and persuasiveness of the membership. In other words, the party would cease to be a traditional political élite and would be neutralized; instead, it would become another, albeit significant, socio-political organization, in competition with others in the allocation of values and resources. The party would enjoy a 'leading' position in this constellation of forces by reason of the superiority of its ideas and the quality of the membership. Here again there was a strong underlying assumption of the high degree of cohesiveness and consensus in Polish society. Furthermore, the reconstituted party would not be Marxist–Leninist even in the formal sense, but would be the repository and aggregate of all socialist traditions in Poland and of the social thought of Roman Catholicism.[7] The demands of the Polish reformers and their redefinition of the leading role were far more radical than anything else seen in post-war Eastern Europe, including the Czechoslovak reform programme. But in common with the ideas current in Prague, the Poles too were determined to return to the mainstream of European socialism and to jettison what was seen as the alien, Russian burden of Leninism.

For the West European communist movement, the Polish events represented a serious challenge. On the one hand, it was difficult for them to reject the manifestly popular and socialist character of Polish aspirations, especially its anti-bureaucratic thrust; on the other hand, the continued links between West European communism and lingering loyalty to the Soviet Union as an article of faith and of identity made the open assimilation of the Polish experience equally problematical. In general, whilst the Western Eurocommunist parties adopted a rather cautious stance towards Solidarity and developments before 13 December, the military *putsch* transformed attitudes. The Italian party, together with the Spanish, British, Swedish and Belgian parties, condemned the takeover; the French party proved to be rather more equivocal and appeared to be offering a measure of support for Jaruzelski. The membership of the Italian party tended to line up with the leadership and only a small minority of 8.6 per cent accepted the Soviet view that Poland had been in the grip of counter-revolution prior to the *putsch*, while a further 10.3 per cent regarded the *coup* as positive because Poland had become ungovernable.[8] It could certainly be argued that the Polish crisis was an unwelcome challenge for the West European communist movement, both in its timing and in its substance. It came at a point when the impetus of Eurocommunism appeared to be on the decline and the ideological and intellectual concepts embodied in Eurocommunism were in need of re-evaluation. In particular, the long-standing dilemma remained unresolved: for a coherent Eurocommunist position to achieve legitimacy, it would have to offer its own, non-Soviet analysis of the past and present in Eastern Europe. Any analysis of this kind, which would have to include a radical critique of 'real existing socialism', would provoke a breach with the Soviet

Union. But a breach would then bring into question the very identity of the West European communist parties as communist, given that the definition of communist had been appropriated by Moscow and could be laid down solely in Leninist terms. The Polish challenge could not, therefore, be met head on without such a breach, something which no West European party was ready to face; hence the rather *ad hoc* responses, the evaluation of individual instances rather than the entire process which provided the context for such instances, and the condemnation of single acts of repression rather than a systematic analysis of the nature of Soviet-type societies. Intellectual consistency by the Eurocommunists would unquestionably have led them to the conclusion that the socio-political order in the Soviet world had little or nothing in common with socialism. Any public declaration of this nature would really have put the fat in the fire.

Notes

1 I have looked at some of the implications of the Eurocommunist-East European relationship in 'Eurocommunism: a Central European Perspective', in Roger Kanet (ed.), *Soviet Foreign Policy and East-West Relations* (New York, 1982).

2 *L'Unità*, 9 April 1982, offers one analysis of the Solidarity programme.

3 The Polish events generated an enormous literature. Among the more valuable are Neal Ascherson, *The Polish August* (London, 1981) and Jean Woodall (ed.), *Policy and Politics in Contemporary Poland* (London, 1982); two useful surveys are Kevin Ruane, *The Polish Challenge* (London, 1982) and Alex Pravda, 'Poland 1980: from Premature Consumerism to Labour Solidarity', *Soviet Studies*, 34 (2) (1982), pp. 167-99.

4 In writing this section, I have relied on Marcin Król, 'Pologne: une révolution différente', *Commentaire*, 3 (12) (1980-1), pp. 537-44, and Maciej Pomian-Srzednicki, *Religious Change in Contemporary Poland: Secularization and Politics*, (London, 1982).

5 There are two English-language texts of the Solidarity programme: *Labour Focus on Eastern Europe*, 5 (1-2), pp. 3-14, and in *The Bulletin* of the Information Centre for Polish Affairs (UK), no. 16/81 (4 November 1981). The former is translated from the French version in *L'Alternative*, no. 14 (1982) and the latter is taken from BBC Monitoring; neither is wholly satisfactory and I have used both for this analysis.

6 See, for example, Adam Michnik, 'Ce que nous voulons et ce que nous pouvons', *L'Alternative*, no. 8 (1981), pp. 5-13.

7 In addition to previously cited works, I also used George Kolankiewicz, 'The Politics of Socialist Renewal' and 'Employees Self-Management and

Socialist Trade Unions', both in Woodall, op. cit., pp. 56-75 and 129-47; furthermore, I have benefited from the many discussions I have had on Polish topics with George Kolankiewicz during the 1980-82 crisis.

8 *L'Espresso*, 21 March 1982.

Appendix

The four major West European communist parties - a guide

In the following pages the main features of the communist parties of Italy, France, Spain and Portugal are presented in tabular form. The election results are from *Keesing's Contemporary Archives*, the membership figures and newspaper circulation figures are mainly from *Le Monde* party congress reports. The 'Checklist of Communist Parties and Fronts, 1980' in *Problems of Communism*, March–April 1981, places these figures in the context of a comparison with other communist parties. These figures were compiled and checked by Nicholas Kaufman.

Italy: PCI

General secretary: Enrico Berlinguer
Membership: 1978   1.79 million
         1977   1.83 million

Traditional strongholds

These are in central and north Italy, notably Emilia-Romagna (48.2 per cent 1980), Tuscany (46.4 per cent), Umbria (45.2 per cent) and Lombardy. Throughout the 1970s the PCI controlled the first three and in 1975 it gained Liguria, Piedmont and Lazio, although losing them in 1980. Yet it was still the largest party in Liguria in 1980.

Either alone or with the PSI the PCI controls nearly all the major towns north of Naples, including Rome, Naples, Turin, Florence, Bologna where it supplies the mayors.

Newspaper

L'Unità. Third highest daily circulation. First Sunday circulation.

Union

CGIL. In 1969 32 per cent of the CGIL executive were affiliated to PCI; this was the last year when dual office holding was allowed.

Government involvement

The 'historic compromise' was first aired by Berlinguer in 1972. In 1976 the PCI agreed to abstain in Parliament and in return gained the speakership of the Chamber of Deputies and seven parliamentary committee chairmanships. In December 1977 the PCI joined the government majority for the first time but they withdrew on 31 January 1979. 49/94 provinces have administrations of the left, including 18 with PCI presidents. In autumn 1980 a number of regions were without a government when the Christian Democrats refused to co-operate with the PCI. The former relented in December 1980.

Elections		*PCI vote* %	*Seats*
Regional	June 1975	33.4	247/720
General	June 1976	34.4	227/630
Partial local (large communes)	April 1977	28.8	
Partial local (medium communes)	May 1978	26.5	
Presidential	8 July 1978	33.5*	
General	3–4 June 1979	30.4	201/630
European	10–11 June 1979	29.6	
Regional	June 1980	31.5	233/720

* of electoral college

France: PCF

Secretary-general: Georges Marchais
Membership: 1980   750,000
              1978   630,000
              1976   543,000
              1974   330,000

Traditional strongholds

These are centred in the Paris 'Red belt' and the 'midi rouge' although in the 1981 general election PCF seats were halved in the former. The 'midi rouge' comprises Bouches-du-Rhône, Languedoc, Hérault and Gard. Also strong in Limoges, Corrèze and the Nord region.

Newspaper

L'Humanité. Circulation: 1981   90,000
  1978   149,900
  1976   124,000

Union

GCT. At 2.5 million the membership of this communist-dominated union makes up half of France's union strength. More than half of CGT top officials also PCF or close.

Government involvement

From June 1981 four ministers, including one minister of state, have been included in the government of François Mitterrand. In March 1977 there were 309 PCF mayors out of 1229 municipalities.

Elections		PCF vote %	Seats
General	March 1978	20.56	86/491
Departmental	March 1979	22.5	
European	June 1979	20.52	19/81
Partial senate	September 1980	(no change)	23/300
Presidential	May 1981	15.37	
General	June 1981	16.18	43/491
			(plus 1 affiliated Deputy)

Spain: PCE

General secretary: Gerardo Iglesias
Membership: 1981   80,000
          April 1977   PCE legalized
          1973   5,000

Traditional strongholds

The main area of influence is Catalonia where the PSUC (the Catalonian Communist Party) gained 19 per cent of the vote in the March 1980 municipal elections. Elsewhere the PCE is relatively strong in Madrid, Andalusia, Valencia and Asturias, particularly in the industrial towns like Madrid and Barcelona.

Newspaper

Mundo Obrero (weekly).

Union

CC.OO (Comisiones Obreras). The largest trade union, it is hegemonic in Catalonia and particularly strong in Asturias, Madrid and Andalusia.
In 1980 it gained 30.7 per cent in works' council elections, as against 35 per cent in 1978 when it had 2 million registered members.
The PCE controls the national executive of the CC.OO - in 1976 21/27 on the executive were members of PCE - and many of its city executives.

Government involvement

The PCE was party to the Pact of Moncloa in October 1977, which was an economic and political agreement to facilitate parliamentary government. The PCE pushed for, but failed to achieve, a government of national consensus in which it would be included. The PSUC secured 2/12 seats in the Executive Council of the Catalan 'Generalitat' in December 1977. After the April 1979 municipal elections the PCE, together with the PSOE, controlled nine provinces. (Provincial assemblies were formed on the basis of these elections.)

Elections		Place	Vote %	Seats
General	June 1977 PCE + PSUC	3rd	9.2	20/350
General	1 March 1979 PCE + PSUC	3rd	10.0	23/350
Provincial	March 1980			
	Catalonia: PSUC	3rd	19.0	25/135
	Basque Provinces: PCE	7th	3.9	1/60
General	28 October 1982	4th	3.9	5/350

NB: Although weak nationally, the PCE is more influential in local politics. Housewife and neighbourhood associations are communist-controlled and the CC.OO is the dominant trade union organization.

Portugal: PCP

Secretary-general: Dr Alvaro Cunhal
Membership: December 1980   188,500
                 1976   100,000–120,000
                 1975   75,000–100,000

Traditional strongholds

Large estate areas of middle and south especially in Alto Alentejo in eastern-central Portugal and Baixo Alentejo in south. Matched by PSP in Alentejo in south-east. Also strong (15–20 per cent vote) in industrial areas around Lisbon and Setubal. Less than 5 per cent in north.

Newspaper

Avante (party weekly). *O Diario* (communist-leaning daily). Circulation: 68,000

Union

Intersyndical. Membership: 232 affiliated trade unions (271 total). 1980, *c.* 1,250,000 (1,613,135 total).

Government involvement

1 15 May 1974   (PM – Palma Carlos): 2 ministers.

2 12 July 1974   (PM - Vasco Goncalves): 1 minister.
3 25 May 1975   (PM - Vasco Gonçalves): 2 ministers + 1 MDP.
4 April 1975   (PM - Vasco Gonçalves): 2 ministers + 1 MDP.
25 November 1975: Attempted coup, PCP implicated.
16 July 1976: Soares (first socialist government), no ministers.

Elections		PCP vote %	Seats
Constituent Assembly	April 1975 PCP (12.53%) MDP[†] (4.12%)	16.65	30/250
General	April 1976 (no MDP)	14.65	40/263
Presidential	June 1976	7.58	
General	2 December 1979 APU* PCP (44) MDP (3)	19.00	47/250
Municipal	16 December 1979 APU	50/305 Town councils	
General	October 1980 APU PCP (39) MDP (2)	16.9	41/250
Presidential	December 1980 PCP withdraw to support Eanes (56.43%)		

* United People's Alliance; PCP + MDP.
† Portuguese democratic movement, closely associated with the PCP.

Index